UVU Comparative Mormon Studies

Comparative Mormon Studies at Utah Valley University is an interdisciplinary program designed to support the academic study of Latter-day Saint culture, theology, literature, and history. Housed in UVU's Religious Studies Program, it offers courses, lectures, conferences, workshops, and other activities with a focus on comparative studies, interreligious understanding, and cross-cultural dimensions of Mormonism. This series is designed to feature the scholarly work of this program and related activities.

The Expanded Canon

The Expanded Canon
Perspectives on Mormonism & Sacred Texts

Edited by
Blair G. Van Dyke
Brian D. Birch
Boyd J. Petersen

Greg Kofford Books
Salt Lake City, 2018

Copyright © 2018 Greg Kofford Books
Cover design copyright © 2018 Greg Kofford Books, Inc.
Cover design by Loyd Ericson

Published in the USA.

All rights reserved. No part of this volume may be reproduced in any form without written permission from the publisher, Greg Kofford Books. The views expressed herein are the responsibility of the authors and do not necessarily represent the positions or views of Greg Kofford Books or Utah Valley University.

Hardcover ISBN: 978-1-58958-637-6
Paperback ISBN: 978-1-58958-638-3
Also available in ebook.

Greg Kofford Books
P.O. Box 1362
Draper, UT 84020
www.gregkofford.com
facebook.com/gkbooks
twitter.com/gkbooks

Library of Congress Cataloging-in-Publication Data

Names: Van Dyke, Blair G., editor. | Birch, Brian D., editor. | Peterson, Boyd J., 1962- editor. | Utah Valley University. Comparative Mormon Studies, sponsoring body.

Title: The expanded canon : perspectives on Mormonism & sacred texts / edited by Blair G. Van Dyke, Brian D. Birch, Boyd J. Peterson.

Description: Salt Lake City : Greg Kofford Books, 2018. | "UVU comparative Mormon studies." | Includes index. | "Among the most distinctive and defining features of Mormonism is the affirmation of continuing revelation through modern day prophets and apostles. An important component of this concept is the acknowledgement of an open canon--that the body of authoritative scriptural texts can expand as new revelations are made available and presented to the membership for ratification. This volume brings together both Mormon and non-Mormon scholars to examine the place, purpose, and meaning of the LDS Standard Works (Christian Bible, Book of Mormon, Doctrine and Covenants, and Pearl of Great Price) in the Mormon tradition, as well as the extra-canonical sources that play a near-scriptural role in the lives of believers. Approaching LDS scripture from a variety of disciplines, methodologies, and perspectives, these scholars offer new insights into both the historical and contemporary understandings of Mormon continuing revelation."--Provided by the publisher.

Identifiers: LCCN 2018028212| ISBN 9781589586376 (hardcover) | ISBN 9781589586383 (pbk.).

Subjects: LCSH: Mormon Church--Sacred books. | Church of Jesus Christ of Latter-day Saints--Sacred books. | Revelation--Mormon Church.

Classification: LCC BX8621 .E97 2018 | DDC 289.3/2--dc23

LC record available at https://lccn.loc.gov/2018028212

CONTENTS

Scriptural Abbreviations Guide ... vii
Introduction ... ix

1. The Triangle and the Sovereign:
   Logics, Histories, and an Open Canon ... 1
   David Frank Holland

2. Beyond the Canon:
   Authoritative Discourse in Comparative Perspective ... 25
   Brian D. Birch

3. On the Literal Interpretation of Scripture ... 47
   James E. Faulconer

4. Reading Women Back into the Scriptures ... 59
   Claudia L. Bushman

5. The Book of Mormon as Post-Canonical Scripture ... 73
   Grant Hardy

6. Reading from the Gold Plates ... 85
   Richard Lyman Bushman

7. History and the Claims of Revelation:
   Joseph Smith and the Materialization of the Golden Plates ... 93
   Ann Taves

8. "The Book Which Thou Shalt Write":
   The Book Of Moses As Prophetic Midrash ... 121
   David Bokovoy

9. The Ascendancy and Legitimation of the Pearl of Great Price ... 143
   Brian Hauglid

10. Pivotal Publishing Moments For The Book Of Mormon ... 157
    Paul C. Gutjahr

11. Relishing the Revisions:
    The Doctrine & Covenants and the Revelatory Process ... 171
    Grant Underwood

12. Spiritualizing Electronic Scripture In Mormonism ... 185
    Blair G. Van Dyke

13. The Art of Scripture and Scripture as Art:
    The Proclamation on the Family and the Expanding Canon   207
    Boyd J. Petersen and *David W. Scott*
14. Patriarchal Blessings in the Prophetic Development
    of Early Mormonism   227
    Gordon Shepherd and *Gary Shepherd*

Contributors   251
Index   255

SCRIPTURAL ABBREVIATIONS GUIDE

Parenthetical scriptural references in this volume use standard LDS abbreviations.

Hebrew Bible

Gen.	Genesis
Ex.	Exodus
Lev.	Leviticus
Num.	Numbers
Deut.	Deuteronomy
Josh.	Joshua
Judg.	Judges
Ruth	Ruth
1 Sam.	1 Samuel
2 Sam.	2 Samuel
1 Kgs.	1 Kings
2 Kgs.	2 Kings
1 Chr.	1 Chronicles
2 Chr.	2 Chronicles
Ezra	Ezra
Neh.	Nehemiah
Esth.	Esther
Job	Job
Ps.	Psalms
Prov.	Proverbs
Eccl.	Ecclesiastes
Song	Song of Solomon
Isa.	Isaiah
Jer.	Jeremiah
Lam.	Lamentations
Ezek.	Ezekiel
Dan.	Daniel
Hosea	Hosea
Joel	Joel
Amos	Amos
Obad.	Obadiah
Jonah	Jonah
Micah	Micah
Nahum	Nahum
Hab.	Habakkuk
Zeph.	Zephaniah
Hag.	Haggai
Zech.	Zechariah
Mal.	Malachi

New Testament

Matt.	Matthew
Mark	Mark
Luke	Luke
John	John
Acts	Acts
Rom.	Romans
1 Cor.	1 Corinthians
2 Cor.	2 Corinthians
Gal.	Galatians
Eph.	Ephesians
Philip.	Philippians
Col.	Colossians
1 Thes.	1 Thessalonians
2 Thes.	2 Thessalonians
1 Tim.	1 Timothy
2 Tim.	2 Timothy
Titus	Titus
Philem.	Philemon
Heb.	Hebrews
James	James
1 Pet.	1 Peter
2 Pet.	2 Peter
1 Jn.	1 John
2 Jn.	2 John
3 Jn.	3 John
Jude	Jude
Rev.	Revelation

Book of Mormon

1 Ne.	1 Nephi
2 Ne.	2 Nephi
Jacob	Jacob
Enos	Enos
Jarom	Jarom
Omni	Omni
W of M	Words of Mormon
Mosiah	Mosiah
Alma	Alma
Hel.	Helaman
3 Ne.	3 Nephi
4 Ne.	4 Nephi
Morm.	Mormon
Ether	Ether
Moro.	Moroni

Doctrine and Covenants

D&C	Doctrine and Covenants
OD	Official Declaration

Pearl of Great Price

Moses	Moses
Abr.	Abraham
JS–M	Joseph Smith–Matthew
JS–H	Joseph Smith–History
A of F	Articles of Faith

Joseph Smith Translation

JST	Joseph Smith Translation

INTRODUCTION

Among the most distinctive and defining features of Mormonism is the affirmation of continuing revelation through modern-day prophets and apostles. An important component of this concept is the acknowledgement of an open canon—that the body of authoritative scriptural texts can expand as new revelations are made available and presented to the membership for ratification.

I

The Book of Mormon was the first public manifestation of the new faith of the Latter-day Saints. The publication presented a sweeping narrative of ancient civilizations in the Americas who descended from Jewish refugees that fled from the city just prior to the Babylonian conquest. The tale covers a thousand-year history and contains sermons, war chronicles, and prophecies culminating in the appearance of Jesus Christ in the new world, his establishment of the Christian church, and the eventual apostasy and destruction of these pre-Columbian Christians.

After publishing the Book of Mormon in 1830, Joseph Smith sent missionaries out to proclaim the new gospel with the book as evidence that God had again spoken to humanity and established a second witness to the Bible. Surprisingly, the Book of Mormon was not initially used as a source of theological clarification but rather as a manifestation of the power and relevance of God. Nevertheless, Smith declared the book to be the "keystone of our religion" and proclaimed that "a man would get nearer to God by abiding by its precepts, than by any other book."[1]

In addition to the Bible and the Book of Mormon, two other books of scripture were added to the canon, namely the Doctrine and Covenants and the Pearl of Great Price. The Doctrine and Covenants is a collection of writings consisting primarily of revelations to Joseph Smith in the early days of the movement. These revelations cover a wide range of issues and

---

1. Joseph Smith et al., *History of the Church of Jesus Christ of Latter-day Saints*, ed. B. H. Roberts, 7 vols., 2nd ed. rev. (Salt Lake City: Deseret News, 1957 printing), 4:461.

events—from mundane instructions to lengthy visions of the afterlife. Its pages also contain the blueprint for Church government, descriptions of the nature of God, and Church declarations on specific issues.

Finally, the Pearl of Great Price was the most recent addition to the LDS canon and was ratified by the Church in 1880. It contains a variety of documents, including portions of Joseph Smith's translation of select books of the Bible, a translation of ancient Egyptian scrolls that came into Smith's possession in 1835, excerpts from Joseph Smith's official history, and the Articles of Faith—which contain the central tenets of Mormon belief.

These four volumes constitute the "Standard Works" of the Church of Jesus Christ of Latter-day Saints and, as such, function as the authorized canon in the affairs of the Church. Though this canon may be enlarged, formal ratification by the membership of the LDS Church is required.

II

Continuing revelation has been among the most challenging aspects in Mormonism's relationship with the wider Christian community. Given the centrality and "sufficiency" of the Bible in Protestant life, the idea of scripture beyond the Bible has been both beyond the pale of acceptability and a heightened source of tension between these groups.

The rejection of the Book of Mormon, for example, was not due primarily to its theological content but to the foundational idea among mainstream Christians that the Bible contains all that is sufficient to bring human beings to salvation. Protestants have traditionally affirmed the doctrine of *sola scriptura*—that scripture is the supreme authority in matters of faith and practice. The Westminster Confession of Faith (1646), for example, states that the "whole counsel of God concerning all things necessary for His own glory, man's salvation, faith and life, is either expressly set down in Scripture, or by good and necessary consequence may be deduced from Scripture: unto which nothing at any time is to be added, whether by new revelations of the Spirit, or traditions of men."[2] Associated with biblical sufficiency is the denial of new revelation since the close of the apostolic period. This is specified in the Westminster Confession and reaffirmed in a variety of Protestant documents in the intervening centuries. Important for American evangelical Christians is the 1978 Chicago Statement on Biblical Inerrancy, which declares the New Testament "now

---

2. Henry Bettenson and Chris Maunder, eds., *Documents of the Christian Church*, 4th ed. (New York: Oxford University Press), 306.

closed inasmuch as no new apostolic witness to the historical Christ can now be borne."[3]

The Protestant emphasis on scripture was informed by their reaction to the traditional Catholic understanding of the relationship between "sacred scripture" and "sacred tradition." Though Catholics agree that the canon is closed and public revelation ceased with the Apostles, they maintain that the teachings of the Catholic Church have authoritative status alongside the Bible. This tradition transmits the Word of God "to the successors of the apostles so that, enlightened by the Spirit of truth, they may faithfully preserve, expound and spread it abroad by their preaching."[4]

Because the biblical canon was developed *within* the context of the early Christian Church, scripture cannot appropriately stand outside of it as an independent source of authority. This issue has been a key point of contention between Catholic and Protestant theologians since the earliest days of the Reformation. The Second Vatican Council reasserted the Catholic position that scripture and tradition "merge into a unity and tend toward the same end," and thus should be "accepted and honored with equal sentiments of deviation and reverence."[5]

Interestingly for Latter-day Saints, the Catholic catechism affirms that the Catholic Church "does not derive her certainty from the holy Scriptures alone," but through the *living tradition* that preserves what the apostles were taught by Jesus Christ and the Holy Spirit.[6] Though additional *public* revelation has ceased, the activity of the Spirit in the Church continues through a growth of understanding regarding that which has already been received.[7]

---

3. "The Chicago Statement on Biblical Inerrancy" (International Council on Biblical Inerrancy, 1978). Located in archives of the Dallas Theological Seminary at http://www.library.dts.edu/Pages/TL/Special/ICBI_2.pdf.

4. *Catechism of the Catholic Church*, 2nd ed. (Rome: Libreria Editrice Vaticana, 2000), Part I, Chapter 2, Article 2.

5. *Dei Verbum* (Dogmatic Constitution on Divine Revelation), 2, 9; http://www.vatican.va/archive/hist_councils/ii_vatican_council/documents/vat-ii_const_19651118_dei-verbum_en.html.

6. *Catechism of the Catholic Church*, Part I, Chapter 2, Article 2.

7. Catholicism maintains an important distinction between public and private revelation. Public revelation consists of Scripture and Tradition and is binding on all Christians, while private revelation includes spiritual manifestations to individuals.

III

Joseph Smith was captivated by questions of biblical authority. The religious crisis that led to his vision of God was fueled by competing and inconsistent appeals to the Bible. The cacophony of voices made it impossible for him to rely exclusively on the text. In the hotly contested environs of his youth, he reported that Christian preachers "understood the same passages of scripture so differently as to destroy all confidence in settling the question by an appeal to the Bible" (JS–H 1:12).

As a result, Smith's religious experiences became his foundational authority. Upon reporting his First Vision to a local Methodist minister, Smith was rebuffed and told "that there were no such things as visions or revelations in these days; that all such things had ceased with the apostles, and that there would never be any more of them" (JS–H 1:21).

What makes this story especially intriguing is that Smith reported being "greatly surprised" by the minister's response. Though the merits of visions and the "gifts of the spirit" were hotly debated among nineteenth-century revivalists, the idea that revelation had ceased had long been established and was commonplace among the Christian establishment.

Smith's momentous vision and the rise of Mormonism occurred in this contested space. The traditional boundaries of religious experience and scriptural canon were being challenged in ways theretofore unseen. David Holland points out that "such commands and revocations drove a wedge between an evolving church and those who held a fast and fundamentalist commitment to the earlier revelations."[8] Shakers, Seventh-day Adventists, and other groups were producing new revelations and matching texts, but none of these matched the Latter-day Saints in their scope and impact.

The Book of Mormon provides a clear and authoritative rejection of biblical sufficiency. It narrates the story of a vision given to an ancient American prophet Nephi, who records the voice of God: "Wherefore, because that ye have a Bible ye need not suppose that it contains all my words; neither need ye suppose that I have not caused more to be written" (2 Ne. 29:10). For Mormons, the expanded canon functioned not only across time but across also culture. Nephi later records God telling him:

> For behold, I shall speak unto the Jews and they shall write it; and I shall also speak unto the Nephites and they shall write it; and I shall also speak unto the other tribes of the house of Israel, which I have led away, and they shall

---

8. David Holland, *Sacred Borders: Continuing Revelation and Canonical Restraint in Early America* (New York: Oxford University Press, 2011), 157.

write it; and I shall also speak unto all nations of the earth and they shall write it. (2 Ne. 29:12)

Though Mormonism has yet to mine this capacious application of scripture, the theological space is available to develop an even more expansive "canon outside the canon."

IV

At present, Latter-day Saints relate to their canon in ways similar to other traditions. It is carefully regulated within the confines of ecclesiastical structures, and there is a clear line of demarcation between the Standard Works and other authoritative texts within the Church. However, *canon* and *scripture* have been neither synonymous nor co-extensive within LDS discourse. There are expansive applications of the term in which much of the authoritative discourse of Church leaders is considered scripture. A popular and provocative example can be found in Brigham Young's statement that "I have never yet preached a sermon and sent it out to the children of men, that they may not call scripture."[9] Though Young is well-known for his mercurial declarations, this statement (and others like it) have been given currency by more recent LDS leaders who employ them to emphasize the importance of the teachings of living prophets and apostles.

Ezra Taft Benson's 1980 sermon, "Fourteen Fundamentals in Following the Prophet," offers us a noteworthy case in point. Among the featured points of his address was the idea that the "living prophet is more vital to us than the Standard Works." Benson recalled a story from the early days of the Church in Kirtland in which a church leader opined publicly that "those who give revelations" should do so according to the "written word of God." In response—and at the behest of Joseph Smith—Young stood up and declared that "when compared with the living oracles those books are nothing to me. . . . I would rather have the living oracles than all the writing in the books."[10]

---

9. Brigham Young, January 2, 1870, *Journal of Discourses*, 26 vols. (London and Liverpool: LDS Booksellers Depot, 1854–86), 13:95.

10. Ezra Taft Benson, "Fourteen Fundamentals in Following the Prophet," February 26, 1980, devotional address given at Brigham Young University, https://speeches.byu.edu/talks/ezra-taft-benson_fourteen-fundamentals-following-prophet/. Benson quotes Brigham Young, *Report of the Semi-Annual Conference of the Church of Jesus Christ of Latter-day Saints*, October 1897 (Salt Lake City: Church of Jesus Christ of Latter-day Saints, semi-annual), 18–19.

One challenge with this expansive approach, however, lies in determining precisely which extra-canonical discourse ought properly to count as scripture. Given the textured history of LDS teaching and the desire for doctrinal consistency, the teachings most eligible are those which are highlighted and emphasized by contemporary leadership.

Other church leaders have emphasized a more restrictive approach that focuses more exclusively on the primal authority of the Standard Works. This approach is found in the influential writings of Joseph Fielding Smith and Bruce R. McConkie, and it was especially amplified by Harold B. Lee, who declared bluntly that if a teaching by a church leader in any way "contradicts what is in the scriptures, it is not true. This is the standard by which we measure all truth."[11] McConkie was equally declarative: "Even the writings, teachings, and opinions of the prophets of God are acceptable only to the extent they are in harmony with what God has revealed and what is recorded in the standard works." It follows for McConkie that when church leaders speak explicitly in the name of God, their teaching "will without any exception be found to be in harmony with the standard works."[12]

This lends itself to a more Protestantized concept of LDS scripture and canon, in which the canon itself is foundational in *determining* which contemporary discourse can rightly be considered scripture. The Westminster Confession, for example, states that the "supreme judge by which all controversies of religion are to be determined, and all decrees of councils, opinions of ancient writers, doctrines of men, and private spirits, are to be examined, and in whose sentence we are to rest, can be no other but the Holy Spirit speaking in the Scripture."[13] Though these two positions are not mutually exclusive, each has developed a lasting sensibility that resonates differently among Latter-day Saints.

V

Joseph Smith challenged not only biblical sufficiency but also infallibility. Because it was said to be the product of direct revelation, the Book of Mormon is understood to be more pristine than the Bible—so much

---

11. Harold B. Lee, "Using the Scriptures in Our Church Assignments," *Improvement Era*, January 1969, 13.

12. Bruce R. McConkie, *Mormon Doctrine*, 2d. ed. (Salt Lake City: Bookcraft, 1966), 111.

13. Bettenson and Maunder, *Documents of the Christian Church*, 306.

so that Joseph Smith deemed it "the most correct of any book on earth."[14] Though the Bible has in no way lost its status as authoritative scripture, its correctness is qualified to the extent that it was "translated correctly." The issue for Smith was not in the fallibility of the original authors, but with the transmission of the texts across the centuries.

Among Smith's many prophetic endeavors, he engaged in an intermittent and ultimately uncompleted project of producing a "new translation" of the Bible. Though the project resulted in nearly five hundred pages of text, it consisted primarily of minor revisions, corrections, and amplifications. Exceptions include the production of entirely new portions of Genesis and Matthew, each of which has contributed to the overall trajectory of Mormon thought.[15]

Noteworthy here is the freedom Smith felt in relation to the texts he encountered—both in the form of received scripture and his own prophetic productions. Though Smith referred to the Book of Mormon, the Book of Abraham, and his work on the Bible as "translations," they do not neatly fit the common use of the term. Kathleen Flake characterizes Smith's experience as "an interpretive response to the text" involving the agency required to "rewrite the prophets."[16]

Revisions to his own revelations also demonstrate some sense of freedom and adaptation—and in some cases contain theological significance. Examples can be seen in the development of the Doctrine and Covenants from his revelations dictated and copied into the Book of Commandments and Revelations. In these instances, Smith appeared more interested in preserving the meaning of the revelation rather than the language. He warned colleagues to "be careful not to alter the *sense* of any of them for he that adds or diminishes the prop[h]ecies must come under condemnation

---

14. Smith, *History of the Church*, 4:461.

15. See Thomas C. Wayment, ed., *The Complete Joseph Smith Translation of the Old Testament: A Side by Side Comparison with the King James Version* (Salt Lake City: Deseret Book, 2009); Robert J. Matthews, *Joseph Smith's Translation of the Bible: A History and Commentary* (Provo, UT: Brigham Young University Press, 1975); and Scott Faulting and Kent P. Jackson, *Joseph Smith's Translation of the Bible* (Provo, UT: Maxwell Institute for Religious Scholarship, 2011).

16. Kathleen Flake, "Translating Time: The Nature and Function of Joseph Smith Narrative Canon," *Journal of Religion* 87, no. 4 (October, 2007): 507–8. See also Heikki Raisanen, "Joseph Smith as Creative Interpreter of the Bible," *International Journal of Mormon Studies* 2 (Spring 2009): 1–22.

writen therein."[17] According to Grant Underwood, this approach allows these revelations to be both "fully human and fully divine." By preserving the "sense" of the revelation, there remains "ample room for regarding as inspired both the earliest wording of, as well as the revisions to the texts."[18] This approach exemplifies efforts among Latter-day Saint scholars to properly account for the data in formulating theologies of revelation and scriptural production.

Despite its rejection of inerrantism, Mormonism leans strongly toward literalist readings of its scripture, which continues to be presented as a perspicuous account of both history and doctrine. Latter-day Saints have thus been loath to accept efforts to demythologize or otherwise downplay the historicity of its sacred narratives.[19]

This volume is a collection of essays designed to explore various dimensions of Mormon scripture. Consistent with other volumes in this series, our aim is to advance the academic study of Mormon theology by promoting quality scholarship from a variety of disciplines and perspectives.

Brian D. Birch
Boyd J. Petersen
Blair G. Van Dyke

---

17. Joseph Smith, letter to William W. Phelps, July 31, 1832, in Dean C. Jessee, ed., *Personal Writings of Joseph Smith*, rev. ed. (Salt Lake City: Deseret Book, 2002), 273; emphasis added.

18. Grant Underwood, "Revelation, Text, and Revision: Insight From the Book of Commandments and Revelations," *Brigham Young University Studies* 48, no. 3 (2009): 80.

19. "Demythologization" is the term employed by Rudolf Bultmann to challenge theological accounts of the New Testament that rely on the historical accuracy of the texts. Central to Bultmann's account is the *kerygma*, or proclamation, of the gospel and its transformative power. See Bultmann, "New Testament and Mythology: The Problem of Demythologizing the New Testament Proclamation," in *New Testament Theology and Other Basic Writings*, ed. Shubert M. Ogden (Philadelphia: Fortress Press, 1984), 1–44. Contrasting LDS approaches can be found in Paul Y. Hoskisson, ed., *Historicity and the Latter-day Saint Scriptures* (Provo, UT: Religious Studies Center, 2001).

1

THE TRIANGLE AND THE SOVEREIGN: LOGICS, HISTORIES, AND AN OPEN CANON

David Frank Holland

In 1973 the American Broadcasting Company began airing a new series of three-minute animated segments called "Schoolhouse Rock." The program introduced a hip new pedagogy that used popular music and cartoon images to teach everything from the legislative process to the parts of speech.[1] One of the first episodes of what would be a remarkable twelve-year run was titled "Three Is a Magic Number," which conveyed to bed-headed kids across the country a rather unlikely but nonetheless groovy lesson in numerology:

> Somewhere in the ancient, mystic trinity
> You get three as a magic number
> The past and the present and the future
> Faith and hope and charity
> The heart and the brain and the body…
>
> It takes three legs to make a tripod or to make a table stand
> It takes three wheels to make a vehicle called a tricycle
> Every triangle has three corners
> Every triangle has three sides
> No more, no less
> You don't have to guess…

Only in the '70s. Yet, as the ditty suggests, the sense of triangulated certainty it asserts does seem to have a kind of timeless resonance.

Writing about the importance of ancient African faiths as a necessary buffer to the colliding cosmologies of Christianity and Islam in his native Nigeria, the scholar of religion Jacob K. Olupona invoked an old Yoruba

---

1. Monica Hesse, "When "Rock" schooled us," *Washington Post*, January 5, 2013, C01.

proverb: *Adiro meta ki yebe sina!*—the three-legged hearth does not fail![2] In his treatment of the ancient roots of American political culture, legal scholar John W. Welch has noted and defended the "tripodic" nature of the United States' governing tradition, pointing out that the three branches of the federal government (which themselves reflect the triangulated balance of the British Constitution) rest on three cultural legacies (Greek, Roman, and Hebrew) and that within each of these three is another series of "triadic" principles—for instance, the Greek citizen's commitment to rationality, individuality, and liberty. Similarly to Olupona's Yoruba adage, Welch has observed, "Only when all three legs of these three traditions upon which the American state stands remain equally strong and of the appropriate length does the tripod not topple over."[3] Whether such analysis reveals triadic realties in the classical sources, or the appeal of triangular structures in the minds of modern observers, the fact remains the same: in the search for clarity and stability amidst complexity, triangles have an unmistakable allure.

Welch may have been particularly attuned to this triadic promise as a devout Latter-day Saint. Indeed, Mormon doctrines and practices seem especially interested in triangular balance, from the three figures of the Godhead, to the three witnesses of the Book of Mormon, to the three classes of the Young Women's program. In ways superficial (the Latter-days Saints have bound the scriptures of the Restoration into a volume colloquially known as a "triple combination") and more substantive (epistolary statements from the First Presidency appear over three authorizing signatures) in the revelatory culture that swirls around Mormons, three can indeed be the magic number. The historian of American religion and former LDS bishop Spencer Fluhman has thoughtfully counseled his congregants to see their quest for God's truth as a "triangulated" process involving ancient scripture, living prophets, and personal inspiration.[4] Though his engagement with this idea is more historically conscious (and his articulation of it more precisely intentional than one would likely find in most meetinghouses across the time and territory of Mormonism),

---

2. Jacob K. Olupona, "Bonds, Boundaries, and Bondage of Faith: Religion at the Crossroads in Nigeria," *Harvard Divinity Bulletin* (Summer/Autumn 2013): 27.

3. John W. Welch, "Three Foundational Roots of American Law and Government," presented at the J. Reuben Clark Law Society Annual Conference in Washington DC, February 2013. Cited with permission.

4. Personal correspondence with the author.

Fluhman has, I contend, put his finger on one of the most essential and one of the most fraught realities of the Latter-day Saint experience.

Three Messengers of the Divine

Mormons speak freely and reverently of all three of Fluhman's revelatory media. The typical Latter-day Saint talk or testimony will invoke any combination of Spirit, scripture, and prophetic leadership without suggesting a necessary hierarchy of authority among them. A verse from the Pentateuch can be cited in exactly the same sense as a statement from the most recent General Conference, and both share the epistemological spotlight with the speaker's own spiritual experiences. The notion that these organs of divine truth may conflict with each other—through anything more substantive than, say, a mistranslation of scripture—does not form a common aspect of the Latter-day Saints' devotional discourse (A of F 8). As one of their "Articles of Faith," Mormons declare their belief in "all that God has revealed, all that He does now reveal, and we believe that He will yet reveal many great and important things pertaining to the Kingdom of God" (A of F 9). This phrasing of inclusive revelatory faith is read by Latter-day Saint adults and memorized by their children. Tellingly, in the Mormon religious curriculum for children, in which music plays a very prominent role, LDS youth sing anthems imploring them to follow the living prophets, to listen to their personal promptings, and to search the scriptures. As suggested by these songs, Latter-day Saints do not grow up thinking about how to adjudicate potential tensions among these messengers of the divine; indeed, the possibility of tension is effectively avoided. Each confirms the others. God simply speaks through all three.[5]

Adults occasionally get a more clearly delineated message. While rhetoric from the central leadership of the Church largely mirrors the members' tendency to avoid discussion of revelatory conflict among these sources (and thus typically skirts questions about a hierarchical ordering of revelatory media), there is and has been an unmistakable strain of official discourse that calls on members to trust "the Brethren" as a standard by which to test other revelations. Typically this is proffered in a rather carefully nuanced form. For example, Spencer W. Kimball, a venerated leader of the Church in the mid-twentieth century, taught that one's per-

---

5. See, for instance, Duane E. Hiatt, "Follow the Prophet"; Merrill Bradshaw, "The Still Small Voice"; Jaclyn Thomas Milne, "Search, Ponder and Pray," in *Children's Songbook* (Salt Lake City: LDS, 1989), 110, 106, 109.

sonal revelations—if true and valid—would always be in alignment with the "whole program" of what the Church was teaching; Kimball saw the belief that one had received revelations that were superior to those enjoyed by the leadership of the church as evidence that one was in the final stages of apostasy.[6] The current Latter-day Saint apostle Dallin H. Oaks has quoted and reinforced elements of Kimball's position.[7] At times, however, the revelatory authority of the church president has been declared with somewhat less nuance. As recently as 2010 two ecclesiastical authorities stood in relatively close sequence in a General Conference of the Church and delivered messages about the primacy of the Church president, stating: "The living prophet is more vital to us than the standard works. . . . The living prophet is more important to us than a dead prophet. . . . The prophet tells us what we need to know." This was hardly an anomalous declaration: they were both quoting a frequently cited address from thirty years earlier, which took for *its* authority a prophetic discourse of eight decades before that, which took as *its* source an impromptu speech delivered in the "early days" of the church.[8] The sentiment persists.

But it is not the only position on the matter. In his memoirs, Hugh B. Brown—a member of the First Presidency of the Church from 1963 to 1970—expressed his awareness of "certain statements that whatever the brethren say becomes the word of God," but, Brown warned, "this is a dangerous practice to apply to all leaders and all cases." Brown insisted that although members are "bound to sustain and support the brethren in the positions they occupy so long as their conduct entitles them to that . . . we also have only to defend those doctrines of the church contained in the four standard works. . . . Anything beyond that by anyone is his or her

---

6. Spencer W. Kimball, *The Teachings of Spencer W. Kimball*, ed. Edward L. Kimball (Salt Lake City: Bookcraft, 1982), 458.

7. Dallin H. Oaks, *In the Lord's Way* (Salt Lake City: Deseret Book Company, 1991), 69–71.

8. Claudio R. M. Costa, "Obedience to the Prophets," *Ensign*, November 2010, 11–13; Kevin R. Duncan, "Our Very Survival," *Ensign*, November 2010, 34–36; Ezra Taft Benson, "Fourteen Fundamentals in Following the Prophet," BYU Speeches, February 26, 1980, https://speeches.byu.edu/talks/ezra-taft-benson_fourteen-fundamentals-following-prophet/; Wilford Woodruff, *Report of the Semi Annual Conference of the Church of Jesus Christ of Latter day Saints*, October 1897 (Salt Lake City: Church of Jesus Christ of Latter day Saints, semi annual), 18–19 (hereafter cited as *Conference Report*).

own opinion and not scripture."⁹ If Brown's position might be qualified by the fact that he was notably liberal in a rather reactionary era, it should be recognized that one of his most conspicuously conservative apostolic contemporaries—Joseph Fielding Smith—said essentially the same thing. Both Smith and Brown indicated that the canonized scripture was a test of prophetic teachings.¹⁰

In turn, that canonized scripture teaches that personal experiences with the Holy Ghost will confirm the truthfulness of the holy writ, a principle that dominates familiar Mormon testimonies of faith (Moro. 10:3–5). According to LDS Church leaders from Brigham Young to Hugh B. Brown, the Spirit is also an arbiter of the truthfulness of statements by living prophets. "Let every man and woman know, by the whisperings of the Spirit of God to themselves, whether their leaders are walking in the path the Lord dictates or not," Young advised.¹¹ Brown put a sharp edge on his statement about the relationship of personal revelation to prophetic declaration: "No one should accept a statement and base his or her testimony upon it, no matter who makes it, until he or she has, under mature examination, found it to be true and worthwhile; then one's logical deductions may be confirmed by the spirit of revelation to his or her spirit, because real conversion must come from within."¹² His statement about spiritual verification is unusual for its precision but hardly unique in its sentiment. In the mid-twentieth century, another member of the First Presidency, J. Reuben Clark, notably insisted that the witness of the Holy Ghost in the body of the Saints must verify whether a particular statement from the prophet actually constitutes the will of the Lord or not.¹³ More boldly even than Young, Brown, and Clark, in 1891 the LDS apostle George Q. Cannon declared, "It is indeed our right and privilege to have the companionship of the Holy Spirit of the Lord, and we need it. Even children may have it if they will, and need not be left to walk alone on earth. Every woman should win and keep it for herself, and never try to walk by another's light.

---

9. Hugh B. Brown, *An Abundant Life: The Memoirs of Hugh B. Brown*, ed. Edwin P. Firmage (Salt Lake City: Signature Books, 1999), 123–25.

10. Joseph Fielding Smith, *Doctrines of Salvation*, comp. Bruce R. McConkie, 3 vols. (Salt Lake City: Bookcraft, 1954–56), 3:203–204.

11. W. D. Davies, "Reflections on the Mormon 'Canon,'" *Harvard Theological Review* (January–July 1986): 52.

12. Brown, *Abundant Life*, 140.

13. J. Reuben Clark, *Selected Papers: On Religion, Education and Youth*, ed. David H. Yarn Jr. (Provo, UT: Brigham Young University Press, 1984), 102.

If she puts her whole trust in another, even if he be her husband and a good man, he will surely some time fail her. Let her learn to stand alone so far as human aid is concerned, depending only on God and the Holy Ghost." In some tension with other Church leaders who have excused the Church president from this sort of spiritual scrutiny, Cannon added, "Do not, brethren, put your trust in man though he be a Bishop, an Apostle, or a President; if you do, they will fail you at some time or place."[14]

Thus all three media of Mormon revelation have had their advocates—Church leaders who have insisted on the power of Spirit, the scriptures, or themselves to check and legitimate their revelatory counterparts. One need not spend much time in Mormon sources before realizing the elusiveness of any one revelatory source as the definitively supreme referent. There is some strain, however, between this triadic arrangement in which each medium of revelation seems to claim a validating authority over the others and the sentiment, long trumpeted in Latter-day Saint discourse, about a "church of order." That phrase is almost always invoked in reference to the authority of *living church leaders*. A sermon by the nineteenth-century apostle Orson Pratt may be representative in this regard. "The Church of Jesus Christ is a Church of order," Pratt declared, "in which it is necessary that some persons have authority to teach and counsel and preside." But then Pratt went on in the rest of the sermon to call on all the Saints to seek their own revelations, going so far as to place the apostles in the same category as the laity, insisting that most women and men—including himself and many of his brethren—were living below their full revelatory privileges.[15] In Pratt's sermon the order of an authoritative structure existed but was ultimately overshadowed by the promise of a universally revelatory theology. Clearly, however, that relationship can be reversed. Both within the Church and among critics from without, statements about the sovereign authority of the living prophets have received much play. In 1978 the president of the LDS women's auxiliary, Elaine S. Cannon, stated the following: "Personal opinions may vary. Eternal principles never do. When the Prophet speaks, sisters, the debate is over."[16] Her phrase was approvingly picked up in an address by a member of

---

14. George Q. Cannon, "Knowledge of and Dependence on God," *The Latter-day Saints' Millennial Star*, October 26, 1891, 673–74.

15. Orson Pratt, May 11, 1878, *Journal of Discourses*, 26 vols. (London and Liverpool: LDS Booksellers Depot, 1854–86), 25:144–48.

16. Elaine Cannon, "If We Want To Go Up, We Have To Get On," *Ensign*, November 1978, 108.

the First Presidency a year later and has appeared in at least one church manual and any number of debates about church governance since. Such statements have lent themselves to the sense—among internal participants and external observers—that in the Mormons' triangle of revelation, not all sources are equal.[17]

To the extent that Latter-day Saints embrace a tripartite manifestation of divine authority and simultaneously demonstrate an impulse to see one of these as the supreme revelatory referent, they reflect a longstanding historical pattern of thought that extends well beyond the story of Mormonism. In conflicting impulses that simultaneously seek to diversify ways of knowing while—for the sake of order—identifying an ultimate arbiter, Latter-day Saints have had much company.

The Insistent Demands of Sovereignty

An appeal to three interrelated ways of knowing has had a recurring resonance in the Anglo-American culture in which the Latter-day Saint movement took root. Three was the magic number a long time before the cartoon characters of "Schoolhouse Rock" declared it so. In the era of the American Revolution, for instance, the founding figure Benjamin Rush advocated for the model made by the Scottish School of Common Sense for a triangular epistemological "marriage" of the physical senses, human reason, and credible testimony.[18] The matter of *religious* epistemology—the question of how one ascertains *divine* truth—appears similarly shaped by this tripodic appeal. The man considered by many to be the primary theological architect of Anglicanism, the sixteenth-century churchman Richard Hooker, has been recognized for resisting both Catholic reliance on Rome and a rigid Puritan dependence on scripture; he ostensibly did so by emphasizing a "tripartite" reverence for the Bible, human reason,

---

17. N. Eldon Tanner, "The Debate Is Over," *Ensign*, September, 1979, 2; *Aaronic Priesthood Manual 1* (Salt Lake City: Church of Jesus Christ of Latter-day Saints, 2002). The manual was accessed through www.lds.org. I am indebted to the website "Mormon Coffee," http://blog.mrm.org, for originally alerting me to these references. Interestingly, they are quoted much more frequently by sources antagonistic to the Church than they are within the Church. The perception of prophetic sovereignty has been a matter of profound interest on both sides of that divide.

18. Leigh Eric Schmidt, *Hearing Things: Religion, Illusion and the American Enlightenment* (Cambridge: Harvard University Press, 2000), 167.

and the historical practice of the church.[19] In a survey text on American Christianity, for instance, Hooker is cited for his "threefold model of scripture, tradition, and reason."[20] The Latter-day Saints' revelatory bases of ancient text, living prophets, and personal inspiration thus hardly constitute the first triangulated search for the divine.

However, as the voluminous research on Richard Hooker has shown, the magic of three can prove somewhat illusory, fading beneath the glare of close scrutiny. Recent scholarship has indicated that careful attention to Hooker's famed Anglican *via media* reveals him to have actually given ancient scripture "authoritative primacy" and, thus, that he was more like the Reformed biblicists than he may superficially appear. For Hooker, as for his Reformed contemporaries, not all sources of divine truth were created equal. Scripture still sat atop the hierarchy of religious knowledge; one leg of the tripod carried the preponderance of the epistemological weight for things relating to salvation. That believers have tried to attribute a "three-legged stool" to Hooker—but that his writings do not in fact fully support such a construction—demonstrates the theoretical appeal and the actual elusiveness of true triangular balance.[21]

Triangles are not, of course, the only geometry of faith. In 1964 the Methodist scholar Albert C. Outler perceived in John Wesley's theological method an addition to Hooker's triad—the evangelical element of "experience"—creating what came to be called the "Wesleyan quadrilateral," in which four sources (scripture, tradition, reason, and experience) determined doctrine. Eventually, however, Outler himself feared that such a formulation ran the risk of misrepresenting Wesley's actual approach. These were not *equal* sources of authority in Wesley's mind, Outler corrected; in the end, and always, scripture was "pre-eminent." The evolution of the Methodists' views of the Wesleyan quadrilateral over the last half century suggest just how attractive the promise of multilateral approaches to divine

---

19. Michael Brydon, *The Evolving Reputation of Richard Hooker: An Examination of Responses, 1600–1714* (Oxford: Oxford University Press, 2006), 1–6.

20. Christopher H. Evans, *Histories of American Christianity: An Introduction* (Waco, TX: Baylor University Press, 2013), 30.

21. Brydon, *Evolving Reputation*, 5–6; Ian S. Markham, J. Barney Hawkins IV, Justin Terry, Leslie Nunez Steffensen, eds., *Wiley-Blackwell Companion to the Anglican Communion* (Oxford: Wiley-Blackwell, 2013), 557; John N. Wall, *A Dictionary for Episcopalians* (Lanham, MD: Rowman Littlefield, 2007), 127.

truth can be and how difficult it is to find such an approach that does not, upon close inspection, actually privilege one source above the others.[22]

Nonetheless, the appeal continues. In process of writing this chapter, I serendipitously opened up a mailer from the Dharma Realm Buddhist University in Ukiah, California, that described its pedagogical ethos in the following terms: "The text, teacher, and student form a triangular relationship of inquiry where authority rests with not one exclusively but through all in concert." Perhaps the DRBU pulls this off harmoniously, but if they do so they are bucking some pretty powerful historical trends. A strategy in which three authorities carry equal weight is attractive in the abstract but challenging to find or sustain in practice. Triangulation, in this sense, may appear to be a source of stability, but the fact is that it can be quite volatile as the various sources vie for primacy. Like the Roman triumvirate depicted in Shakespeare's *Antony and Cleopatra*, the rule of three may raise as many questions as it answers. The history of the traditional Christian doctrine of the Trinity demonstrates both the mythic appeal of triunity and the vulnerabilities of such a formulation; the endless recurrence of Arian, Socinian, and various Unitarian heresies evidences the ways in which a certain logic both underwrites and undermines the appeal of three. There is both something appealing and repulsive about the triad. *Someone*, the anti-Trinitarian heretics endlessly insist, must have come first. *Somebody*, they reason, must be in charge. There must be a true sovereign.

The tension between the appeal of multiplicity and the demands of sovereignty appears beyond the religious realm. In the political culture of the Founding era, for instance, a phrase, partially in Latin, frequently recurred in the writings of political theorists: *imperium in imperio* is a solecism in politics, they kept saying.[23] This phrase and its various permutations were intended to convey the idea that the notion of multiple sovereign powers, multiple ultimate authorities, coexisting in the same community was grotesque if not simply impossible: a contradiction in terms, an effort to divide

---

22. Albert C. Outler, ed, *John Wesley* (New York: Oxford University Press, 1964); Albert C. Outler, "The Wesleyan Quadrilateral—in John Wesley," Thomas A. Langford, "The United Methodist Quadrilateral: A Theological Task," and Ted A. Campbell, "The 'Wesleyan Quadrilateral': The Story of a Modern Methodist Myth," all in Thomas A. Langford, ed., *Doctrine and Theology in the United Methodist Church* (Nashville: Kingswood, 1991), 75–88, 154–61, 232–44.

23. The historian Bernard Bailyn has called this "one of the most commonplace phrases of eighteenth-century political theory." See Bailyn, *Ideological Origins of the American Revolution* (Cambridge: Harvard University Press, 1967), 206.

the indivisible. In place of "solecism" they sometimes used the term "monster," suggesting that an *imperium in imperio* violated the laws of nature, something like a beast with two heads that could not long live.[24] It was against this longstanding axiom of their political culture that Federalists had to defend a constitution that seemed to invest multiple levels of government with some supreme decision-making powers. The historian Jack Rakove has written of this maxim that in the orthodoxies of early American political philosophy, "two sovereign authorities could not coexist within one polity; one or the other had to be supreme; and because power itself was dynamic, the loser in the competition must expect its authority to continue to atrophy." This truism, Rakove wrote, "was so commonplace that it needed no further attribution" than simply to state it.[25]

This idea that—like matter flowing into a vacuum—power irresistibly seeks one supreme instrument has a certain compelling rationale to it. The Federalists conceptually got around this by investing sovereignty in the body of citizens known somewhat fictively as "the People," who could then apportion out their decision-making powers to national, state, or local authorities as they wished. Thus, despite appearances, the Founders did not really divide sovereignty, they merely relocated it such that its decision-making power could both retain its necessary unity and be variously delegated. This, James Wilson argued, was the only conceptual foundation on which the federal Constitution could be comprehended.[26] Like Richard Hooker and John Wesley, the American Founders have been recognized for enshrining divided and balanced authorities when all the while they did not really disturb the basic logic of an indivisible sovereignty. Sovereign power still had one source.

The general ethos of the Protestant Reformation underscores this point. For all Protestantism did to decentralize religious authority in the western world, its logic and rhetoric actually also did much to reinforce this principle of sovereignty's indivisibility. Churches divided, but

---

24. See, for instance, Alexander Hamilton in *Federalist #15*: "They seem still to aim at things repugnant and irreconcilable; at an augmentation of federal authority, without a diminution of State authority; at sovereignty in the Union, and complete independence in the members. They still, in fine, seem to cherish with blind devotion the political monster of an *imperium in imperio*." *The Federalist* (New York: Modern American Library, 2000), 88.

25. Jack N. Rakove, *Original Meanings: Politics and Ideas in the Making of the Constitution* (New York: Knopf, 1996), 182.

26. Rakove, 190.

Scripture rose to fill the hegemon's seat. As with the appeal to the People in the Constitution's federal solution or as with the Revolution's imperially divisive cry of "No king but Jesus," the logic of the Reformation split institutions but did not actually split sovereignty; rather, as in the other cases, it pushed sovereignty back and more thoroughly concentrated it in its purest, safest source. What the People's constitution was to the Founders' republic, the Lord's scriptures were to the Reformers' church. The same rhetorical process that had so remarkably elevated the "Bible alone" as the sovereign religious authority—not only for Calvinists, but for the likes of Richard Hooker and John Wesley as well—highlighted the basic notion that whatever was supreme must be "alone." To declare *sola Scriptura* was to promote the logic of *sola* as well as the sanctity of *Scriptura*.

Any number of Protestant thinkers have taken pains to argue that cries of the "Bible alone" do not actually mean there are no other authorities to which a Christian could appeal; they mean, instead, that the Bible is the final say, the ultimate determinant, not really alone but above. Consider the language of the widely respected evangelical theologian Donald G. Bloesch: "The Bible alone, not the church, is the supreme norm of faith, and yet this norm is not effective apart from the church. The Bible is the sovereign authority, the church the subordinate authority."[27] In citing Bloesch, the evangelical scholar Kevin Vanhoozer—professor of systematic theology at the Trinity Evangelical Divinity School—has compared church tradition to "*many* witnesses. . . . The task of theology is to cross-examine the witnesses in order to offer proximate judgments under the ultimate authority of the presiding judge: the Spirit speaking in the Scriptures."[28] Here again we see the tension: the appeal of multiple sources, a commitment to one final arbiter. But perhaps even more striking is the assumption in such statements of the *either/or* relationship of church and scripture in that competition for theological sovereignty. Bloesch's and Vanhoozer's late twentieth-century logic resembled the thinking that drove famed sixteenth-century Protestant apologist William Whitaker: "[I]s the voice of the church," Whitaker asked, "indeed the rule of faith? Does scripture follow the voice of the church, or the contrary?" He pressed in on his opponent with this insistence that one or the other must be true. Answering his own question, he stated,

---

27. Donald G. Bloesch, *Holy Scripture: Revelation, Inspiration and Interpretation* (Downers Grove: InterVarsity Press, 1994), 156.

28. Kevin J. Vanhoozer, *The Drama of Doctrine: A Canonical-Linguistic Approach to Christian Theology* (Louisville: Westminster John Knox Press, 2005), 234.

> [S]ince it is canonical scripture, therefore the church can do no otherwise than declare it to be scripture. Thus the church is not the rule, but a thing directed by the rule. The scripture itself is the rule of faith. . . . [T]he church ought to be governed by scripture.[29]

The logic of sovereignty has had a long Protestant history.

In some of this Reformation rhetoric this question of pre-eminence in authority in part came down to the matter of which entity verified the other. In other words, do Christians receive a book of scripture because the church sanctions it, or do they receive a church because the scriptures sanction it? The implication of such discussions seemed to be that whichever provided the original rule of judgment necessarily carried the superior power; that is, by bringing its counterpart into existence as an authority within the faith, the verifying entity retained the powers of creator over creature.[30] This is not unlike the constitutional argument of whether the states provided the original sanction for the federal government. With different emphasis but similar logic, William Chillingworth's *The Religion of Protestants a Safe Way to Salvation*, wherein he established the Protestants' *imperium* with the memorable phrase "the Bible only, is the Religion of Protestants," likewise emphasized the hierarchical relationship between the proof and the thing proved; he insisted that because Catholics defended the truthfulness of their church by appeals to scripture, then even they had inadvertently but unavoidably placed scripture in the position of greater trust. By so doing, Chillingworth told his Catholic readers, you "tacitly confess, that yourselves are surer of the truth of the Scripture than of your church's authority. For we must be surer of the proof than of the thing proved, otherwise it is no proof."[31] The upshot of all this Protestant discourse and reasoning is that either church or scripture must be the singular rule of faith. Their bet, obviously, was on the latter.

Key components of this logic persisted in the New World, where the ideal of *sola Scriptura* seemed more practically attainable. Elisha Williams, a one-time rector of Yale College and an early critic of creedalism, wrote of the creeds in his eighteenth-century argument for the rights of private judgment and stated that if a person "is to be governed and determined

---

29. William Whitaker, *A Disputation on Holy Scripture against the Papists* (Cambridge: Cambridge University Press, 1968), 350–58.

30. See, for instance, the extended passage of Thomas Forrester, *A Review and Consideration of Two Late Pamphlets* (Edinburgh: N.p., 1706), 80–81.

31. William Chillingworth, *The Works of W. Chillingworth* (London: B. Blake, 1836), 465–66.

by the Opinions and Determinations of any other, the Scriptures cease to be a Rule to him, and those Opinions or Determinations of others are substituted in the Room thereof." Williams offered a stark logic: if one accepts the authority of a creed, the scriptures can no longer be seen as the Rule by which truths are determined. In such renderings, scripture is the Christian's rightful *imperium*, and the claim of "any other" authority to direct the opinion or faith of the individual believer threatened the essence of scripture's supreme status.[32] Now the very creeds that had posited the supremacy of scripture faced pressure from their own arguments. The ideal alone exerted steady pressure. By the end of the eighteenth century, Americans were particularly determined to make the ideal real.[33] Though Luther's call for *sola Scriptura* must be understood in the context of its time, in which scripture was hardly the only resource to which sixteenth-century reformers appealed, the zero-sum logic of the phrase seemed to churn toward the singularity of sovereignty in the early United States. Such a claim for the sovereignty of scripture was closely related to another claim: that the scriptures verified themselves. If they are to be alone in power, their proofs must be internal, otherwise the external verifier would necessarily become a rival for the sovereign's seat. In the late eighteenth century, the American preacher Benjamin Bennet observed that the argument that Scripture carries "its own proof" could be traced back to the earliest figures of the Reformation and was an assertion on which they laid "so great weight."[34]

This is precisely, however, where some Catholics cried foul. Perhaps their counterargument became clearest in the writings of an American Catholic convert critiquing the very sort of biblical evangelicalism that a figure like Williams represented. As a marker of the depth to which this thinking was rooted, consider Orestes Brownson's argument about the natural tendency of Protestantism to descend into atomized individualism, a point he made most directly in his essay "Protestantism Ends in Transcendentalism." Here, adopting what he saw as Chillingworth's logic that the thing "proposed" can never be of a higher order than the thing

---

32. Elisha Williams, *The Essential Rights and Liberties of Protestants* (Boston: S. Kneeland and T. Green, 1744), 9.

33. Mark A. Noll, *America's God: From Jonathan Edwards to Abraham Lincoln* (New York: Oxford, 2002), 373.

34. Benjamin Bennet, *Discourse on the Credibility of the Scriptures* (New Brunswick: Abraham Blauvelt, 1795), 173–74. See also Forrester, *A Review and Consideration*, 80–81.

"which proposes," Brownson turns that logic back on Protestantism, with its famed emphasis on the rights of private judgment.

> If we take the Bible to be the word of God on the authority of private judgment, and its sense on the same authority, as Protestants do and must, then we assume private judgment to be competent to decide of itself what is and what is not the word of God, what God has revealed and what he has not revealed, has commanded and has not commanded, and therefore competent to decide what we are to believe and what we are not to believe, and what we are to do and what we are not to do. But this is to assume the whole for private judgment, and therefore to assume its unrestricted right.[35]

In other words, if private judgment is the adjudicator and in that sense the creator of scripture—howsoever much it may verify the authority of the scriptures—in the process of assuming the role of legitimator, it checks the authority of the thing legitimated. Thus, one of the challenges in establishing biblical sovereignty is the problem of verification: if the Bible is the sovereign measure of truth, how do we know the Bible is true and how do we know its meaning? If something else verifies the truth and meaning of the Bible—be it the Church or individual reason or the Holy Spirit—does not the church or the individual's reason or the Spirit thus become the true rule by which the divine revelation is measured? As Chillingworth might have said it: Can the authority of a sovereign securely rely on an inferior proof?

Verifier and Verified

This suggestion that the verifier retains power over the verified can be tested in a particularly illustrative way in the history of American revelatory movements. Take, for instance, the curious case of a piece of Shaker scripture, Philemon Stewart's 1843 *A Holy, Sacred and Divine Roll and Book; From the Lord God of Heaven, to the Inhabitants of Earth*. Stewart's work offered a transcript of a divine revelation that had been recited to him by ministering angels. At a time of intense millenarian excitement throughout the United States, the *Sacred Roll* clarified the Shakers' distinctive views on the millennium. The history of the *Roll's* rapid ascent and descent within the United Society of Believers in Christ's Second Appearing underscores this point about the primacy of creator over creature. Stewart's book of revelations was received some seven decades after

---

35. Orestes Brownson, *The Works of Orestes A. Brownson*, ed. Henry F. Brownson, 20 vols. (Detroit: Thorndike Nourse, 1882–87), 6:125–26.

the establishment of the United Society in North America. Indeed, it appeared at a time of particular strength, prominence, and vitality for the society. The *Sacred Roll* quickly received the endorsement of the Shaker leadership, which set to work publishing and distributing copies of it. In an important sense, the church created this scripture; that is, the church's approval gave it its scriptural status. As Stewart learned, however, what the church gives it can also take away. As Stewart's personal behavior caused a rift between him and the leadership of the United Society, his *Sacred Roll* eventually fell from grace and ceased to function canonically within the movement. The church thus preceded the scripture, functioned as the verifier of its divine status, and thereby retained the power of creator over the creature. The conclusion is inescapable: the Society was the sovereign.[36]

If we once again move outside the strictly religious realm and look instead at the political history of the United States, we find a complementary dynamic. Indeed, it was precisely on this same reasoning that the concept of constitutional ratification rested. Founders, by their very nature, pose a problem for republics. A republic, we are often told, must be a government of laws and not of men. The problem is that men and women make the laws, and the creators will always bear a potentially dangerous relationship to the creature. It is difficult to maintain an ideal of equality before the law when some of those who are supposed to be its subjects are also its source. Constitutionalism is intended to be a way out of this predicament. By enshrining a "fundamental law" that was not created by the standing branches of government, those that manage the day-to-day affairs of state cannot claim the rights of creation over a constitution to which they too are purely subject. This, then, in theory becomes a government of law and not of men and women. The problem, however, is that someone, somewhere had to create that fundamental law. Constitutionalism helps by setting the problem of creation at further remove, but it can never fully eliminate it. One could attribute the ultimate source of the fundamental law to God or the People, but someone, somewhere had to channel those supreme authorities. Eventually, we have to deal with the founders. Sparta's Lycurgus legendarily got around this problem by establishing the supreme law and then never returning to the polis: "[T]he end of life would be a consummation of his happiness, while for his fellow citizens it would be a guardian of the blessings he had secured for them during his lifetime, since they had sworn to use

---

36. Stephen J. Stein, "Inspiration, Revelation, and Scripture: The Story of a Shaker Bible," *Proceedings of the American Antiquarian Society* 105 (October 1995): 347–76.

his constitution until he returned."[37] Similarly the procedure of ratification addressed this problem by calling into session special ratifying conventions that would dissolve once the work of ratification was done. That is, after bringing the fundamental law into existence, they then ceased to exist, leaving the constitution in its unrivaled place, with no extant creator above it, only subjects below it. The verifier of the verified disappears, placing its creation all alone in the sovereign's place.

Imagine then, for a moment, a counterfactual. What if the ratifying conventions remained perpetually in session? What if Lycurgus never left? Would it change the way we view the Constitution, if its creator remained prominently present, continually capable of acting again at will? Evidence suggests that it likely would.[38] And perhaps in just such a conception lies a source for the sense among Protestants that the mere existence of an ecclesiastical entity that can claim creative status over the scriptures necessarily challenges the sovereignty of those texts. Many have experienced those stereotypical LDS-evangelical discussions in which Mormonism is accused of having insufficient reverence for the Bible, some of which has to do with specific exegetical disagreement, but some of which lies in the fact that where evangelical Protestantism believes the primitive apostolic church compiled a canon and then disbanded—leaving the Bible exercising an unrivaled constitutional role for Christendom—claims like those of the Latter-day Saints seem to reconvene the ratifying convention and keep it unendingly in session. If the verifier persists, the scriptures cannot truly be sovereign. In such logic, Congress and Constitution could not both be sovereign any more than a living prophet and canonical scripture. Whichever entity finds itself in a subordinate position must see its authority atrophy—exactly what evangelicals claim happens to scripture in denominations that place too much emphasis on the authority of a magisterium. They have been known to accuse Catholics of such a thing, though the Catholic Church denies the charge. As Charles Cardinal Journet has written, "As long as they [the Apostles] were living, the Church was, through them, 'in the act of revealing' and above the 'revealed' Sacred Scripture. But at the

---

37. Plutarch, *Lives That Made Greek History*, ed. James S. Romm, trans. Pamela Mensch (Indianapolis: Hackett, 2012), 25.

38. Donald Lutz has suggested that constitutions which are too easily amendable lose the veneration of the people. See Lutz, "Toward a Theory of Constitutional Amendment," in *Responding to Imperfection: The Theory and Practice of Constitutional Amendment*, ed. Sanford Levinson (Princeton: Princeton University Press, 1995), 237–74.

death of the Apostles, the Church lost this privilege: she ceased to be above Scripture."[39] What, then, of a church in which apostles continue to live?

In both the history of the American republic as well as in the history of Protestant Christianity, one can perceive a running tension. In each narrative, a general fear and suspicion of concentrated power became a telltale feature of the culture. Hence, an impulse to divide authority. However, that instinct repeatedly collided with the immovable logic of sovereignty's indivisibility. To accommodate these paradoxical presences within their respective mental worlds, the American founders multiplied the levels of subordinated government while reifying the sovereignty of a sacralized constitution (or, the People, to the extent that the Constitution was amendable), just as Protestant reformers decentralized the locus of ecclesiastical authority while reifying the supremacy of inerrant scripture (which they saw as unamendable). In each case there is both the urge to divide and a logic of unity. This history of the ideational forces that informed early American culture may help us make sense of a Latter-day Saint movement that posits three sources of revelatory authority and yet has continually reflected a tendency to put one of these sources above the others. In their insistence on the triad and their impulse toward a final arbiter, Mormons share much with their contemporaries. But their ongoing struggles with this tension also suggests something distinctive about the Latter-day Saint experience.

The Mormon Question of Verification

In Latter-day Saint culture, which principle prevails? Triangulation or sovereignty? And if sovereignty, then what fills the role of the sovereign? To get at these questions, let us return one more time to the question of the verifier. In Mormon discourse, perhaps the most frequently cited verifier of divine truth is the personal enlightenment of the Spirit. When pushed on this or that question of faith, Mormons have become quite renowned for falling back on their own individual experiences as the ultimate defense of their beliefs: "I know the Church is true because the Spirit has testified to my soul"—a familiar refrain in LDS discourse. The foundation for that logic rests on certain passages in the New Testament and Book of Mormon. The language of the Book of Mormon is particularly expansive in this regard: "And by the power of the Holy Ghost ye may know the

---

39. Charles Journet, *The Theology of the Church* (San Francisco: Ignatius Press, 2004), 120.

truth of all things" (Moro. 10:5). Perhaps the most common sequence of faith that Latter-day Saints describe reads as follows: The Spirit testifies of the truthfulness of the Book of Mormon, and once one knows that the Book of Mormon is true, every other aspect of the Latter-day Saint faith—including the authority of the living prophets—falls into place. As this same sequential formulation is repeated again and again at pulpits and in classrooms around the Church, it places personal inspiration in the position of the ultimate verifier, the original arbiter. All epistemological certainty leads back to the sense of individual conviction that Latter-day Saints traditionally call personal revelation. If the Book of Mormon and thus the modern-day prophets derive their status from the private inspirations of individual members—if they are sustained as prophetic because millions of Mormons *feel* them to be so—they would, of necessity, remain dependent for their authority on the direct spiritual experiences of the laity. As William Chillingworth said, "For we must be surer of the proof than of the thing proved, otherwise it is no proof." That relationship of verified to verifier indicates that if there were a conflict between one's direct inspirations and something declared either in scripture or by living prophets, one could not override the revelations that come immediately to the souls of church members without undermining the very source of the authority on which the other two rest. Among Latter-day Saints, personal revelation to the membership clearly enjoys the logical prerogatives of the verifier.

Note, though, that the Latter-day Saints' appeal to the Spirit often rests on the authority of the scriptures. They seek the witness of the Holy Ghost about whether the Book of Mormon is divine in part because the Book of Mormon has instructed them to do just that. In their famously energetic proselytizing efforts, Latter-day Saints may appeal to the Bible rather than the Book of Mormon: James 1:5 is often seen as the ur text of the Mormon Restoration, and Latter-day Saints often read that verse as an endorsement of personal inspiration. When proselytizing a Christian and telling her to trust the Spirit as her guide, an LDS missionary will often use the Bible to build her case. Even a cynical interpretation, which holds that the Church has appealed to the Bible so frequently merely for the sake of its effort to gain recognition as a Christian faith, simply demonstrates the fact that a proselytizing religion has to appeal to a common authority. It is thereby subject to the same sort of logic to which William Chillingworth held Rome. Consider again the language of Hugh B. Brown's pitch for the sovereignty of the Standard Works: Latter-day Saints are obligated "only to defend those doctrines of the church contained in the four standard works." The idea of defense implies a necessary engagement with an external audience. A revelatory church without grand aspirations of growth may not have the same need to reify the authority of shared scripture; Latter-day Saints have no such option. An evangelistic movement must, at least at times, cite the scriptures as the ultimate verifier, even if it is only to establish the authority of Spirit. But if scripture is necessary to prove the propriety of personal revelation, or the truthfulness of the living prophets, scripture can ascend to the sovereign's throne.

Scripture and Spirit each have a powerful logic on their side in claiming their place as the ultimate verifiers of truth among Latter-day Saints. Either of the two following stories would be familiar in a LDS expression of faith: one, the Spirit told me the Book of Mormon was true, the Book of Mormon confirmed the divine calling of the prophet, the prophet told me to seek the Spirit; two, the Scriptures told me to trust the Spirit, the Spirit confirmed the divine call of the prophets, the Prophets told me to read the Scriptures. In these reinforcing circuits of logic it appears that either Spirit or scripture can serve as the originating and, thus, dominant divine referent in the search for truth. What is rarely heard among Latter-day Saints, however, is a sequence that starts with living prophets. Something else, something beyond the prophets themselves, typically proves their legitimacy first. Enjoying neither the direct subjective power of the personal spiritual experience nor the historical and communal heft of canonized scripture, living prophets may have the most tenuous logical claim on the prerogatives of the ultimate verifier. Why, then, does so much Mormon rhetoric seem to afford the ecclesiarchy a kind of revelatory primacy? Perhaps the question suggests the answer. Maybe in order to maintain the prophets' comparable status with one's personal inspirations and the canonical scriptures, the Church community intuitively emphasizes their position. Perhaps the very rhetoric that appears to elongate one leg of the tripod to disproportionate lengths actually seeks to extend it to an equal level. Ironically, it may be the demands of triangular balance that generate such strong rhetoric in favor of the living prophets' ultimate authority.

Somewhat contradictorily, this emphasis on prophetic power is likely also a reflection of organizational realities. While the Spirit and the scriptures may have powerful logics on their side in the contest for revelatory authority, they have little institutional muscle. And thus they have little capacity to cohere or manage or define a church. The Spirit and the scriptures do not excommunicate members or issue temple recommends or edit church magazines. These things are done by the institutional church, and the institutional church is headed by living prophets and apostles. Thus, one may claim the prerogative of personal revelation or scriptural interpretation vis-à-vis ecclesiastical authority, but if the inspirations and interpretations one proclaims are deemed by local authorities to be too clearly in conflict with the position of the Church as laid out by its apostolic leadership, one ceases to be a member of the Mormon communion. Personal inspiration and canonical scripture can exercise a kind of sovereignty for the individual, but they are thoroughly diffused and thus neutralized at an institutional level. The status of prophets and apostles might rest on the *collective* inspirations or scriptural studies of the membership, but the revelations and interpretations of any *one* member have little power church-wide. When Latter-days Saints declare that the president of the Church is the only one who can announce revelation to and for the whole church, that is not merely a theological ideal; it is an inescapable organizational reality. In considering the Mormon tendency to recognize a triad but speak about a sovereign, it may be the strange combination of institutional reality with the demands of tripodic balance that inflates such strong language in favor of the living prophets' ultimate authority, ratcheting up the rhetorical activity in one corner of the triangle.

And yet among Latter-day Saints, while rhetoric generated by both leadership and laity celebrates the revelatory prerogatives of a living prophet, there is still something that prevents the full claiming of hegemony. As a case in point, consider the sermons of Ezra Taft Benson—who served as a member of the Quorum of the Twelve Apostles for forty years before becoming president of the church in 1985. Benson is likely the most frequently cited source for those looking to reify the supreme authority of the living prophet. His 1980 discourse, "14 Fundamentals in Following the Prophet," serves as the evidentiary backbone of any number of arguments on the topic. Much less quoted, however, is a conference address from 1963—"Be Not Deceived"—in which Benson made similar assertions, including some of the most aggressive about the authority of the living prophets. "There is only one man on the earth today who speaks for the Church," Benson declared. His "words have an even more immediate importance than those of the dead prophets. When speaking under the influence of the Holy Ghost his words are scripture." What this earlier speech demonstrates, however, is the way in which the triangle doggedly appears even in the midst of language that seems to affirm prophetic sovereignty. These statements are actually made in the context of his offering "three short tests" for determining divine truth. In this series, appeals to the living prophet constitute the "second test"; Benson begins not with the Church president but with the canonized scripture. Moving to test two, he cited Brigham Young on the primacy of the living prophets over historical scriptures. And then he concluded with the direct guidance of the Holy Ghost, referencing living prophets and canonical scripture to prove the importance of personal inspirations. Benson summarized,

> These then, are the three tests: The standard works; the inspired words of the Presidents of the Church, particularly the living Presidents; and the promptings of the Holy Ghost. . . . God has not left us in darkness regarding these matters. We have the scriptures ancient and modern. We have a living prophet, and we may obtain the Spirit.

The speech opens with a homage to the living prophet, but it ends up constructing an epistemological triadic framework in which each revelatory source seems to have its particular claims on primacy; those claims even appear to cross and contradict each other in forming a nexus of divine forces.[40] The appearance of a prophetic sovereign, the persistent reality of a revelatory triangle: thus is the story of Mormonism.

The Implications of the Open Canon

This—at long last—brings us to the Latter-day Saints' expanded canon. At first blush, nothing seems to highlight the prerogatives of the living prophets more than the idea that the canon is open. What could better demonstrate the sovereignty of living oracles than the power to rewrite canonized scripture? But here, through the history of the Latter-day Saints, we see something like the reverse image of the one we see in Richard Hooker's three-legged stool or John Wesley's quadrilateral. Whereas the narratives of those concepts demonstrate the appeal of multiple authorities but the stubborn reality of the sovereign scriptures, Latter-day Saint history demonstrates the appeal of singular sovereignty in the person of the prophet but the stubborn reality of multiple voices. Contrary to common perception, the implications of the Mormon's open canon flow in the direction of multiplicity: what is typically seen as proof of prophetic hegemony—the expanded canon—may actually demonstrate the persistence of the triangle. And it does so not through anecdotal evidence or pulpit rhetoric, but through the historically rooted structures of the faith.

As historically demonstrated, a revelation to a latter-day prophet does not become officially canonical—that is, included in the Standard Works—

---

40. Ezra Taft Benson, "Be Not Deceived," *Conference Report*, October 1963, 15–19.

on its own merits or simply by virtue of its association with the leaders of the Church. Rather, it becomes canonized by the vote of the membership. And in this process, we see all three points of the triangle demonstrating their authority. First, and most obviously, that a revelation which might be a candidate for canonization has always come through a president of the Church suggests the potential primacy of the living prophet. Second, that such a revelation would seek canonization suggests that inclusion in the canonical scriptures gives the revelation an authority that exceeds that of the prophet's voice alone; by definition, the process of adding to the Standard Works indicates that canonical scripture is more authoritative than mere prophetic discourse. Third, that this canonization cannot take place until the members of the church vote to sustain it affirms the notion that the experience of the Holy Ghost in the hearts of the Church members is the ultimate judge of whether the prophet is speaking for heaven in any particular instance. As George Q. Cannon explained in presenting revised versions of the Standard Works to a General Conference in 1880, "it has been deemed wise to submit these books with their contents to the conference, to see whether the conference will vote to accept the books and their contents as from God, and binding upon us as a people and as a church." The president of the Church, Joseph F. Smith, then moved that "we"—the membership of the Church—accept the scriptures, submitting his motion to a vote of the laity.[41] Thus, in the Mormons' doctrine of an open canon, the triad is profoundly reinforced. That the vote for these proposed canonized additions has historically been characterized as unanimous—and perhaps seen as *pro forma*—may speak to any number of possibilities: an instinctive deference by members to the notion of institutional sovereignty or that the Spirit in the hearts of the members really does harmonize with the vision of the prophet. But that such a vote is formally necessary insists that sovereignty rests somewhere other than with the revelator.

What, then, of indivisible sovereignty? In their triangular circuits of verification, are Latter-day Saints absolved of its historical and logical demands? That they feel those demands is quite apparent in the amount of language in LDS discourse that essays to place the prophet in the sovereign's seat. The logic of indivisibility cannot be easily ignored. Its challenge is ever present; the triangle is always in conversation with the sovereign. Perhaps this challenge will do—or has done, or is doing—for Mormons what the problem of federalism did for the United States' founding

---

41. "Fiftieth Semi-Annual Conference," *The Latter-day Saints Millennial Star*, November 15, 1880, 724.

generation. Committed to the pluralization of governmental power but confronted by the inescapable logic of sovereignty, advocates of the new constitution were compelled to make an important conceptual shift, to place sovereignty not in the hands of federal, state, or local governments, but in the hands of "the People"—the original source. Such a reorientation toward "popular sovereignty" allowed the logic of an undivided *imperium* to obtain while also allowing for a diversity of government expressions that could function at a variety of levels. Much of this shift was initially rhetorical, but as the eminent historian Edmund Morgan has shown, reality eventually had to close the gap with rhetoric.[42] So the Latter-day Saints' triadic faith in scripture, prophets, and personal revelation may necessitate a similar reorientation away from the various claims of these three media and toward the undivided sovereignty of the God—the original source—who has declared the prerogative to speak through any of these subordinate avenues at any time. In explaining why sometimes the Lord has called people to position as apostles and revelators only to have them fall from grace, George Q. Cannon suggested the following: "Perhaps it is His own design that faults and weaknesses should appear in high places in order that His Saints may learn to trust in Him and not in any man or men."[43] Cannon meant to privilege personal revelation above blind trust in church leaders, but the implication of his emphasis on human frailty underscores the idea that each medium of the divine—living prophets, canonized scripture and personal inspiration—involves faulty humans and thus forms an earthen vessel: mortal imperfection—past, present and personal—abounds. Amid the recurrent agreements among these authorities, their sometimes tense struggles may remind Latter-day Saints of their foundational doctrine that ultimately none of these exercise true sovereignty but rather collectively and imperfectly point to the God whose will they approximate. Equilateral triangles tend to point upwards. But in order for the distinctive culture of Mormon revelation to produce this profoundly theocentric result, and the devotional implications it may carry, the faithful must be candidly conscious of the true complexity of the revelatory faith they hold. They must know their history and their doctrine. They must recognize the triangle and the sovereign for what they are. Then they may know if the Yoruba were right.

---

42. Edmund Morgan, *Inventing the People: The Rise of Popular Sovereignty in England and America* (New York: Norton, 1988).

43. Cannon, "Knowledge of and Dependence on God," 674.

2

BEYOND THE CANON: AUTHORITATIVE DISCOURSE IN COMPARATIVE PERSPECTIVE

Brian D. Birch

What power shall stay the heavens? As well might man stretch forth his puny arm to stop the Missouri river in its decreed course, or to turn it upstream, as to hinder the Almighty from pouring down knowledge from Heaven upon the heads of the Latter-day Saints.
Revelation to Joseph Smith, 1839

Let me say first that we have a great body of revelation, the vast majority of which came from the prophet Joseph Smith. We don't need much revelation. We need to pay more attention to the revelation we've already received.
Gordon B. Hinckley, 1997

During the heat of the 2012 presidential campaign, *The Washington Post* published an article on Mormonism and race that ignited a new round of discussions among Latter-day Saints regarding doctrinal authority. Randy Bott, a popular religion professor at Brigham Young University, was interviewed by Jason Horowitz and expressed longstanding (and relatively offensive) views on the theological rationale for the LDS Priesthood restriction. These included explanations related to a hierarchy of races such that those of black African descent were not prepared for the priesthood, and because they were not prepared, God was actually protecting them from the consequences of abusing this power. Said Bott: "You couldn't fall off the top of the ladder, because you weren't on the top of the ladder. So, in reality the blacks not having the priesthood was the greatest blessing God could give them."[1] The response from LDS Church Headquarters

---

1. Randy Bott, quoted in Jason Horowitz, "The genesis of a church's stand on race," *Washington Post*, February 28, 2012, https://www.washingtonpost.com/politics/the-genesis-of-a-churchs-stand-on-race/2012/02/22/gIQAQZXyfR_story.html.

was swift. The next day, the Church posted a statement on its Newsroom website, which read in part:

> The positions attributed to BYU professor Randy Bott in a recent *Washington Post* article absolutely do not represent the teachings and doctrines of The Church of Jesus Christ of Latter-day Saints. BYU faculty members do not speak for the Church. It is unfortunate that the Church was not given a chance to respond to what others said.[2]

What makes this case intriguing is the fact that the institution issued an extremely rare public response to *one of its own* veteran Church Education employees (the group specifically charged with maintaining currency with, and fidelity to, the teachings of the Church). More relevant for our purposes is the fact that it highlights second-order questions regarding the regulation of doctrinal authority, specifically the extent to which one may justifiably draw upon the history of LDS authoritative discourse in shaping contemporary application:

- What ecclesiastical structures, categories, and criteria are in place for dealing with doctrinal diversity, historical inconsistencies, and the public expression of doctrinal nuance?
- How do contemporary dynamics within Mormonism compare to, and contrast with, other traditions dealing with similar issues?
- How does one properly choose between competing authoritative criteria?

Continuing Revelation

Among the distinguishing features of The Church of Jesus Christ of Latter-day Saints is its affirmation of *continuing* revelation through living prophets and apostles. At the Kirtland Temple dedication in 1836, the Saints proclaimed in song that "the veil o'er the earth is beginning to burst." Throughout the course of his prophetic career, Joseph Smith produced a "new translation" of the Bible, three additional volumes of scripture, and a wealth of uncanonized accounts of revelatory activity. The exuberance of the early Church is exemplified in Joseph Smith's 1839 revelation, in which he records the voice of God: "What power shall stay the heavens? As well might man stretch forth his puny arm to stop the

---

2. "Church Statement Regarding 'Washington Post' Article on Race and the Church," Mormon Newsroom, February 29, 2012, http://www.mormonnewsroom.org/article/racial-remarks-in-washington-post-article.

Missouri river in its decreed course, or to turn it upstream, as to hinder the Almighty from pouring down knowledge upon the heads of the Latter-day Saints" (D&C 121:33).

As the prophet to the "dispensation of the fulness of times," Joseph Smith is understood by Mormons to have restored the "fulness" of the Christian gospel present in the first-century church. This meant that the restoration project developed beyond Christian primitivism to include the "restoration of all things," including the "whole doctrine of redemption" contained in the revelation of Jesus. Applying the "restitution of all things" (Acts 3:21) to the mission of Joseph Smith, "the Church teaches that every gospel truth and blessing, and all priesthood authority, keys, ordinances, and covenants necessary for mankind's eternal salvation have been, or will be, restored in this dispensation."[3]

Nevertheless, of the hundreds of pages of revelations recorded by Smith, most were produced in a relatively short period of time. By the time of the 1835 publication of the Doctrine and Covenants (some four years prior to the revelation referenced above), early spontaneity had given way to more discrimination and caution in the scope and distribution of revelation.[4]

The death of Joseph Smith in 1844 accelerated the transformation of continuing revelation from *charismatic* to increasingly *bureaucratic*. Though Latter-day Saints affirm that the prophetic office was perpetuated through Brigham Young and his successors, the position has functioned more in terms of a presiding officer than a charismatic medium. Since Smith's 1844 martyrdom, the Church has produced four publicly recognized and officially sanctioned revelations. In the case of the 1978 priesthood revelation, for example, the Church offered a brief statement that the revelation came to President Spencer W. Kimball "after extended meditation and prayer in the sacred rooms of the holy temple." Thus, in contrast to many of the revelations through Joseph Smith, contemporary revelation is understood to come primarily in forms other than theophanies and divine utterance.

Of course, most of these observations are nothing new. As far back as 1963, sociologist Thomas O'Dea characterized early Mormon leadership a prime example of the "routinization of charisma"—a concept made famous by Max Weber in his *Theory of Social and Economic Organization*.

---

3. Cory H. Maxwell, "Restoration of all Things," *Encyclopedia of Mormonism*, 4 vols. (New York: Macmillan Publishing, 1992), 3:1218.

4. See Thomas O'Dea, *The Mormons* (Chicago: University of Chicago Press, 1963), 162.

O'Dea argued that, given the tensions between democratization and authority present among the early Latter-day Saints, it was "important for Mormonism to control and contain the very prophetic charisma upon which it was based."[5]

What makes this issue worth exploring now, I believe, are the ways in which the trend continues toward the domestication of revelation both in form and dissemination. In 1997, for example, and to the surprise of many Latter-day Saints, President Gordon B. Hinckley declared in two different news interviews:

> Now we don't need a lot of continuing revelation. We have a great, basic reservoir of revelation. But if a problem arises, as it does occasionally, a vexatious thing with which we have to deal, we go to the Lord in prayer. We discuss it as a First Presidency and as a Council of the Twelve Apostles. We pray about it and then comes the whisperings of a still small voice. And we know the direction we should take and we proceed accordingly.[6]

> Let me say first that we have a great body of revelation, the vast majority of which came from the prophet Joseph Smith. We don't need much revelation. We need to pay more attention to the revelation we've already received.[7]

This sensibility was further solidified by the Church in a late 2011 Newsroom commentary entitled "Divine Revelation in Modern Times." Acknowledging the range of revelatory activity in the Bible, the document nevertheless affirms that "Mormons generally believe that divine guidance comes quietly, taking the form of impressions, thoughts, and feelings carried by the Spirit of God."[8] At one point, the terms "inspiration" and "revelation" were used synonymously in connection to the experience of the leadership in governing the affairs of the Church. Other points reaffirmed

---

5. See Max Weber, *Theory of Economic and Social Organization* (New York: The Free Press, 1947), sections iv and v; and O'Dea, *The Mormons*, 156.

6. "Compass Interview with Prophet Gordon B. Hinckley," *Compass*, November 9, 1997, transcript at http://www.abc.net.au/compass/intervs/hinckley.htm. See also Hinckley's interview for the Frontline and American Experience documentary *The Mormons*, transcript at "Interview: Gordon B. Hinckley," The Mormons, PBS.org, http://www.pbs.org/mormons/interviews/hinckley.html.

7. Quoted in Don Lattin, "SUNDAY INTERVIEW -- Musings of the Main Mormon / Gordon B. Hinckley," *San Francisco Chronicle*, April 13, 1997, http://www.sfgate.com/news/article/SUNDAY-INTERVIEW-Musings-of-the-Main-Mormon-2846138.php.

8. "Divine Revelation in Modern Times," Mormon Newsroom, December 12, 2011, http://www.mormonnewsroom.org/article/divine-revelation-modern-times

in the document include the connection between revelatory authority and ecclesiastical office:

> Church leaders are blessed with revelation in their capacity as Church leaders, just as individuals are enlightened in the context of their own lives. Revelation permeates the Church —bottom, top and in between. . . . Like a river guided by its banks, revelation received by Church leadership flows through an orderly channel. Doctrinal, administrative and policy questions, for example, are carefully weighed against historical precedent. The foundational revelations and teachings of the Church serve as the basis for decision-making. Church leaders work outward from the already established foundation of scripture, teachings, practices and traditions and chart a course for the future.[9]

Again, these distinctions are not novel within Mormonism. However, their careful explication and the particular emphasis on "precedent" and "tradition" invites us to compare this approach to Catholic teaching on doctrinal authority and the centuries of debate associated with these issues.

The Deposit of the Faith

In particular, the choice of the word "reservoir" has intriguing resonances with the Catholic concept of "deposit" (*depositum fidei*). The "deposit of faith" is understood in Catholic life as "the body of saving truth entrusted by Christ to the Apostles and handed on to them to be preserved and proclaimed." Catholic ecclesiology is necessarily backward looking. The deposit is something that is "guarded" and "expounded" in the application of what has *already* been revealed in the incarnation, resurrection, and ascension of Jesus Christ. All dogma, theology, and Church teachings must find their ultimate ground in this deposit.[10]

Of the deposit, the Catholic Church affirms that it "listens to it devoutly, guarding it scrupulously and explaining it faithfully in accord with a divine commission and with the help of the Holy Spirit. It draws from this one deposit of faith everything which it presents for belief as divinely revealed."[11] Thus, the activity of God in the Church does not include new "public" revelation, but rather preserves what in "finality" and "comple-

---

9. "Divine Revelation."

10. Second Vatican Council, *Dei Verbum (Dogmatic Constitution of the Church)*, sec. 10, http://www.vatican.va/archive/hist_councils/ii_vatican_council/documents/vat-ii_const_19651118_dei-verbum_en.html.

11. Second Vatican Council, sec. 10.

tion" has already been revealed in Jesus Christ. The ecclesiastical mechanism through which this is accomplished is the magisterium, the teaching authority of the church. The college of bishops, in communion with the Pope, establish and regulate official doctrinal discourse.[12] The emphasis on *public* revelation is crucial here. Catholics do not deny what they call "private" or "particular" revelation; rather, what they deny is that the Church as a whole will receive new revelation necessary for salvation.[13]

Though Latter-day Saints continue to orient themselves in anticipation of new revelatory knowledge, contemporary discourse (as we have seen) tends toward the preservation of existing revelation rather than the anticipated production of the new. Hinckley's statements above take us back to earlier statements from George Q. Cannon at the turn of the twentieth century. Speaking of the Mormons, he says that "[w]e have been blessed as a people with an abundance of revelation. Some have deceived themselves with the idea that because revelations have not been written and published, therefore there has been a lessening of power in the Church of Christ. This is a very great mistake." He adds that the Church "has been continually led by the spirit of revelation," though "the men who have held the keys have not always felt led to write revelations as the Prophet Joseph did."[14]

However, the task of sifting previous revelatory truth from human imperfection has been a challenging task. Though Joseph Smith distinguished his revelations from other forms of preaching and commentary, it was not easy to tell in every case where revelation ended and human interpretation began. Smith himself declared that "a Prophet is not always

---

12. An immense challenge for the Catholic Church has been the long and involved debate regarding the precise relationship between bishops, popes, and councils. The Second Vatican Council, well-known for its inclusiveness, retained papal infallibility, though it worked on the areas around the doctrine to give greater recognition to the laity and the collegial relationship between pope and bishops.

13. Catechism 67 states: "Throughout the ages, there have been so-called 'private' revelations, some of which have been recognized by the authority of the Church. They do not belong, however, to the deposit of faith. It is not their role to improve or complete Christ's definitive Revelation, but to help live more fully by it in a certain period of history." *Catechism of the Catholic Church*, 2nd ed., (Washington, DC: United States Catholic Conference, 2011), section 67, http://www.usccb.org/beliefs-and-teachings/what-webelieve/catechism/catechism-of-the-catholic-church/epub/index.cfm.

14. George Q. Cannon, *Report of the Semi-Annual Conference of the Church of Jesus Christ of Latter-day Saints*, October 7, 1899 (Salt Lake City: Church of Jesus Christ of Latter-day Saints, semi-annual), 64.

a Prophet only when he is acting as such."¹⁵ But it has not always been entirely clear exactly when the prophets have been speaking "as such."

Elder D. Todd Christofferson acknowledged this point in his April 2012 General Conference address entitled "The Doctrine of Christ." Echoing an earlier Newsroom commentary, he declares that "[n]ot every statement made by a Church leader, past or present, necessarily constitutes doctrine. A single statement made by a single leader on a single occasion often represents a personal, though well-considered, opinion, but is not meant to be officially binding for the whole Church."¹⁶ Thus, LDS leadership has tended to downplay or ignore historical idiosyncrasies and focus instead on the discourse of the current prophet. This approach is expressive of the optimistic and progressive nature of Mormon thought. The faithful believe that continuing revelation will shake off errant teachings of the past as the Church majestically rolls forward.

However, an important qualifier to this was articulated in the October 2013 General Conference by President Dieter F. Uchtdorf, in which he very publicly acknowledged that there have been times when Church leaders have said or done things which "were not in harmony with our values, principles, or doctrine."¹⁷ He quickly followed this up with an affirmation that in spite of these mistakes, "the eternal truth of the restored gospel found in the Church of Jesus Christ of Latter-day Saints is not tarnished, diminished, or destroyed."¹⁸ Uchtdorf's comments gesture toward the idea that dubious teachings can, have been, and will continue to be identified and tossed overboard. In most cases, this "tossing" has taken the form of omission rather than explicit identification of errant teachings and corrective information. To follow the Catholic use of the Latin, this could be identified as *magisterium via neglectum*.

And this takes us back to the notion that revelation "permeates the Church—bottom, top and in between." In his landmark speech in 1954, J. Reuben Clark of the LDS First Presidency attempted to navigate these questions. "We can tell when the speakers [Church leaders] are 'moved upon by the Holy Ghost' only when we, ourselves, are 'moved upon by the

---

15. Joseph Smith, Journal, December 1842–June 1844; December 21, 1842–March 10, 1843, The Joseph Smith Papers, http://www.josephsmithpapers.org/paper-summary/journal-december-1842-june-1844-book-1-21-december-1842-10-march-1843/178.

16. D. Todd Christofferson, "The Doctrine of Christ," *Ensign*, May, 2012, 86–90.

17. Dieter F. Uchtdorf, "Come Join with Us," *Ensign*, November 2013, 21–24.

18. Uchtdorf, 24.

Holy Ghost.' In a way, this completely shifts the responsibility from them to us to determine when they so speak."[19]

Clark believes, like Uchtdorf, that dubious teachings will be ferreted out "by the testimony of the Holy Ghost in the body of the members." This principle resonates with another Catholic concept known as *sensus fidei* (sense of the faithful). The idea here is that Christ fulfills his purposes "not only through the hierarchy who teach in His name and with His authority, but also through the laity whom He made His witnesses and to whom He gave understanding of the faith (*sensus fidei*)."[20] Appealing to the New Testament promise that the Holy Spirit will always be with the Church, *Dei Verbum* further specifies that the "entire body of the faithful, anointed as they are by the Holy One, cannot err in matters of belief. They manifest this special property by means of the whole peoples' supernatural discernment in matters of faith."[21] This discernment is said to be "exercised under the guidance of the sacred teaching authority, in faithful and respectful obedience." It is through this discernment that "the people of God [adhere] unwaveringly to the faith given once and for all to the saints."[22]

A practical illustration can be seen in Pope John Paul II's 2004 letter to the Inquisition Symposium in which he draws the distinction between the "*authentic* 'sensus fidei'" and what he calls the "*prevailing mentality*" of a given period. He acknowledges that the passage of time allows the Church to receive a "more profound awareness" of their fidelity to the deposit of faith. So, though the sensus fidei may be invoked as a "just judgment on the *past* of the life of the Church;" it may not serve as a corrective to current magisterial teaching.[23] Pope Benedict XVI cemented this point in his 2012

---

19. J. Reuben Clark, "When Are the Writings or Sermons of Church Leaders Entitled to the Claim of Scripture?" (speech, Brigham Young University, Provo, UT, June 7, 1954); republished in *Dialogue: A Journal of Mormon Thought* 12, no. 2 (Spring 1979): 68–69.

20. Second Vatican Council, *Lumen gentium (Dogmatic Constitution on the Church)*, 35, http://www.vatican.va/archive/hist_councils/ii_vatican_council/documents/vat-ii_const_19641121_lumen-gentium_en.html.

21. Second Vatican Council, sec. 12.

22. Second Vatican Council, sec. 12.

23. John Paul, "Letter of John Paul II to Cardinal Roger Etchegaray on the Occasion of the Presentation of the Volume 'L'Inquisizione,'" June 15, 2004, https://w2.vatican.va/content/john-paul-ii/en/letters/2004/documents/hf_jp-ii_let_20040615_simposio-inquisizione.html; italics added. See also the "Instruction on the Ecclesial Vocation of the Theologian - *Donum Veritatis*,"

address to the International Theological Commission. "Today," he states, "it is particularly important to explain the criteria that make it possible to distinguish the authentic *sensus fidelium* from its counterfeit. It is certainly not a kind of public ecclesial opinion and invoking it in order to contest the teachings of the Magisterium would be unthinkable, since the *sensus fidei* cannot be authentically developed in believers, except to the extent in which they fully participate in the life of the Church, and this demands responsible adherence to the Magisterium, to the deposit of faith."[24]

Returning to J. Reuben Clark, a comparable dynamic is present in his address. He affirms that "adventurous expeditions" by LDS Church leaders will be ferreted out by the Holy Ghost "*in the body of the members,*" and that "in due time" the Church will know which of these have been set aside and which are genuinely revelatory.[25] He is equally as emphatic, however, that the President of the LDS Church is in the privileged position of authority when it comes to the production of new revelation or binding interpretations of scripture or doctrine.[26]

All of this brings us to acknowledge the reciprocal dynamic present in both traditions when it comes to questions of authority and receptivity. Though each appeals to the receptivity of the faithful, a sensible question

---

which states that "the believer can still have erroneous opinions since all his thoughts do not spring from faith. Not all the ideas which circulate among the People of God are compatible with the faith. This is all the more so given that people can be swayed by a public opinion influenced by modern communications media." Available at http://www.vatican.va/roman_curia/congregations/cfaith/documents/rc_con_cfaith_doc_19900524_theologian-vocation_en.html, 35.

24. "Address of His Holiness Benedict XVI to the International Theological Commission on the Occasion of its Annual Plenary Assembly," December 7, 2012, http://www.vatican.va/holy_father/benedict_xvi/speeches/2012/december/documents/hf_ben-xvi_spe_20121207_cti_en.html. Related to the *sensus fidei* is the concept of the *sensus fidelium* (or *consensus fidelium*), which is understood to be the collective sense of the faithful. "This convergence (consensus) plays a vital role in the Church: the *consensus fidelium* is a sure criterion for determining whether a particular doctrine or practice belongs to the apostolic faith." International Theological Commission, "*Sensus Fidei* in the Life of the Church," 2014, http://www.vatican.va/roman_curia/congregations/cfaith/cti_documents/rc_cti_20140610_sensus-fidei_en.html.

25. Clark, "When are the Writings," 73–74; emphasis added.

26. Clark quotes from Doctrine and Covenants 50:22: "Wherefore, he that preacheth and he that receiveth, understand one another, and both are edified and rejoice together."

involves the extent to which this receptivity can be said to actually *regulate* Church teaching as opposed to merely *affirming* authoritative discourse; though regulation and affirmation are not mutually exclusive, there is the *potential* for conflict as we have observed on occasion in both Mormonism and Catholicism. Each tradition has mechanisms in dealing with wayward teachings such that the "*sensus fidei*" can be interpreted and regulated precisely *through* authoritative discourse.

In the case of Catholicism, legalistic distinctions have provided a way to address the messiness and confusion of centuries of theological interpretation, cultural influences, and denominational schism. However, from the perspective of newer and more atheological traditions such as Mormonism, doctrinal legalism can cut both ways. It can help to bring clarity out of chaos, but it can also lead to intramural mischief. Conversely, however, the absence of theological precision has its own challenges, including the avoidance of inconsistencies and other vicissitudes that come with the affirmation of continuing revelation.

Bootstrapping Religious Authority

What is the locus of ecclesiastical authority? Who decides? How is it regulated in the life of the church? For Catholics, these questions have been ripe for debate since the fourteenth century. The conciliar controversies created deep divisions in the church and led to delicate relations between bishops, popes, and the laity they serve. The conciliarists argued that ultimate religious authority resided in the collective body of the Church, and further that the "mystical union" between Christ and the faithful was mediated through councils involving the entire church. An uneasy truce was eventually established wherein the Pope retained supremacy, but did so in relation to councils.

This landscape shifted in the First Vatican Council (1869–70) in which papal infallibility was declared a doctrine of the church and, to the dismay of the conciliarists, not subject to the consent of the laity. When the Pope speaks *ex cathedra* on matters of faith and morals, *Pastor aeternus* declared, his teachings are "irreformable of themselves and not from the consent of the Church."[27] Conciliarists were livid. The centuries-old

---

27. First Vatican Council, *Pastor aeternus*, accessed June 5, 2018, http://www.vatican.va/archive/hist_councils/i-vatican-council/documents/vat-i_const_18700718_pastor-aeternus_la.html.

mechanism put in place to check papal power had now been leveraged to elevate and enshrine it.

The Second Vatican Council (1962–65) retained papal infallibility, though it worked on the areas around the doctrine to given greater recognition to the laity and the collegial relationship between pope and bishops. The Catechism of the Catholic Church states that the "task of interpreting the word of God authentically has been entrusted solely to the Magisterium of the Church, that is, to the Pope and to the bishops in communion with him."[28] The Magisterium refers to the teaching authority of the Church, and there are distinctions and levels within the magisterium that allow for the sifting of Catholic teaching in the effort to identify the purest forms of doctrinal teaching. The key distinction lies between the *ordinary* and *extraordinary* magisterium. The extraordinary magisterium is "infallibility certain" and applies specifically to the body of teachings as defined by (1) the pope speaking *ex cathedra* on matters of faith or morals, or (2) by an explicit solemn definition of bishops together in ecumenical council.

The ordinary magisterium is subdivided between non-infallible and infallible levels. Non-infallible teachings are those of bishops and popes not explicitly stated by solemn definition and which occur in their individual offices. This is the category, for example, that applies when the pope is writing or speaking as a theologian in the Church and not in the capacity of his pontifical office.

The most contentious of categories, however, has been the middle level designated as the *ordinary and universal magisterium*. Although the individual bishops do not enjoy the prerogative of infallibility, they nevertheless proclaim Christ's doctrine infallibly whenever—even though dispersed through the world, but still maintaining the bond of communion among themselves and with the successor of Peter, and authentically teaching matters of faith and morals—they are in agreement on one position as definitively to be held.

Corresponding to the degrees of the magisterium is what Catholics call the "levels of assent." As one moves up the scale of authoritative discourse, the demands on the faithful is elevated as well. For example, if a bishop publishes a sermon or letter, it would fall into the category of the ordinary magisterium and would not be considered as a "solemn definition."

---

28. *Catechism of the Catholic Church*, 2nd ed. (Washington, DC: United States Catholic Conference, 2011), section 100, http://www.usccb.org/beliefs-and-teachings/what-webelieve/catechism/catechism-of-the-catholic-church/epub/index.cfm.

The challenge for the Catholic Church, especially since the First Vatican Council, is that it now maintains four forms of infallibility: (1) the Pope speaking *ex cathedra* on matters of faith and moral, (2) solemn definitions of ecumenical councils, (3) universal teaching on faith and morals, and (4) the *sensus fidei*. In an ideal world, the content of each of these would be completely consistent, resulting in the kind of harmony sought after by a church "sustained by the Spirit of truth."[29] The particular challenge at present lies in identifying the content of the final two categories.

For example, the *ordinary and universal magisterium* has created intense debate over the past few decades. As we observed above, it refers to a set of common teachings among bishops that rise to the level of being taught "as one that has to be definitively held." At issue here is the extent to which something can be properly declared as infallible that has not been explicitly defined.[30] Pope John Paul II and Pope Benedict XVI were assertive in their attempts to leverage the *ordinary and universal magisterium* to help quell debate on controversial teachings. The Congregation for the Doctrine of the Faith, for example, declared that "a doctrine can be confirmed or reaffirmed by the Roman Pontiff, even without recourse to a solemn definition, by declaring explicitly that it belongs to the teaching of the ordinary and universal Magisterium as a truth that is divinely revealed."[31]

The debates over birth control and women's ordination in the Catholic Church have been the most public cases in point. In response to inquiries, the Congregation for the Doctrine of the Faith declared in 1995 that the Church has "no authority whatsoever" to confer priestly ordination on women. Their chief rationale was that the teaching had, from the beginning, been "constantly preserved and applied in the Tradition of the Church" and thus "set forth infallibly by the ordinary and universal Magisterium."[32] At issue was the status of Pope John Paul II's apostolic let-

---

29. Second Vatican Council, *Lumen gentium*, 12.

30. See Francis A. Sullivan S.J., *Magisterium: Teaching Authority in the Catholic Church* (New York: Paulist Press, 1983), 119. See also Richard R. Gaillardetz, "The Ordinary Universal Magisterium: Unresolved Questions," *Theological Studies* 63 (2002), 447–71.

31. Joseph Cardinal Ratzinger, "Doctrinal Commentary on the Concluding Formula of the *Professio fidei*," Congregation for the Doctrine of the Faith, 1998, 9, http://www.vatican.va/roman_curia/congregations/cfaith/documents/rc_con_cfaith_doc_1998_professio-fidei_en.html.

32. Joseph Cardinal Ratzinger, "Responsum ad Propositum Dubium Concerning the Teaching Contained in 'Ordinatio Sacerdotalis," Congregation for the Doctrine

ter *Ordinatio Sacerdotalis* in which he declared that the Church's teaching on this point was to be "definitively held" by the Church's faithful.

Earlier debates over artificial contraception appealed to the same categories. Pope Paul VI's 1968 encyclical *Humanae vitae* condemned artificial methods of birth control. Prior to the encyclical, the Papal Commission on Birth Control released its report to the Holy Office and recommended that the Church's position on contraception be relaxed. To the chagrin of the commission, the Pope chose not to follow their recommendation and *Humane vitae* was released shortly thereafter. Debate ensued regarding the authoritative status of the document and appeal was made to the *ordinary and universal magisterium* to defend the definitive nature of the teaching.[33]

Among the most articulate and persistent critics of the encyclical was the theologian Hans Kung, who played an important role in drafting the documents of the Second Vatican Council. In his aptly-titled book, *Infallible?*, Kung uses the events surrounding *Humane vitae* to call into question the very idea of papal infallibility. He states that in every century "the errors of the Church's teaching office have been numerous and indisputable."[34] If one takes a sober look at history, he argues, it is obvious that many teachings that had enjoyed universal consensus have been abandoned. If this has been the case with some teachings, why couldn't the Church give up its traditional teachings on the evils of birth control? For Kung, not only should the Church abandon its teachings on birth control, it should rethink the doctrine of infallibility altogether.

Karl Rahner, another key theologian in Vatican II, argues from a different direction that "not every doctrine taught unanimously by the whole episcopate is of itself infallible, even when it deals with faith and morals or intends to do so."[35] Hence the mere fact that there has been universal consensus is not enough to establish infallibility. Rahner agrees with Kung on the factual point that "many doctrines which were once universally

---

of the Faith, 1995, http://www.vatican.va/roman_curia/congregations/cfaith/documents/rc_con_cfaith_doc_19951028_dubium-ordinatio-sac_en.html.

33. Paul VI, *Humanae Vitae*, July 25, 1968, http://w2.vatican.va/content/paul-vi/en/encyclicals/documents/hf_p-vi_enc_25071968_humanae-vitae.html.

34. Hans Kung, *Infallible? An Unresolved Inquiry* (New York: Continuum Publishing Group, 1994), viii.

35. Karl Rahner, *Commentary on the Documents of Vatican II*, vol. I (New York, Herder & Herder, 1967), 210–11.

held have proved to be problematic or erroneous."[36] However, in Rahner's view, erroneous doctrines are proof that they were not definitively held. Kung disagrees. He believes it is clear that the teaching was intended to be definitively held; and this fact serves as evidence that the doctrine of infallibility is itself very fallible.

Finally, these considerations take us to the question of explicitness. Rahner argues that "mere *de facto* universality of Church doctrine related to the faith is not enough."[37] A formal and public action is required before it can qualify for the ordinary universal magisterium. As we noted above, the administrations of John Paul II and Benedict XVI were explicit in their appeals to the *ordinary and universal magisterium*. It is also noteworthy that the Code of Canon Law requires explicitness: "No doctrine is understood as defined infallibly unless this is manifestly evident."[38] With a two-thousand-year history from which to draw, the effort to identify teachings that properly belong to the *ordinary and universal magisterium* is a monumentally challenging exercise; and yet there is much at stake. If the Church changes its position on women's ordination and birth control, it would be widely seen as nothing less than a reversal of an irreformable teaching. Furthermore, given the appeal to the Holy Spirit in guiding magisterial teaching, it would destabilize a central component of the Church's self-understanding. On the other hand, if it does not change its positions on key social issues, it continues to risk isolation and alienation from a growing ethical consensus in the contemporary world. On this point, we will turn our attention to Mormonism.

Collegiality and Consensus

Similar in ways to the Catholic "collegial exercise of teaching authority," the Latter-day Saint apostles and prophets have operated according to a consensus model of doctrinal teaching. All major decisions regarding the doctrines and practices of the Church are publicly presented as the unanimous will of the First Presidency and Quorum of the Twelve Apostles. Almost all deliberation takes place outside of public view, and only rarely is there anything like a papal commission to offer input regarding doc-

---

36. Karl Rahner, *Sacramentum Mundi*, vol. III (New York: Herder & Herder, 1969), 356.
37. Rahner, *Sacramentum Mundi*.
38. *Code of Canon Law*, can. 749, sec. 3, accessed March 20, 2018, http://www.vatican.va/archive/ENG1104/_P2H.HTM.

trinal matters. In the absence of a recognized body of theologians with whom to consult, LDS apostles possess undisputed teaching and pastoral authority over the Church.[39] Consultation with Latter-day scholars is not unusual, but it almost always occurs informally and in private. On occasion, *ad hoc* subcommittees among church leadership have been formed to address a particular issue or question.[40]

In the absence of widely acknowledged legalistic distinctions, the LDS Church has had to wrestle with ambiguity and uncertainty regarding which teachings are authoritative and definitive for "full faith and fellowship" and which are the "personal opinions" of Church leaders and educators. On May 4, 2007, the Church released a statement entitled "Approaching Mormon Doctrine" as part of an ongoing effort to clarify authoritative doctrinal discourse. The statement was released via the Church's Newsroom and offered six bulleted paragraphs, each of which communicates points previously made in publications and statements by the Church:[41]

> With divine inspiration, the First Presidency (the prophet and his two counselors) and the Quorum of the Twelve Apostles (the second-highest governing body of the Church) counsel together to establish doctrine that is consistently proclaimed in official Church publications. This doctrine resides

---

39. The distinction between teaching and pastoral authority has been an issue of much debate in the Catholic Church. One question involves whether or not Catholic theologians have any kind of teaching authority or if they are to be designated as consultants. See "Instruction on the Ecclesial Vocation of the Theologian" and "Doctrinal Responsibilities: Approaches to Promoting Cooperation and Resolving Misunderstandings between Bishops and Theologians." See also Avery Dulles, "The Magisterium and Theological Dissent" in *The Craft of Theology: From Symbol to System* (New York: Crossroad, 1992), 105–18; and Charles E. Curran, *Loyal Dissent: Memoir of a Catholic Theologian* (Washington, DC: Georgetown University Press, 2006).

40. "Reading committees" were popular prior to correlation to review publications in the interest of seeking consensus among Church leadership. For a helpful look at LDS intra-ecclesiastical deliberation, see Richard L. Sherlock, "We can See No Advantage to a Continuation of the Discussion," *Dialogue: A Journal of Mormon Thought* 13, no. 3 (Fall 1980): 63–78.

41. The Newsroom functions somewhat similarly to the official newspaper of the Vatican, the *Osservatore Romano*: it is an official artery by which the Church makes statements and offers commentary, but it does not enjoy the status of a binding ecclesiastical document.

in the four 'standard works' of scripture, . . . official declarations and proclamations, and the Articles of Faith.[42]

Sitting behind this statement is the ongoing and careful negotiation between traditional resistance to legalistic analysis and the growing need to separate doctrinal wheat from chaff. As we observed in the case of Randy Bott, nowhere has this issue been more evident and relevant than in the debate over the priesthood restriction for members of African descent.

On June 8, 1978, the LDS First Presidency announced that president Spencer W. Kimball had received a revelation that the priesthood should be extended "to all worthy male members of the Church" (OD 2). Thus ended a long and tumultuous period for the Church, which had predictably been the subject of intense criticism regarding this policy. Of particular relevance to our analysis is the struggle to come to terms with the precise categorization of the priesthood ban. Was it a doctrine of the Church or a mere policy? Did it originate in scripture or revelation, thus requiring a new revelation to overturn it? Added to the debate is the complicated admixture of cultural beliefs, scriptural fragments, bureaucratic politics, and folk theology.

The historical origins of the priesthood ban are not clearly documented, but it was not until the years after the Saints' arrival in the Salt Lake Valley that it became an established policy. It derived its unofficial justification from a variety of sources, including the Christian folk belief in a hierarchy of lineages (with Africans at the bottom).[43] Early Mormons shared the idea that they were of a "chosen lineage" and represented the literal gathering of Israel in the last days. According to Mormon sociologist Armand Mauss, a "new element in this evolving doctrinal complex was a linkage of mortal lineage to premortal developments. By the 1850s, the Saints accepted the idea that they had been identified and set aside in a premortal life to enter mortality through Israelite (especially Ephraimite)

---

42. "Approaching Mormon Doctrine," Mormon Newsroom, May 4, 2007, http://www.mormonnewsroom.org/ldsnewsroom/eng/commentary/approaching-mormon-doctrine.

43. Armand Mauss labels two important folk beliefs: "Anglo-Saxon triumphalism" and "British Israelism." See Armand L. Mauss, *All Abraham's Children: Mormon Conception of Race and Lineage* (Urbana: University of Illinois Press, 2003), ch. 2. See also W. Paul Reeve, *Religion of a Different Color: Race and the Mormon Struggle for Whiteness* (New York Oxford University Press, 2015), 38–43.

lineage as a people of 'royal blood.'"[44] Based upon this pre-mortal righteousness, some taught that the "noble" races were entitled to the priesthood ahead of the others. On this view, the African race was eligible only after the others were exhausted. As literal accounts of "royal blood" faded over time, the idea of race hierarchy and pre-mortal status persisted.

Though Joseph Smith had earlier ordained African American men to the priesthood, his scattered statements are variously interpreted. After the arrival in Utah, however, Brigham Young officially instituted the policy of restriction that more or less remained in place until the 1978 revelation. As in the case of *Humane Vitae*, any question of abandoning the policy involved getting clear as to its doctrinal status. If the practice was a policy only, it could be changed as a matter of administrative decision. If it was a doctrine, it was said that only new revelation could overturn it. Evidence for the latter designation came in the form of a 1949 statement from the First Presidency, which is the first official statement on the issue: "The attitude of the Church with reference to Negroes remains as it has always stood. It is not a matter of the declaration of a policy but of direct commandment from the Lord, on which is founded the doctrine of the Church from the days of its organization." The statement also quotes Brigham Young, who had earlier declared that "when all the rest of the children have received their blessings in the holy priesthood, then that curse will be removed from the seed of Cain, and they will then come up and possess the priesthood."[45]

It is clear that many leaders of the church agonized over these issues, and there is evidence of considerable disagreement within their ranks. There is also strong evidence that during the 1950s, President David O.

---

44. Mauss, *All Abraham's Children*, 24. See also Armand L. Mauss, "The Fading of Pharaoh's Curse: The Decline and Fall of the Priesthood Ban Against Blacks in the Mormon Church," *Dialogue: A Journal of Mormon Thought* 14, no. 3 (Autumn 1981): 10–45; Armand L. Mauss, "Mormonism's Worldwide Aspirations and Its Changing Conceptions of Race and Lineage," *Dialogue* 34, no. 3/4 (Fall/Winter 2001), 103–33; Lester E. Bush Jr., "Mormonism's Negro Doctrine: An Historical Overview," *Dialogue: A Journal of Mormon Thought* 8, no. 1 (Spring 1973), 226–93; Lester E. Bush Jr. and Armand L. Mauss, eds., *Neither White Nor Black: Mormon Scholars Confront the Race Issue in a Universal Church* (Salt Lake City: Signature Books, 1984); and Newell G. Bringhurst and Darron T. Smith, eds., *Black and Mormon* (Urbana: University of Illinois Press, 2006).

45. First Presidency Statement, August 17, 1949, excerpt in Russell M. Stevenson, *For the Cause of Righteousness: A Global History of Blacks and Mormonism, 1820–2013* (Salt Lake City: Greg Kofford Books, 2014), 310–11.

McKay desired to overturn it, but that he could not reach consensus with other apostles.[46] McKay did, however, relax specific policies related to racial identification in cases of unclear ancestry. Then in 1969, the Church released another statement; this time expressing a greater degree of agnosticism regarding the ban's doctrinal basis and appealed instead to traditional church teaching. "Joseph Smith and all succeeding presidents of the Church have taught that the Negroes . . . were not yet to receive the priesthood, for reasons which we believe are known to God, but which He has not made fully known to man."[47] Though the statement implicitly references pre-mortal life as an explanation, it avoids elaboration and there is no mention of lineage hierarchy. More recent work has carefully documented the historical challenges involved in tracing the teaching to Joseph Smith. In his landmark work *Religion of a Different Color*, historian Paul Reeve chronicles the development of the issue among Church leadership: "If the ban could be connected to Smith, the reasoning likely went, then it must be of divine origins and thus a restriction mortals could not interfere with."[48] The evidence shows, however, that the connection to Smith was based upon faulty memory, inconsistent accounts, and the perpetuation of unverifiable reports.

The debates over the priesthood ban occasioned more careful reflection among Mormon scholars regarding official vs. unofficial teachings. Mauss, for example, points to the inconsistency between the 1949 statement and the 1978 revelation to argue for the "*principle of parsimony*" in the acceptance and dissemination of LDS doctrinal teaching. The 1949 letter "explicitly endorsed Brigham Young's teaching that blacks would not get the priesthood until all the other descendants of Adam had done so—a position obviously proved wrong by the June 1978 revelation."[49] Because official statements carry with them some degree of fallibility, cau-

---

46. See Mauss, "The Fading of Pharaoh's Curse," 11 and 36n9. Mauss points out that McKay's personal correspondence indicates (1) considerable struggle and (2) that he considered the ban a *policy* rather than as a *doctrine*. See also, Edward L. Kimball, "Spencer W. Kimball and the Revelation on Priesthood," *BYU Studies* 47: 2 (Spring 2008), 5–78; and Gregory A. Prince & Wm. Robert Wright, *David O. McKay and the Rise of Modern Mormonism* (Salt Lake City: University of Utah Press, 2005), 60–106.

47. "Policy State of Presidency," December 15, 1969, *Church News*, January 10, 1970, 2, excerpt in Stevenson, *For the Cause of Righteousness*, 334–35.

48. Reeve, *Religion of a Different Color*, 255.

49. Mauss, "The Fading of Pharaoh's Curse," 44n128.

tiousness should be a virtue "lest again we digest dubious doctrine in the service of temporary policy."[50]

To help clarify these distinctions, Mauss presents what he calls a "scale of authenticity," a heuristic device to assist in the stratification of LDS doctrinal teaching. At the top of the scale is *canon doctrine*, which is the body of the teaching presented as revelation. "The four standard works of the Church (with recent addenda) obviously fall into this highest category of authenticity, but it is difficult to think of anything else that does."[51] Next comes *official doctrine*, which includes statements from the President or First Presidency and includes official Church publications and curricula that fall "under the explicit auspices of the First Presidency."[52] Mauss makes is clear that "there is no assumption of infallibility here, but only that the legitimate spokesmen for the Church are expressing its official position at a given point in time."[53] This category offers us an intriguing comparison to the Ordinary Universal Magisterium and to Rahner's position in particular. In response to their respective crises, both Mauss and Rahner want to underscore that official teaching and widespread acceptance in no way implies infallibility, and they have the historical examples to prove it.

Latter-day Saint ecclesiology does not include the formal category of infallibility. The sister doctrines of continuing revelation and an open canon are said to preclude this possibility. However, the strong emphasis on ecclesiastical authority and the internal policies of the Church have cultivated a form of *practical infallibility*. These policies include the prohibition against public criticism of the Church or its leaders. Those who persistently publicize the errors or weaknesses of Church teaching or authority can be subject to discipline and possible excommunication. In 1993, six Latter-day Saint scholars were excommunicated for charges related to their writings (or related public activities) that were said to challenge Church teachings, policies, or counsel.[54]

---

50. Mauss, 35.
51. Mauss, 32.
52. Mauss, 32.
53. Mauss, 32–33.
54. See Dallin H. Oaks, "Alternate Voices," *Ensign*, May 1989, 27–30; Dallin H. Oaks, *The Lord's Way* (Salt Lake City: Deseret Book, 1991); Richard Ostling and Joan Ostling's, *Mormon America: The Power and the Promise* (San Francisco: Harper SanFrancisco, 1999), ch. 21; Lavina Fielding Anderson, "The LDS Intellectual Community and Church Leadership, A Contemporary Chronology," *Dialogue: A Journal of Mormon Thought* 26, no. 1 (Spring 1994) 7–64; and

Three years earlier, the Vatican was embroiled in a similar controversy with outspoken theologians who questioned, among other things, the authority of magisterial teaching and the diminished role of the theologian in the Catholic Church. This led to the 1990 curial document "Instruction on the Ecclesial Vocation of the Theologian." Issued by the Congregation on the Doctrine of the Faith, the document was an effort to communicate the perspective of the Vatican regarding the obligations of its theologians. Among the instructions was the call for the highest degree of assent—the assent of faith—"even to the teaching of ordinary and universal Magisterium when it proposes for belief a teaching of faith as divinely revealed."[55] In recent years, the LDS church has publicly recognized the permissibility of its members to disagree with policies of the Church. The extent of this permissiveness, however, has not been made clear and the application of formal discipline has been selective.[56]

Returning to Mauss's scale of authenticity, the final two categories are *authoritative doctrine* and *popular doctrine*, respectively. Authoritative doctrine is the category of literature and sermons by Church authorities and educators. These works may or may not be published by official church presses. In 1983, all general authorities of the Church were instructed to include a disclaimer in their books to the effect that "the views expressed in this book do not represent the official position of the Church of Jesus Christ of Latter-day Saints."[57]

The final and most inclusive category is *popular doctrine*, which includes the substantial body of literature containing "apocryphal prophecies," folk theology, and other doctrinal narratives that circulate among the membership independently of official review or approval.[58] For Mauss, the "traditional Negro doctrines" appeared to have begun merely at the level of popular doctrine and, at some point, were incorporated into official discourse. However, the fact that Brigham Young taught them in

---

Philp Lindholm, *Latter-day Dissent: At the Crossroads of Intellectual Dissent and Ecclesiastical Authority* (Salt Lake City: Greg Kofford Books, 2011).

55. "Instruction on the Ecclesial Vocation of the Theologian," 8.

56. See Frank Guliuzza III, "Showdown on Main Street: Salt Lake City, the Mormon Church, and Freedom of Expression," *Teaching Ethics* (Fall 2002): 71–77.

57. Letter to General Authorities, March 22, 1983, LDS Church History Library.

58. See Richley Crapo, "Grass Roots Deviance From Official Doctrine: A Study of Latter-day Saint Folk-Beliefs," *Journal for the Scientific Study of Religion* 26, no. 4 (December, 1987): 465–83.

his official capacity was at least a contributing factor to the ecclesiastical inertia on this issue.

This returns us to the Randy Bott case. Given the categories and analysis presented above, it appears clear that the LDS Church intended to marginalize Bott's ideas by portraying them as a manifestation of unofficial folk theology. However, it needs to be pointed out that his ideas were informed by a strong and persistent tradition in Mormon thought. Though the explicitly racist theology of pre-mortality and race lineage has been abandoned in official discourse, it has had strong currency in LDS Church educational circles and was conventional wisdom among the Latter-day Saints for much of the twentieth century. Though Bott's ideas were anachronistic, the historical record demonstrates that they were far from idiosyncratic.

In fact, it wasn't until two years after Bott's interview that the LDS Church, for the first time, directly, officially, and publicly repudiated the ideas that informed his comments. As part of its Gospel Topics series, the Church released an essay entitled "Race and the Priesthood." The highlight of the document was the long-awaited rejection of racialist theology:

> Today, the Church disavows the theories advanced in the past that black skin is a sign of divine disfavor or curse, or that it reflects unrighteous actions in a premortal life; that mixed-race marriages are a sin; or that blacks or people of any other race or ethnicity are inferior in any way to anyone else. Church leaders today unequivocally condemn all racism, past and present, in any form.[59]

The essay does not detail specific theories, nor does it address the institutional context within which many of these ideas maintained strong currency. It is this latter point that concerns us here. The absence of legalism in Mormon theology has served it well in many respects; but this case does not appear to be among them. The tumult surrounding the LDS priesthood restriction demonstrated the challenges involved in the attempt to merely neglect harmful ideas. It also brought to the foreground the apparent disconnect between the public relations messaging of the Church and the educational culture within the institutional structures of the Church. Efforts are underway to close the gap, but they are in the early stages and will require sustained attention and broad institutional commitment.

---

59. "Race and the Priesthood," Church of Jesus Christ of Latter-day Saints, December 2013, https://www.lds.org/topics/race-and-the-priesthood.

Conclusion

Despite these ongoing challenges, Latter-day Saints share with their Catholic neighbors the theological claim that, despite human failing and historical change, the church (though differently understood by each) has maintained its integrity as the body of Christ and people of God. In *Lumen gentium*, Vatican II declared that "the Church is strengthened by the power of God's grace promised to her by the Lord, so that in the weakness of the flesh she may not waver from perfect fidelity."[60] Rejecting the apostasy and the need for restoration, Catholic teaching maintains that the abiding presence of the Holy Spirit has always been able to overcome political entanglements, misguided teachings, and sinful practices. A similar conviction is present among Latter-day Saints regarding their post-restoration organization. Despite the vagaries of its history, a key feature of contemporary Mormonism is the conviction that the activity of the Holy Spirit will not allow the Church of Jesus Christ to be "led astray" for a second time. In an information and secular age, this conviction will continue to be tested in ways heretofore unseen in the textured and inspiring history of the Latter-day Saints.

---

60. Second Vatican Council, "*Lumen gentium*," 9

3

ON THE LITERAL INTERPRETATION OF SCRIPTURE

James E. Faulconer

My thesis is that all scripture (at least all Jewish and Christian scripture) should be read literally, perhaps only literally. That means that literal reading is appropriate not only to the narrative portions of scripture, but also to such genres as psalmody, legal texts, allegories, and apocalypse. To defend my thesis I will discuss three issues: "What do we mean by *scripture*?" "What is history?" and "What is a literal reading?" Answering those questions will allow me to say why scripture ought always to be read literally.

Scripture

We have to ask what we mean by the word "scripture" because unless we merely define the term by stipulation, it isn't obvious what it covers and what it does not. Christians recognize the New Testament as scripture, but most Christians don't recognize the Book of Mormon as such. Is the Tao Te Ching scripture for Taoists? Might it be reasonable for someone to think of Dante's *Inferno* as scripture? Let me consider this issue by making three overlapping points.

First, to be scripture is to be part of a canon—whether that canon is formally or informally constituted. So we might say something like this about scripture: Scripture is a set of texts that are recognized as authoritative for a particular thought community. To call something scripture is to speak of it in relation to other books, some of which—like it—are canonical, and some of which are not.

A canon is a collection of texts brought together over time by a reflective, historical community. The Hebrew Bible and the New Testament are both excellent examples of canons formed in this way—but so are the less well-defined canons of Western philosophy and those of Japanese literature. So sometimes the canon is formed by an explicit adjudication of relevant authority, and sometimes it is created more informally over time by the choices of authoritative readers. Not every canon has the kind of history and structure that the Bible has, and not every canon is scriptural; but being canonical is necessary, though not sufficient, for something to be scripture.

Second, to speak of something as scriptural is to say that it has a special relation to a community. I might, of course, refer to a book and say, "That book is scripture for me." But the addition of "for me" makes my point: when I speak that way, I am using an analogy or a metaphor. When a person says that a text is scripture, he or she is saying, "That book is scripture *for us*; we who belong to this community recognize this as part of our scriptural canon." In fact, the community may well define itself by that recognition: "We are the believers who accept this text as scripture."

Third, because scriptural texts are canonical, they have authority over those who recognize them. The character of that authority may differ greatly from one religious group to another, but each will be the group that it is at least partly because it finds in its scriptural texts material that is superior for teaching, particularly for teaching moral and spiritual matters. Many Christians insist that ultimately the authority of scripture is an authority given by the Holy Spirit: under the guidance of the Holy Spirit the church has collected the books together that were written by the revelation of the Holy Spirit. But one could believe that something is scriptural—that it has an authoritative moral and spiritual educative function—without believing that it has attained that authority in the way that Christians generally believe their scriptures receive it. What is important is that it has that kind of authority.[1]

So I take the word *scripture* to mean a set of texts selected over time by a particular thought community for their authority in teaching moral and spiritual truth.[2]

History

The question of what we mean by *history* is more difficult. It is probably the most difficult of my three questions, so I've shored it up by placing it between thinking about what the terms *scripture* and *literal* mean.

---

1. Hans-Georg Gadamer says that Gerhard Krüger (*Einsicht und Leidenschaft: Das Wesen des platonischen Denkens* [Frankfurt: Klostermann, 1963]) shows how pre-Platonic Greek thinkers understood their myths as authoritative. See Hans-Georg Gadamer, "On The Problem of Self-Understanding," in *Philosophical Hermeneutics*, trans. David E. Linge (Berkeley, CA: University of California Press, 1976), 51.

2. For more on the question of how to define scripture, see James E. Faulconer, "Paul Ricoeur on Scripture," in a forthcoming festschrift for Louis Midgley.

I have argued elsewhere that if we read a scriptural text as a believing Christian, then we don't read about just the "bare" events that happened, as if there were any a-contextual events.[3] An event, after all, is something that stands out from the unformed flow of time. It stands out to us and in relation to other events. Though we don't want to trust etymology too much, the etymology of the word *event*—*evenir*, "to come out"—suggests the contextuality of the event: it comes to us out of undifferentiated time.

That means that if we read as a believer (which is not the only way one can read; even a believer can read otherwise), then we read about the events that happened as part of God making Himself, His patterns, and His plans manifest in history. That means that from a believing point of view, a history that doesn't include the hand of God isn't a fully true history. But, of course, from a contemporary academic historian's point of view, a true history *cannot* include the hand of God, except perhaps by mentioning it as one of the beliefs held by an actor in history.

Neither of these views of history is one in which the historian reports bare events. Perhaps there are naïfs who think that is what academic historians do, but I doubt that academic historians are among them. Nor is either of these ways of understanding the past in a position to judge the truth or falsity of the other absolutely because each proceeds from a different set of assumptions about what is real, and there is no birds-eye view outside of history from which to choose between them. There is no way for one view to judge the other absolutely because, at least for human beings, no absolute view is possible. In fact, human beings—who live *in* history and are constituted through it—ought not to want such a view from everywhere and nowhere. That is the desire of the Tower of Babel, the desire to leave human limitation behind and reach God on our own power. Multiple histories are always possible. Within that multiplicity the believing historian and the academic historian use two different understandings of history, and in spite of a great deal of overlap, ultimately those two views of history are radically incommensurable. And the question of the difference between them isn't a merely methodological or otherwise technical question. These two views differ because they disagree about what is real, about what is possible.

To think about that claim further, let me offer a rough-and-ready definition of history, as opposed to historiography: History is the horizon of effects that open the world to us. I call that definition rough-and-ready

---

3. James E. Faulconer, "Scripture as Incarnation," in *Faith, Philosophy, Scripture* (Provo, UT: Maxwell Institute, 2010), 151–202.

because, though I think it will do for my purposes, it needs more thought and refinement. For example, were I to go into this in more depth, I would need to explain how this view of history avoids making history into a straitjacket that forces us along a predetermined causal path. To do so I would argue that the effects of history give us possibilities to which we can respond. In a strong sense, the effects of history are the openness of our future. But that isn't a matter for this discussion.

Given that rough-and-ready definition of history as the horizon of effects within which we find ourselves, consider an example: I was baptized into the LDS Church on February 2, 1962. By thinking in primarily general terms, I can say that event in my personal history is the same as it would be in an academic history of my life. To keep things clear, in what follows I will distinguish between history as I have defined it here (the horizon of effects that open the world) and historiography (an account of those effects, their relations to one another, and the openings that they afford). An academic historiographer giving an account of that event and the possibilities it opened in the world would speak of my attending Brigham Young University for an education, of my experiences as an LDS missionary in Korea in the '60s, and perhaps of the ways in which those experiences made me see the world differently. He or she might speak of my career teaching at BYU and would probably include some of my church service. Surely this historiographer would recognize that my baptism made my marriage possible by creating a direction that resulted in that marriage, with the children and grandchildren that have followed. A thoughtful biographer would be likely to write about the attitudes and feelings made possible by my baptism and events subsequent to it.

In contrast, consider a hypothetical biography by a believer.[4] His or her historiography would surely include most of the supposedly same events that the academic biography included. But it would also include events and entities missing from the latter. The most obvious example would be that at certain key points in this second historiography, where the academic writer might very well speak about powerful experiences I had, experiences of intuition or inspiration, the believing historiographer could speak of the manifestations of the Holy Ghost in my life. These are not just two different interpretations of an event in my life. They are two accounts of two different events, two different ways in which one can say

---

4. I don't intend to imply by this that believers cannot be academic historians. I'm talking here about a type, not about particular persons. Believers can certainly write academic histories—but not *as* believers.

that the horizon of the world opened for me. They are two different accounts of what is real. A simple way to make the distinction is to say that, for the academic, what is real is my experience and my psychological response to it; but for the believer what is real is the event, my response, and the Being who initiated my experience. (Neither of those lists exhausts the differences, but they are enough to make the point.)

Because of this different understanding of the real, the believing biographer is certain to write about the past differently than that person would if writing an academic historiography, and vice-versa. And it is imaginable that this difference might even cause the believing biographer to rethink the relation between important documents or events. Perhaps he or she would go so far even as to reconsider their temporal order. Certainly the writer would understand the events of my life differently. It is easy to imagine a believing historiographer writing in a way that, according to an academic one, twists the truth in order to make fully apparent the realities that the believer understands to be manifest in the events in question. But the believer could make the same charge against the academic. Each writes as he or she does to allow the truth of the events in question to show itself, and each could see the other as distorting events in order to show what they want to show, thus masking the real truth of the event.

The difference between these two historiographies is non-trivial. Each reveals a different understanding of history, of the real, of what affects us and makes our present world possible. Every historiography will implicitly reveal what it takes to be real in the world, by showing us that reality in the effects of history.

It is tempting to say, "But there is what happened, and that's the same. We may have different perspectives on it, but it's still the same event." I disagree. History is more complicated than that, which is what makes historiography of any sort more complicated. As Hans-Georg Gadamer says:

> [History] determines in advance both what seems to us worth inquiring about and what will appear as an object of investigation, and we more or less forget half of what really is—in fact, we miss the whole truth of the appearance [i.e., an event]—when we take its immediate appearance as the whole truth.[5]

Of course there must be some sense of sameness to the event of my baptism that the academic historiographer tells of and that which the believing

---

5. Hans-Georg Gadamer, *Truth and Method*, 2nd rev. ed., trans. Joel Weinsheimer and Donald G. Marshall (New York: Continuum, 2004), 300; translation revised.

biographer refers to. But if we think that the "immediate appearance" of an event, what we suppose an eye witness would tell if she only described the physical or social event itself and left out anything not available for documentation, then we miss at least half of that event. Namely, we miss what has allowed us to see the event in the way that we do, the history that has opened the world in this way rather than that.

I hope it is clear that the ultimate incommensurability of believing and academic historiography doesn't mean that the work of the former is metaphorical, at best. Nor does it mean that the work of the latter is, from a believer's point of view, simply false. Both kinds of historiography are about the real world, the world that is, the world that human beings inhabit. And what those historiographies each take to be real overlaps considerably. There's no reason not to suppose that, for the most part, they are talking about two different ways in which the same reality shows itself, a reality that has no ultimate revelation but many possible ones.

People doing both kinds of historiography can talk with each other, though usually today only by adopting the academic historiographer's more parsimonious take on reality. Nevertheless, these two kinds of historiography differ because they are about different ways in which the real reveals itself, different effects in history, and different futures opened by those effects. One historiography includes seeing that world as a world in which God makes Himself manifest in and through history, and the other doesn't. There's no middle ground between those two views.

Reading Literally

That brings me to the third issue: What does it mean to read literally? Medieval thinkers had already thought about the issue, and they divided readings of scripture into two categories, one of which has three subdivisions: We can read literally (in accordance with history), and we can read spiritually. Spiritual reading includes reading scripture as allegorical (a teaching about the church and faith), tropological (the demands scripture makes on individuals), or anagogical (what it teaches about the future of the church). Theologians didn't think that one of these ways of reading necessarily excludes the others. In fact, Thomas Aquinas (1225–74) explicitly argued that any spiritual sense of scripture always comes from its literal sense.⁶ I'm not a Thomist, but my point about reading literally will be similar to his.

Today when we speak of a literal reading we ordinarily mean "in a real or actual sense," in other words "without metaphor, exaggeration, or distortion"⁷ or perhaps more simply "as an accurate historical account," which sounds a lot like the medieval understanding. As you might suspect from what I've already said about history, the problem with that understanding of *literal* is that there is more to thinking that something is in accordance with history than might meet the modern eye. In fact, as I see it, many who purport to be giving literal readings of scripture are actually giving bad academic historiographic readings, using academic historiographer's assumptions about history yet insisting on historiographies that contradict those assumptions.⁸ Those, for instance, who read Genesis 1 as describing a six-day or a six-thousand year physical creation of the universe approach scripture this way: they use the assumptions of academic historiography and science, but force their accounts to contradict those assumptions by injecting bad historiography and science into the accounts.

What, then, would be a better description of a literal reading? Using etymology once again as a tool for thinking about something rather than a proof, think about the word *literal* differently: to read a text literally is to read it "by the letters." Though it isn't without complications to put it this way, we could say that to read literally is to read something exactly as its words say they should be read. That isn't the same as the medieval meaning of the word *literal*, "in accordance with history," though it isn't necessarily disconnected from that medieval idea either. But before turning to the complications that history might inject, think more about the word *literal*.

It probably sounds straightforward to say that a literal reading of a text is one that understands it to say what it says rather than something else. On that view we might say that those who read Genesis 1–3 literally read it something like this:

> There was a six-day period of creation, followed by a day of rest. Then God created Man, and placed him in a garden with numerous trees, one of which was the tree of knowledge of good and evil. God told

---

6. As, for example, in Thomas Aquinas, *Commentary on St. Paul's Epistle to the Galatians*, ch. 4, lec. 7.

7. *Oxford English Dictionary*, 3rd ed., s.v. "literal."

8. See James E. Faulconer, "Myth and Religion: Theology as a Hermeneutic of Religious Experience," in *Faith, Philosophy, Scripture* (Provo, UT: Maxwell Institute, 2010), 72–73.

Man not to eat the fruit of that tree under penalty of death. Then he had Man name the animals. When Man discovered that all of the animals had a mate except him, God put him into an unconscious state, took a bone from his body, and created Woman. At some point a talking serpent challenged Woman to eat of the forbidden fruit, and she succumbed to his temptation. Then she shared what she ate with Man, and the two of them recognized that they were naked. Being embarrassed, they hid themselves in some bushes. When God discovered what they had done, he cursed the serpent to crawl on the ground, and he told Woman that she would have sorrow bearing children. He also cursed the earth so that Man would have difficulty working it. Then Man named Woman "Eve," and after providing Adam and Eve with clothing, God cast them both out into the world outside the garden, remarking that they had become like one of the Gods.

Often when people speak of reading literally, they have something like what I have just said in mind, with the addition to that précis of one more detail: "This is a description of historical events."

I contest that understanding of *literal*. As I see it, the above account of Genesis 1–3 is *not* a literal reading of those chapters, and not because there are details I omitted which others might think essential. It is not a literal reading of the text because it is, at best, a précis of the narrative rather than a reading of what the words of the text say. Indeed, it is a précis of one particular way of reading the chapters. Other interesting and perhaps mutually exclusive précis are possible.

To think more about how to understand the word *literal*, consider only the first few words of Genesis—and I will use English to make things easier for us all. (For my example I will proceed as if the Bible were written in English and the chapters at hand didn't have editorial complexities.) The first five words of Genesis are: "In the beginning God created . . ." To read that phrase literally is to read what its letters say in this particular combination. But the question is, "What do they say?"

Of course one way to answer that question is trivial: I understand those words and the syntax that joins them. Almost any English speaker can do that. A reader can understand that phrase without believing in God. All that is required is a reasonable proficiency in English. But that can't be what we mean by a literal reading, and the moment that we go beyond that, things become complicated.

If we go beyond that trivial meaning, one not uncommon response to how to understand scripture is to speak of it as my subjective response to the scriptural text: I might say, "When I read those first five words of Genesis, I am reminded of the grandeur of God's creation, and I feel small in comparison." Believers often have those kinds of responses to scripture. Those responses aren't insignificant, but they are not only not a literal reading of the text, they aren't really an understanding *of the text*. (Nor are they, I would argue, what the Book of Mormon's Nephi has in mind when he speaks of likening the scriptures to ourselves [1 Ne. 19:23].) So surely that's not what we mean when we talk about understanding scripture literally. Scripture is more than a many-paged Rorschach test.

To read what the words formed by those letters say in the first five words of the Bible requires that I not only be able to grasp their plain English sense. I must also understand those words in relation to other words and ideas, in relation to traditions of reading, and particularly in relation to questions that they raise. I must already have in mind certain things, such as the range of things that the phrase "in the beginning" and the word "created" can mean, what kind of being God is, and what kind of a text we are looking at—historical narrative, ritual retelling, or something else. I must either have these things in mind, or have a question about them. For example, I might be unsure how to understand "in the beginning" and have a question about that.

A literal reading of the text requires that I think about all such questions, including my presuppositions about those for which I believe I have answers. In fact, perhaps the latter are the most important kinds of questions I can ask. There isn't one and only one answer to the questions that arise when we begin to read literally, and the answers to them are so important that denominations are often established on the differences of the answers people give to them.

So, we can answer these kinds of questions in different ways, but we have to sort out the different answers if we are going to understand any particular literal meaning of the phrase under consideration, "In the beginning God created . . ." And we cannot forget that, at the same time, we have to sort out how the meaning of those five words is modified by the meaning of the words that follow them and the things that have been written about them, the textual context. Sorting out such things means identifying the reality of the text in question: Perhaps I need to know what effects have brought *it* into being? In other words, what is the text's historical background? I surely need to know how to understand the realities of which it speaks when it refers to God and to creation, and I need to be able to take them seriously even if I am not a believer. I probably need to think about how others have read the passage I'm looking at, and I surely want to think about what possibilities this passage opens up. In my view, a literal reading is a reading that takes those kinds of questions seriously and puts itself to the task of responding to them.

Conclusion

I hope it is obvious why I think that all scripture should be read literally. But a critic could legitimately ask, "Doesn't this just mean that you think all scripture should be read as literature?" My critic has noticed the connection between the literal and the literary, and worries that I may have turned scripture into little if anything more than great literature.

My answer to the critic's question is yes. Scripture should be read with the same kind of attention and care with which we read literature and with many of the same tools. *Yes, but*: To read scripture literally is not *merely* to read it as literature, looking for interesting insights and clever connections, perhaps going further and finding deep existential import in its stories and messages. Scripture is more than a particular person's expression of how to see the world. Scripture is not only literary in the best and broadest sense of that term, it is also mythical in the scholars' sense of that word. Namely, it is a traditional story that reveals the way in which *a people* see the world. That use of the term *myth* doesn't assume anything about the truth or falsity of the story in question, so it is reasonable to speak of scripture as mythical. Jewish and Christian scripture claims to show us the ways in which the people of this particular diffuse and complicated history have seen and see the world.

But the believer goes still further and asserts that scripture is not only more than literary, it is more than mythical. Scripture is also authoritative and historical. As an authoritative text, scripture speaks not only for the community of believers but also for God. A believer reading scripture encounters more than the wisdom of the tribe. From within that wisdom she hears the voice and call of God, a voice that comes from outside the tribe—and may not be easy to hear. So for the believer, scripture reveals a people's vision of the world and shows a person his or her place in it, offering recognized moral and spiritual education. But more than that, scripture reveals a vision of things that continues to challenge the individual believer as well as the community. It tells us that there is something real that is beyond—more than—the tribe and community's vision.

As an historical text, scripture doesn't say "Here is a story to compete with or replace that of the academic historian." Its business is completely otherwise than that. Instead scripture says "Here is a history of the world in which God reveals Himself," a different world than that in which God does not reveal Himself. Many of the events of scripture may have been edited and rewritten for various purposes. Many may have been shaped by liturgical needs or in response to historical and political events. Many are not historical narratives, so the question of historicity doesn't seem to arise with them. Yet at least in the Jewish and Christian traditions, there is a necessary historical core to scripture as a whole: the structure of reality underlying the scriptures is ultimately historical in the sense I've described rather than only mythical.[9] Whatever the facts about the redactors of the Torah narrative, to Jews it matters that Israel was saved from Egypt. Whatever the history of the manuscripts of the Gospels, to Christians it matters that Jesus was born, died, and was resurrected. However we explain Book of Mormon geography or deal with anomalies in the text, to Mormons it matters that there were Nephites and Lamanites.

Because Judaism and Christianity are historical rather than only mythical religions, even the way in which the divine is exhibited is different for them. Mythical reality tends to be cyclical. But Israelite reality and the reality of those religions that spring from it give us an ongoing history of the world, with a beginning, middle, and end. There is real time in biblical history. Believers locate themselves at a particular point of that history, rather than as only another repetition of a mythical cycle. The patterns that one sees exemplified in scripture are repetitions of "the same thing" in the Kierkegaardian sense of repetition—authentic repetition of an act—rather than mere imitations, over and over again, of the same thing. For those who write and read Judeo-Christian texts as scripture, God reveals Himself in and through history and He does so repeatedly in the same types or patterns, but it is history, not only myth.

If we understand clearly what we mean by the terms *scripture*, *history*, and *literal*, then only a literal reading of scripture makes sense. But the naïve view that we must choose between reading scripture literally or spiritually, that scripture represents the version of history against which academic histories should be measured, and that attention to the richness and detail of scripture are substitutes for attention to its truth will melt away. And so will the equally naïve views that better historiographical methods, more academic training, or less concern with historicity will save us from ourselves. My vote is for the literal reading of all scripture.

---

9. See Brevard Childs, *Memory and Tradition in Israel* (London: SCM Press, 1962), 82.

4

READING WOMEN BACK INTO THE SCRIPTURES

Claudia L. Bushman

I want to read women back into the divine story. It is certainly a challenge, but if our eyes are very sharp, we get an occasional reference. I was recently a guest instructor in an LDS Institute class studying Galatians, discussing circumcision and why it was no longer necessary as a token of Abraham's covenant. Circumcision, as the token of a covenant, was replaced by baptism unto Christ, a covenant much more widely applicable. That new state was available to Jew, Greek, bond, free, male, and that otherwise excluded group, female, doubling the potential pool (Gal. 3:27–29). What is more, all those baptized unto Christ were newly Abraham's seed, heirs according to the promise, and so retrospectively circumcised, as it were. Yes, reading women back into the scriptures is a game we can all play.

Paul, whose letters make up a third of the books of the New Testament, mentioned some women in his evangelizing efforts—Priscilla (Rom. 16:3) and Euodia and Syntyche (Phil. 4:2–3), for instance. They were his fellow laborers in the gospel vineyard. Priscilla helped teach the gospel to Apollos, and it is widely understood that Phoebe conveyed Paul's letter to the Romans.[1] But where are the letters of Priscilla and Phoebe? Did they write letters of encouragement to the members in far-flung branches? Could they write? Were their letters lost? Were they not preserved as Paul's were? Why did the Christian women not write, and if they did, where are their letters?

---

1. See Marg Mowczko, "Did Priscilla teach Apollos?," *Marg Mowczko* (website), September 11, 2010, http://margmowczko.com/did-priscilla-teach-apollos/; and Arland J. Hultgren, *Paul's Letter to the Romans: A Commentary* (Grand Rapids: Wm. G. Eerdmans, 2011), 570.

That is why I am so comforted by the idea of Mormon's cave full of records that Brigham Young referred to.² Early stories suggest that there are roomfuls of writings, shelves full of documents, manuscripts, plates, and scrolls that tell the stories of many believers. And I believe that the women's pages exist, to be opened to view at some time.

---

2. Several accounts posit the final resting place of the gold plates as a cave. These came from Mormon leaders after the westward migration was well under way. One of these accounts is contained in the diary of Elizabeth Kane, a non-Mormon whose husband Thomas was an incalculable political ally and friend to Mormonism for much of the nineteenth century. Elizabeth and others were with Young, Porter Rockwell, and others at Young's St. George, Utah, home on or near the evening of January 15, 1873. She records that after dinner,

> I asked where the plates were now, and saw in a moment from the expression of the countenances around that I had blundered. But I was answered that they were in a cave.... [Oliver Cowdery] had been to the cave, I did not understand exactly whether Oliver Cowdrey was there three times, or whether he accompanied Joseph the third time *he* went there, and Brigham Young's tone was so solemn that I listened bewildered like a child to the evening witch stories of its nurse. Nor do I understand whether the plates were all transcribed by this time or not. (Elizabeth Kane, *A Gentile Account of Life in Utah's Dixie, 1872–73 – Elizabeth Kane's St. George Journal* [Salt Lake City: University of Utah, Tanner Trust Fund, 1995], 75.)

In 1877 Brigham Young himself declared what he said Oliver Cowdery would not disclose in public:

> When Joseph got the plates, the angel instructed him to carry them back to the hill Cumorah, which he did. Oliver says that when Joseph and Oliver went there, the hill opened, and they walked into a cave, in which there was a large and spacious room. He says he did not think, at the time, whether they had the light of the sun or artificial light; but that it was just like day. They laid the plates on a table; it was a large table that stood in the room. Under this table there was a pile of plates as much as two feet high, and there were altogether in this room more plates than probably many wagon loads; they were piled up in the corners and along the walls. (Brigham Young, June 17, 1877, *Journal of Discourses*, 26 vols. [London and Liverpool: LDS Booksellers Depot, 185486], 19:38.)

Heber C. Kimball and Wilford Woodruff also recounted hearing Young discuss the cave. See Heber C. Kimball, September 28, 1856, *Journal of Discourses*, 26 vols. (London and Liverpool: LDS Booksellers Depot, 185486), 4:105; and Woodruff's December 11, 1869, entry in *Wilford Woodruff's Journal, 1833–1898*, ed. Scott G. Kenney, 9 vols. (Salt Lake City: Signature Books, 1984).

Reading women into the Book of Mormon is difficult. We do have Sariah playing her household shrew role, berating Lehi for taking the family on the road and for losing her sons. This colorful episode is the smokescreen that hides the lack of family reaction to the murder of Laban. With Sariah's rant in place, readers do not notice that Nephi records no response from either his brothers on the road or his family back in the tent for his honorific execution of Laban. He may not have mentioned it to any of them. It may not have happened. But that's another story.[3]

Reading women into the Bible is easier, and we have many interesting, dangerous, and glamorous vixens such as Delilah, Salome, and even Jael—who was not above hammering a tent peg into an evil head. Even the good people are compromised, however. Esther saves her people, but she is in a very unfortunate situation; Eve, whom we now consider a heroine, has been vilified for centuries; and so on.

My question is: Can we read women back into the divine story? Can women be considered to have a place in divine matters? Can we find women's writings that we can consider scriptural? I will list some in the restored Church.

I will begin with the possibility of proselytizing missions for women nineteen years old. This change in the age requirement has, at a single stroke, elevated women in the restored church. Henceforth, significant numbers of LDS women will face their maturity better prepared. They will be more likely to live serious lives. They will provide equal numbers of missionary journals. And they will ascend to mission leadership positions, whatever those may be. This move will effect more change than all the proposals and actions of feminists in recent years. The document, which will arguably make as much difference in as many lives as the 1978 proclamation of the extension of the priesthood to all worthy males, should be canonized. No longer will missions for women be offered to the hard-core unmarrieds as they were in my day; the best and brightest young women will seize the opportunity to go. Women in the modern Church, who will serve missions with distinction, are more and more a part of the divine story than ever in history. Where is the provenance? We have President Thomas S. Monson's General Conference talk on October 6, 2012, and

---

3. See my essay on Nephi's killing of Laban in Claudia L. Bushman, "I, Nephi," in *Perspectives on Mormon Theology: Scriptural Theology*, ed. James E. Faulconer and Joseph M. Spencer (Salt Lake City: Greg Kofford Books, 2015), 81–95.

we have newspaper announcements.[4] Is there a preliminary document? I'd like it canonized as a scripture.

We all know that our scriptures have been assembled from bits and pieces, accounts of varying age and purpose. I propose a volume of LDS women's scriptures of the restoration. I want female-friendly scripture, something for us to chew on. This is a proposal in progress, and all plans are open to change. For now I want documents contemporary to their time. I require that the writings be original, dated, and signed. I don't want exegesis, commentary, apologetics, or interpretations. I want to be able to get as close to the original words as possible. The decision of whether to include complete or partial documents remains to be made. But the documents must be as true to themselves and their creation as possible—not as tampered with by editors down the line.

I'm not suggesting canonization for most of these writings—not at this point anyway—but a sort of secondary recognition as family or women's or personal scriptures. We don't want to clutter up our primary canon, which is extensive enough with the four big books. But we should have a body of scripture, with all its strangenesses and contradictions, for females.

For this proposal in progress, I welcome comments, judgments, and additions. For now, I respectfully submit these nominations for consideration for the women's collection.

I

As it happens, we have an extensive Mormon female writing, a woman's narrative account of the early Church that describes life as surely as Nephi describes his life and times. This narrative—a family history—is a widely available account that the Church uses as a basic text; I think you could almost say as scripture, although there are those who have complained of it, as they have of the Bible, that human errors have crept in. Many of you know by now that I am describing Lucy Mack Smith's account, the one that she narrated to Martha Jane Knowlton Coray after the murder of her sons. This account deals with Lucy's history as well as her son Joseph's. It was edited and abridged by early publishers and is

---

4. "Young Women Prepare for Option of Missionary Service," *LDS Church News*, December 13, 2012, https://www.lds.org/church/news/young-women-prepare-for-option-of-missionary-service.

currently available in half-a-dozen different versions.⁵ The parts of Lucy's memoirs that Church leaders have liked most—and are available nowhere else—have been copied into dozens of Church lesson manuals and thousands of Sacrament Meeting talks. If we did not have that document we would know little of Joseph's early life or of early Church history and pre-history. We would not know about Joseph's leg operation, of the social overreaching that caused the Smiths to build a better house than they could afford and to lose their whole farm, of Father Smith's dreams, and of Joseph taking Emma with him to the Hill Cumorah to get the gold plates. This is certainly family scripture, household scripture. It is used as scripture by the Church. Why has it been so roughly treated?

I submit that had this account been available earlier, before Joseph's untimely death, or written by Alvin or Joseph Smith Sr., it would have been accorded more authority. The Smith ladies, Emma and Lucy, were on the outs with the Church's new leadership, so much so that approval of Lucy's book was then impossible. Still it is the backbone of LDS writings, almost as hefty and significant as the Book of Mormon itself. The scholars of the Joseph Smith Papers Project at the Church History Department have prepared an online edition of the original rough copy and fair copy, both with careful transcriptions and facsimiles of each page.⁶ That book, in its original form, must lead the list.

II

We do have a genuine female scripture, from the 1830 dawn of the Church's organization, and this one—section 25 of the Doctrine and

---

5. Editions include Orson Pratt, ed., *Biographical Sketches of Joseph Smith, the Prophet, and His Progenitors for Many Generations by Lucy Mack Smith, Mother of the Prophet* (Liverpool: S. W. Richards, 1853); Preston Nibley, ed., *History of Joseph Smith By His Mother Lucy Mack Smith* (Salt Lake City: Bookcraft, 1954); Scott F. Proctor and Maurine J. Proctor, eds., *History of Joseph Smith by His Mother: Revised and Enhanced* (Salt Lake City: Deseret Book Co., 1996); R. Vernon Ingleton, comp., *History of Joseph Smith by His Mother Lucy Mack Smith: The Unabridged Original Version* (n.p.: Stratford Books, 2005); Lavina Fielding Anderson, ed., *Lucy's Book: Critical Edition of Lucy Mack Smith's Family Memoir* (Salt Lake City: Signature Books, 2001).

6. Early manuscripts of Lucy Smith's memoir can be read on *The Joseph Smith Papers* website at http://josephsmithpapers.org/paperSummary/lucy-mack-smith-history-1844-1845 and http://josephsmithpapers.org/paperSummary/lucy-mack-smith-history-1845.

Covenants—is canonized. This scripture justifies the importance of women and lays out a plan for them as expansive as anything anyone has come up with since. Emma Smith, to whom this scripture is directed, is told to be a scribe for her husband and to compile a hymnbook, directions familiar to Latter-day Saints. But she is also told that she will be "ordained" to "expound scriptures, and to exhort the church," general directions that expand our understanding of women's work. She is told that her time shall be given to "writing, and to learning much" (D&C 25:7–8). On the home front she is not told to serve nutritious meals. She is not told to keep her house in order. She is not told to take good care of her children. Emma had no living children at the time this scripture was recorded. Instead, she is told to comfort her husband and not to murmur—instructions to build her marriage relationship. The section expands the number of women being spoken to as it says, "This is my voice to all" (D&C 25:16). I don't think women could ask for a better scripture for their direction. I do think that it could be better implemented.

III

Joseph's instructions and intentions are also clearly stated in the 1842 Minutes of the Relief Society, recently made widely available through the Joseph Smith Papers Project. These minutes were recorded on-site by Relief Society secretary Eliza R. Snow and are her best effort to keep up with the activity of the meetings and the six sermons that Joseph Smith delivered to the Relief Society women.[7]

There are some problems about the content of the minutes, such as painful references to the current times, questions about what blessings and opportunities were actually given to the women, and questions about authority and priesthood. But surely these original minutes of the Church's first auxiliary, recorded by the poetess of the restoration, in the presence of the prophet and in the sound of his voice, in our new age of full disclosure, could count as scripture. Again, I won't require canonization, but these minutes should rank as high as or higher than conference

---

7. The Relief Society Minute Book can be found on the *Joseph Smith Papers* website at http://josephsmithpapers.org/paperSummary/nauvoo-relief-society-minute-book. See also Sheri Dew and Virginia H. Pearce, *The Beginning of Better Days: Divine Instruction to Women from the Prophet Joseph Smith* (Salt Lake City: Deseret Book, 2012), which contains a transcription of the six sermons of Joseph Smith contained in the minutes.

talks. That they are confusing and contradictory to some of the things we are taught today should not deter us from valuing these minutes. Many of our doctrines operate over a continuum of meaning and understanding. We should keep the range in front of us. So the minutes go into my compendium. We find in them such instructions and comments from Joseph Smith as these:

> If you live up to your privileges, the angels cannot be restrain'd from being your associates—females, if they are pure and innocent can come into the presence of God.[8]
>
> The object of the Society—that the Society of Sisters might provoke the brethren to good works in looking to the wants of the poor—searching after objects of charity, and in administering to their wants—to assist; by correcting the morals and strengthening the virtues of the female community, and save the Elders the trouble of rebuking; that they may give their time to other duties etc. in their public teaching.[9]
>
> Respecting the female laying on hands, he further remark'd there could be no devils in it if God gave his sanction by healing—that there could be no more sin in any female laying hands on the sick than in wetting the face with water—that it is no sin for any body to do it that has faith, or if the sick has faith to be heal'd by the administration.[10]
>
> He exhorted the sisters always to concentrate their faith and prayers for, and place confidence in those whom God has appointed to honor, whom God has plac'd at the head to lead—that we should arm them with our prayers.—that the keys of the kingdom are about to be given to them, that they may be able to detect every thing false—as well as to the Elders.[11]
>
> This Society shall have power to command Queens in their midst—I now deliver it as a prophecy that before ten years shall roll around, the queens of the earth shall come and pay their respects to this Society—they shall come with their millions and shall contribute of their abundance for the relief of the poor—If you will be pure, nothing can hinder.[12]
>
> The female part of community are apt to be contracted in their views. You must not be contracted, but you must be liberal in your feelings.[13]

---

8. Page numbers for quotations from Dew and Pearce, *The Beginning of Better Days*, 107.
9. Dew and Pearce, 89.
10. Dew and Pearce, 104.
11. Dew and Pearce, 106.
12. Dew and Pearce, 108.
13. Dew and Pearce, 109–10.

I now turn the key to you in the name of God and this Society shall rejoice and knowledge and intelligence shall flow down from this time—this is the beginning of better days, to this Society.[14]

Sisters of this Society, shall there be strife among you? I will not have it—you must repent and get the love of God. Away with selfrighteousness.[15]

And, of course, there's more.

IV

Zion's poetess, Eliza R. Snow, proclaimed the existence of a Heavenly Mother. Her poem has been set to music as the popular Latter-day Saint hymn "O My Father." This doleful song is the only hymn that I know of that purports to be revelation. Snow noted the origin of the idea as coming from an otherwise undocumented conversation with Joseph Smith. This verse, however, references reason rather than prophetic authority, saying, "Truth is reason; truth eternal Tells me I've a mother there"[16]—that is, a Mother in Heaven. This revelation has been accepted by generations of Church leaders, but no one knows what to do with it. We have seen a lot of doctrinal creation by the women who seek to call their own Heavenly Mother to life.

V

The transcripts of the Mass Meeting against the passage of the United States Congress's anti-polygamy Cullom Bill in 1870 presented many of the finest Mormon women in rich, thundering religious and patriotic rhetoric: "Notwithstanding the inclemency of the weather, the Tabernacle was densely packed with ladies of all ages, old, young, and middle aged."[17] The women sounded like prophets preaching from the mountain top as they met to speak against the bill then being considered in Congress which would strengthen the national anti-bigamy laws already on the books. The words of the Utah women, like the denunciations of Old Testament prophets, stand as scriptural pinnacles in the annals of Mormon history. The bill

---

14. Dew and Pearce, 110.
15. Dew and Pearce, 123.
16. "O My Father," *Hymns of The Church of Jesus Christ of Latter-day Saints* (Salt Lake City: The Church of Jesus Christ of Latter-day Saints, 1985), 292.
17. *Proceedings in Mass Meeting of the Ladies of Salt Lake City, To Protest Against the Passage of Cullom's Bill., January 14, 1870* (Salt Lake City: n.p.), 1.

was defeated. Although we might not exactly champion this issue today, we warm to the inspiring and scriptural style. Here is some of what they said:

> Sarah N. Kimball: "We have been driven from place to place, and why? Simply for believing in and practicing the counsels of God as contained in the gospel of Heaven. . . . 'We are not advocating woman's rights, but man's rights.' The bill in question would not only deprive our fathers, husbands, and brothers of enjoying the privileges bequeathed to citizens of the United States, but it would also deprive us, as women, of the privilege of selecting our husbands, and against this we most unqualifiedly protest."[18]

> Mrs. Levi Riter: "We are here to express our love for each other, and to exhibit to the world our devotion to God, and Heavenly Father, and to show our willingness to comply with the requirements of the gospel; and the law of celestial marriage is one of its requirements that we are resolved to honor, teach, and practice, which may God grant us strength to do. ['Amen!' from the audience.]"[19]

> Eliza R. Snow: "Our enemies pretend that in Utah woman is held in a state of vassalage; that she does not act from choice but by coercion; that we would even prefer life elsewhere were it possible for us to make our escape. What nonsense! . . . I will now ask this intelligent assembly of ladies, Do you know of any place on the face of the earth where woman has more liberty and where she enjoys such high and glorious privileges as she does here as a Latter-day Saint? 'No!' The very idea of women here in a state of slavery is a burlesque on good common sense. The history of this people, with a very little reflection, would instruct outsiders on this point; it would show at once that the part woman has acted in it could never have been performed against her will. . . . [T]he women in this church have performed and suffered what could never have been borne and accomplished by slaves."[20]

> Harriet Cook Young: "Every woman in Utah may have her husband, the husband of her choice. Here we are taught not to destroy our children, but to preserve them; for they, reared in the path of virtue and trained in righteousness, constitute our true glory."[21]

> Mrs. Miner: "Let Senators and Representatives, and all our would-be benefactors know that we, the daughters of Zion, uphold our brethren by our faith and prayers; that we have no wrongs for the outside world to right. We need no champion nor will we accept of one!"[22]

---

18. *Proceedings*, 1.
19. *Proceedings*, 2.
20. *Proceedings*, 4–5.
21. *Proceedings*, 6.
22. *Proceedings*, 8.

VI

Edward W. Tullidge's 1877 book *The Women of Mormondom* offers two good reasons for inclusion. This version of the Mormon story includes many women's autobiographical accounts from the 1870s, caused to be written for this volume by Eliza R. Snow. Tullidge uses these first-hand accounts to tell, in first person, about historical LDS events. These are personal testimonies of the restoration by the significant women who crossed the plains as young women, who were the first wives of significant men, and who welcomed in other wives. Such women as Vilate Kimball, Bathsheba W. Smith, Abigail Leonard, Prescindia Huntington Smith Kimball, and many others, have their say.

The book is also nominated for Tullidge's apocalyptic view of Mormon women, praising them highly and saying such inexplicable and unexpected things as:

> The women . . . did their full half in founding Mormondom.[23]

> Mormonism has restored woman to her pinnacle.[24]

> Woman is heiress of the Gods. She is joint heir with her elder brother, Jesus the Christ; but she inherits from her God-Father and her God-Mother. . . . The God-Father is not robbed of his everlasting glory by this maternal completion of himself. It is an expansion both of deity and humanity. They twain are one God![25]

Or his intriguing picture of the women helping the missionaries in foreign lands:

> The elders riveted the anchor of faith by good gospel logic, and their eloquent preachers enchanted the half-inspired mind with well-described millennial views, but the sisters, as a rule, by the nicest evangelical diplomacy brought the results about. They agitated the very atmosphere with their magical faith in the new dispensation; they breathed the spirit of their own beautiful enthusiasm into their neighborhood, they met the first brunt of persecution and conquered it by their zeal; they transformed unbelief into belief by their personal testimonies . . . they enticed the people to hear their elders preach, and did more to disturb the peace of the town than could have done the

---

23. Edward W. Tullidge, *The Women of Mormondom* (New York: Edward. W. Tullidge, 1877), 68.
24. Tullidge, 177.
25. Tullidge, 192–93.

town-crier; they crowded their halls with an audience when without their sisterly devising those halls had remained often empty and cold.²⁶

To which I say, gosh! Really? And finally, "The Mormon women, as well as men, hold the priesthood. To all that man attains, in celestial exaltation and glory, woman attains. She is his partner in estate and office."²⁷ This book raises questions, but its very rich biographical materials plus his sensational commentary, easily equaling the books of John or Revelation in their challenges to comprehension, set up much food for thought. This is writing to chew on.

VII

Next is Emma Smith's February 1879 firsthand testimony of the translation of the Book of Mormon. Part of Emma's interview with her son Joseph Smith III, this document is probably the best firsthand testimony of Joseph Smith's translation of the Book of Mormon—and it is by a woman who was there and who maintained that testimony long after she might have changed her mind. In this interview Emma does deny that her husband was involved in polygamy or "spiritual wifery"—a claim most historians consider untruthful—but she includes a very specific and detailed account of her husband translating the Book of Mormon. Here are some of her statements.²⁸

> I know Mormonism to be the truth, and believe the Church to have been established by divine direction. I have complete faith in it. In writing for your father I frequently wrote day after day, often sitting at the table close by him, he sitting with his face buried in his hat, with the stone in it, and dictating hour after hour with nothing between us. . . . He had neither manuscript nor book to read from. . . . If he had had anything of the kind he could not have concealed it from me. . . . The plates often lay on the table without any attempt at concealment, wrapped in a small linen table cloth, which I had given him to fold them in. I once felt of the plates, as they lay on the table, tracing their outline and shape. They seemed to be pliable like thick paper, and would rustle with a metallic sound when the edges were moved by the thumb, as one does sometimes thumb the edges of a book.²⁹

---

26. Tullidge, 266–67.
27. Tullidge, 487.
28. Quoted in Dan Vogel, *Early Mormon Documents*, vol. 1 (Salt Lake City: Signature Books, 2002), 534–43. Quotations are taken from the published version.
29. Vogel, 541.

> Joseph Smith ... could neither write nor dictate a coherent and well-worded letter, let alone dictating a book like the Book of Mormon. And, though I was an active participant in the scenes that transpired, and was present during the translation of the plates, and had cognizance of things as they transpired, it is marvelous to me, "a marvel and a wonder," as much so as to any one else. ... My belief is that the Book of Mormon is of divine authenticity—I have not the slightest doubt of it. I am satisfied that no man could have dictated the writing of the manuscripts unless he was inspired, for, when acting as his scribe, your father would dictate to me hour after hour, and when returning after meals, or after interruptions, he would at once begin where he had left off, without either seeing the manuscript or having any portion of it read to him. This was a usual thing for him to do. It would have been improbable that a learned man could do this; and, for one so ignorant and unlearned as he was, it was simply impossible.[30]
>
> I have been called apostate; but I have never apostatized, nor forsaken the faith I at first accepted, but was called so because I would not accept their new fangled notion.[31]

This is great scripture.

VIII

Now I get into spongy territory. I would like to include something from Susa Young Gates, the prolific daughter of Brigham Young. She writes with an attractive prophetic sureness, but I have not found one specific document to include.

Woman's Exponent, the little newspaper, became the voice of the Relief Society containing the writings of leaders, the official directions for local organizations, synopses of sermons, and much else. There is certainly important and useful spiritual narrative and instruction here. But, if we include the whole newspaper, we will have to take *The Young Woman's Journal* and the *Relief Society Magazine*. We already accord high status to the *Ensign* magazine. I don't want to edit sources, and I wouldn't want to include the whole LDS journalistic output. We can't admit the *Deseret News* and certainly not the *Salt Lake Tribune*. So, for now, the *Woman's Exponent* is out.

I am not including *Representative Mormon Women*, by Augusta Joyce Crocheron. That's a useful volume but is full of representations by Crocheron, not by the voices of women themselves. I'm not including Amy Brown Lyman, Alice Louise Reynolds, Elaine Cannon, Belle Spafford, or

---

30. Vogel, 542.
31. Vogel, 543.

Barbara Smith. Maybe they are just not old enough to sound like scripture to me. I have a big blank from the early twentieth century on. But we might notice that the restored scriptures of the Church thinned out quite a bit in the twentieth century too. I am still reading for good submissions.

IX

I would add one more sure entry, which may call into question some of my earlier rules for inclusion, and that is Chieko Okazaki's *Lighten Up*. The gospel according to Chieko, a complete course of study for the good life, full of homely examples and useful parables, provides an up-to-date Christianity especially for women. She was the greatest orator in the Church in these later years, the best teacher, and the one who speaks to women in all their LDS diversity. Here are a few of her many, many quotable comments:

> In our diversity, we manifest the pure light of Christ. Let us know each other, help each other, and love each other.[32]
>
> In principles, great clarity. In practices, great charity.[33]
>
> God wants you—not somebody else, not you in ten years, not a perfect you, but you right now.[34]
>
> We don't have to be in a sacred place for spiritual things to happen.[35]
>
> I strongly feel that we should expect struggles and imperfections in this life. The most realistic expectation we can make of ourselves is to do our best. We should not expect to control outcomes, either for ourselves or for our children.[36]
>
> I have had a sense that many mothers are wandering in just . . . a wilderness, burdened with guilt that they have accepted but of which they are innocent. It is true that much is expected of Latter-day Saint women. Mothers bear a great responsibility. But guilt is a burden they need not pick up. They need not make themselves responsible for the deficiencies of society.[37]
>
> Three ideas for a brighter life: First, you have permission to make mistakes. Second, accept what life gives you. And third, trust in the Lord's love for you.[38]

---

32. Chieko N. Okazaki, *Lighten Up* (Salt Lake City: Deseret Book, 1993), 16.
33. Okazaki, 17.
34. Okazaki, 69.
35. Okazaki, 73.
36. Okazaki, 78.
37. Okazaki, 91.
38. Okazaki, 103.

That one goes in even if I have to change the rules. We must grab and hold on to whatever we can from the past. At this point, I think more women than men are writing their own stories, their own family scriptures. Women might not feel the authority, but in this dispensation, they are feeling increasing justification. We cannot tell in advance what is going to make it into the canon. Such approval takes hundreds of years and sometimes strange accidents. But we do know that others besides the prophet receive revelation. All who have the Holy Ghost can prophesy. In our canonized books, all kinds of people make scripture. Prophets come out of the wilderness. Young boys get visitations. Women get revelation and write what will be scripture too. It takes a long time to turn our stories into gold, but if we do not write them down, they will never even become paper plates.

We should all be scriptorians, even as we should all be artists. We should not only study scripture, we should write it. It is good to know the scriptures of the past, but our responsibility is to create the scriptures of the future. We should give voice to such insight and revelation as come to us. We do not mean to usurp the president of the Church, but we have a responsibility to speak for our families, our wards, and for our other stewardships. I hope we will.

5

THE BOOK OF MORMON AS POST-CANONICAL SCRIPTURE

Grant Hardy

There is no question that the Book of Mormon was an important part of nineteenth-century America, and many students of American religious history have at least briefly mentioned its reception during that time period—that is, how people understood and responded to its message. Others have looked at the role the Book of Mormon has played in the history of the Latter-day Saints, from relative neglect during the first decades of Mormonism (aside from its continuing function as tangible evidence of Joseph Smith's prophetic calling) to a new Church-wide emphasis in the 1980s under President Ezra Taft Benson.

These are important perspectives, and there is still more work to be done in terms of American history and denominational studies. For instance, Laurie Maffly-Kipp's Penguin anthology of American sacred writings offers a promising avenue for additional comparative studies.[1] In this chapter, I will examine the Book of Mormon in the context of world scripture. If we broaden our view outward from America, and even from Christianity, it may allow us to ask new questions and make new observations about a text that is, in many ways, quite remarkable.

The first thing to note is that even though new scripture is produced regularly, very little of it has a continuing authoritative role within a long-term religious community. I would estimate that within the last thousand years, there are only about a dozen books or collections of writings that could be judged to have attained world scripture status. These might include the Zen classics *Biyan Lu* (*Blue Cliff Record*, twelfth century) and *Wumenguan* (*Gateless Gate*, thirteenth century), the Jewish *Zohar* (thirteenth century),

---

1. Laurie F. Maffly-Kipp, ed., *American Scriptures: An Anthology of Sacred Writings* (New York: Penguin, 2010). See also Eran Shalev, *American Zion: The Old Testament as a Political Text from the Revolution to the Civil War* (New Haven: Yale University Press, 2013), which offers another exciting comparative perspective.

the Baha'i sacred writings, and the *Ofudesaki* of the Japanese Tenrikyo sect (both from the nineteenth century). The twentieth century saw the Cao Dai scriptures in Vietnam, Sun Myung Moon's *Divine Principle*, Li Hongzhi's *Zhuan Falun*, and the writings of L. Ron Hubbard, though the staying power of the last three is still an open question.

The most successful new scripture of the last millennium, in terms of number of believers and world-wide reach, is the *Adi Granth* of the Sikhs, dating to 1604, with about 26 million adherents. The second most successful is the Book of Mormon, with about half as many believers. (Latter-day Saints don't often brag "We're number two!" but it is a notable accomplishment nonetheless.) Of course, if we extend our survey back another three and a half centuries, we catch the Qur'an, which greatly surpasses everything that comes after.

So if we examine the Book of Mormon in the context of world scripture, looking for similarities and differences, what kinds of features or characteristics are most noticeable? I'll start with five that seem pretty obvious, and then I'll try to sharpen the question a bit.

Five Basic Observations

(1) To begin with, the Book of Mormon takes the form of a lengthy, coherent, integrated, history-like narrative. This is an uncommon genre in world scripture, and it is nearly unique in world scripture produced in the last thousand years, which for the most part consist of commandments, devotional poetry, doctrinal expositions, community regulations, scriptural commentary, or prophecy. (The Doctrine and Covenants is much more typical of recent scripture than the Book of Mormon.) Whatever else the Book of Mormon may be, it is a work of theological exposition. Yet producing new scripture is an unusual way to do theology—as opposed to writing commentaries or doctrinal disputations or systematic treatises—and embedding theological thought within thick narrative is rarer still.

(2) A second unusual feature is that when the Book of Mormon was published in 1830 it was accepted immediately by believers as canonical and complete. This is quite rare in the history of religions. It took centuries for the canons of Hinduism, Buddhism, Judaism, Christianity, and Daoism to be firmly established. Gerald Sheppard, of the University of Toronto, once observed that:

> In examining religious scriptures as "canons," one may generalize that the founding leaders of religions almost never compose for their disciples a

complete scripture. The one obvious exception is that of the third-century Mani, founder of Manichaeism. There are usually substantial periods after the death of a leader or founder when oral and/or written traditions function authoritatively as canonical, in the sense of representing a scripture without specific dimension.[2]

Mani argued for the superiority of his religion by noting that he had written down and collected his revelations personally rather than leaving this task to his disciples, but today the Manichaean canon of seven scriptures exists only in fragments. A better example of an exception, at least in terms of being more accessible, is the Book of Mormon.

(3) Not only was its canonical status set from its first appearance, its form was relatively fixed as well. The textual history of the Book of Mormon is remarkably clear compared with most other sacred books. The Book of Mormon today is, apart from its grammar, essentially the same book that Joseph Smith first dictated, as can be seen from Royal Skousen's meticulous reconstruction of the earliest text.[3] This situation is quite different from other relatively recent sacred books such as the Qur'an, the *Adi Granth*, and the scriptures of Baha'i, to say nothing of the writings of Emanuel Swedenborg, Nakayama Miki (the founder of Tenrikyo), or Mary Baker Eddy, all of which took shape and acquired authoritative status over the course of decades.[4] The Book of Mormon is also distinct from other LDS scriptures. For various editions of the Doctrine and Covenants from 1835 to 1981, decisions were made about which of Joseph Smith's revelations to include and exclude, sometimes with substantive revisions to the documents themselves. The writings in the Pearl of Great Price were first collected and published in England in 1851, with additions in 1878 followed by formal canonization by church vote in 1880. That's the more common pattern.

---

2. Gerald T. Sheppard, "Canon," in the *Encyclopedia of Religion*, ed. Lindsay Jones, 2nd ed., 15 vols. (Detroit: Thomson Gale, 2005), 12:1408.

3. See Royal Skousen, ed., *The Book of Mormon: The Earliest Text* (New Haven: Yale University Press, 2009); and Royal Skousen, *Analysis of Textual Variants of the Book of Mormon*, 6 vols. (Provo, UT: Foundation for Ancient Research and Mormon Studies, 2004–9).

4. To be fair, I should clarify that in the case of the Qur'an, although it took two or three decades to codify and organize the written version after Muhammad's death, the original oral recitations revealed to the Prophet were considered authoritative from the beginning.

(4) It is also worth noting that in March 1830, when the Book of Mormon was first published, there was no Mormon church in existence (the Church was formally organized about two weeks later). Instead of a community of believers coming to accept the book as authoritative, the book created a religious community; those who viewed the Book of Mormon as equivalent to the Bible joined the movement and were soon known as "Mormonites," named after their distinctive scripture. This is unusual, though it was also the case with Christian Science, Scientology, and Falun Gong.

(5) Like Muslims and Sikhs, Latter-day Saints ended up with a fairly limited canon of several hundred pages, which has not been significantly expanded since the death of its founder. By contrast, Baha'is and Scientologists believe that all the writings of their founders are scripture, which in the case of the Baha'is runs to about a hundred volumes (fifteen times the length of the Old and New Testaments combined).

A More Exclusive Notion of Canon

David Holland has written an important study of the desire for new revelation in antebellum America, one that places the Book of Mormon within the mainstream of Christian theology rather than at the margins of folk magic or hermetic traditions. Yet in his discussion of Puritans, Deists, Evangelicals, African-American prophets, Adventists, and Transcendentalists, he focuses on an expansive, generic meaning of *canon*, which downplays the radical nature of Mormon scripture.[5]

Again, we might turn to Gerald Sheppard, who has suggested that we use the term "Canon 1" to refer to authoritative traditions, either written or oral, that are seen as binding in matters of faith and practice. These are the newly revealed instructions and injunctions that Holland so ably documents. "Canon 2," on the other hand, consists of a discrete, widely acknowledged collection of authoritative writings.[6] In Christianity, only the Old and New Testaments count as Canon 2. Later sermons, dreams, visions, prophecies, or inspired utterances might be accepted by some believers as coming from God, but they are rarely put forward as equivalent to the words of the Bible. That is to say, it would be a remarkable thing if some Christian group published an edition of the Bible that included ad-

---

5. David Holland, *Sacred Borders: Continuing Revelation and Canonical Restraint in Early America* (New York: Oxford University Press, 2011), 36.

6. Sheppard, "Canon," 12:1407–10.

ditional books after the book of Revelation.[7] Yet this is exactly what most Latter-day Saints carry to church every week in "quadruple combinations," with the Bible, the Book of Mormon, the Doctrine and Covenants, and Pearl of Great Price all bound within a single, leather-clad volume.

I don't know that anyone else in antebellum America wanted to challenge the exclusive authority of the Bible in quite this way, with the possible exception of the Shakers—whose *Sacred Roll* was first published in 1843 with an angelic instruction to keep a copy "sacred in the pulpit of their house of worship . . . to be used accordingly."[8] But the new Shaker scripture was a rather late development that was pushed to the margins of Shakerism within just a few years.[9] The Book of Mormon, by contrast, was central to Joseph Smith's religion from the beginning.

The Book of Mormon itself emphatically announced its status as Canon 2 when it reported God himself as declaring:

> Thou fool, that shall say: A Bible, we have got a Bible, and we need no more Bible. . . . Wherefore murmur ye, because that ye shall receive more of my word? Know ye not that the testimony of two nations is a witness unto you that I am God, that I remember one nation like unto another? . . . And I do this that I may prove unto many that I am the same yesterday, today, and forever; and that I speak forth my words according to mine own pleasure. . . . Wherefore, because that ye have a Bible ye need not suppose that it contains all my words; neither need ye suppose that I have not caused more to be written. . . . For behold, I shall speak unto the Jews and they shall write it;

---

7. James Charlesworth probably overstates things in his observation that "when one considers that global Christianity includes the Falasha and the Mormons, the concept of canon loses its inherent and traditional meaning," yet his two examples inadvertently highlight how unusual the LDS position is. The Falash Mura are descendants of Beta Israel, or Ethiopian Jews. They converted to Christianity in the nineteenth century and have kept some of the additional Jewish scriptures that were unique to their ancestors, but today they number only about 25,000 adherents. James H. Charlesworth, "Writings Ostensibly Outside the Canon," in *Exploring the Origins of the Bible: Canon Formation in Historical, Literary, and Theological Perspective*, ed. Craig A. Evans and Emanuel Tov (Grand Rapids: Baker Academic, 2008), 58. For Beta Israel scriptures, see Wolf Leslau, trans., *Falasha Anthology* (New Haven and London: Yale University Press, 1951).

8. *A Holy, Sacred, and Divine Roll and Book* (Canterbury, NH: The United Society, 1843), 11.

9. Holland, *Sacred Borders*, 129–41; Stephen J. Stein, "Inspiration, Revelation, and Scripture: The Story of a Shaker Bible," *Proceedings of the American Antiquarian Society* 105, no. 2 (1996): 347–76.

and I shall also speak unto the Nephites and they shall write it. . . . And it shall come to pass that the Jews shall have the words of the Nephites, and the Nephites shall have the words of the Jews. (2 Ne. 29:6–13)

In other words, God promises forthcoming revelations, and specifically the Book of Mormon, that will have equal authority with the Bible. Did other Americans in the nineteenth century understand that message? It appears that they did. The earliest extant public notice of the forthcoming scripture, in June 1829 (nine months prior to the publication of the Book of Mormon), referred to it as a "Golden Bible," a term that was frequently repeated, indicating that readers at the time understood the book's audacious ambitions to take its place as a second Bible.[10]

This observation suggests that the Book of Mormon might usefully be compared to other examples of what I'll call "post-canonical canon"—that is, new sacred texts that attempt to find a place within, or to supersede, canons that have been closed for some time. The Book of Mormon wants to reopen the biblical canon something along the lines of the relationship between the New Testament and the Hebrew Bible, or the Qur'an and the Jewish and Christian scriptures, or the way in which the *Adi Granth* and the Baha'i texts challenge the Qur'an. In each case there is a particular sort of textual self-awareness, a desire to adapt and incorporate the strengths of one's predecessor, while at the same time pointing out and remedying deficiencies. All these books are self-consciously defensive about their status as scripture and their relationship to earlier canonical texts.

Comparisons with Other Post-canonical Canons

The ways in which New Testament writers cited passages from the Septuagint as proof texts, or borrowed its phrases, or reinterpreted terms such as the "new covenant" of Jeremiah 31 or the political notion of *messiah* are well-studied. The relationship between the Book of Mormon and the King James Bible has received much less scholarly attention, surprisingly. A couple of quick observations: (1) It is odd, given the affinity of early Mormonism with Protestantism, that while the Book of Mormon laments the deletion of "plain and precious" truths from the Bible (1 Ne. 13), it does

---

10. *The Wayne Sentinel* (Palmyra, New York), June 26, 1829. This article, in both facsimile and transcript, is available at Matthew Roper and Sandra A. Thorne, eds., "19th-Century Publications about the Book of Mormon (1829–1844)," a website hosted by the Harold B. Lee Library at Brigham Young University, http://contentdm.lib.byu.edu/cdm/compoundobject/collection/BOMP/id/188/rec/1.

not also accuse the Catholic Church of making unauthorized additions; that is to say, Nephite prophets seem unaware of the controversy surrounding the Apocrypha. (2) The presence of Christian terms and concepts throughout the Book of Mormon, which appear rather anachronistic, represent an attempt to renegotiate the boundary between the Old and New Testaments.

Some nineteenth-century Americans recognized parallels between the Qur'an and the Book of Mormon, but few knew both texts well enough to make insightful comparisons.[11] John M'Chesney, for example, observed in 1838:

> Here we have both the book of Mormon, and the Alcoran [Qur'an] before us. They both breathe the same spirit—are both in the same style—twins were never more alike, except that the book of Mormon exhibits more of the low vulgar than the Alcoran; and if they were both bound in the same volume, you would hardly be able to distinguish by their spirit the difference.[12]

"Low vulgar" may be in the eye of the beholder, but the two books are structurally quite distinct. The Qur'an is presented as a transcript of God's direct revelation, in the first-person voice, whereas the Book of Mormon—like the Bible—is an account of various revelatory experiences, written by human beings who were trying to communicate God's will in particular, historical circumstances. Yet the claim that the Qur'an offers more direct access to God is mirrored somewhat by the Book of Mormon's contention that, unlike the Bible's messy compilation, canonization, transmission, and translation, the Nephite record passed directly from the hands of its authors to Joseph Smith, who subsequently produced a miraculous translation by the gift of God—claims that answered many of the complaints of Deists and other critics at the time.

The two books are also very different functionally. The Qur'an was intended to supersede the Bible. While Muhammad acknowledged the revealed status of the Torah, the Psalms, and the Gospel (a book, now lost, that had been revealed to Jesus), he taught that after the death of the prophets the sacred words had been distorted, emended, and augmented; hence the need for a new revelation. But since the Qur'an is perfect, there is little reason for Muslims to study the corrupt text of the Bible. By con-

---

11. J. Spencer Fluhman, "An 'American Mahomet': Joseph Smith, Muhammad, and the Problem of Prophets in Antebellum America," *Journal of Mormon History* 35, no. 3 (Summer 2008): 23–45.

12. James M'Chesney, *An Antidote to Mormonism* (New York: Burnett & Pollard, 1838), 18, http://contentdm.lib.byu.edu/cdm/compoundobject/collection/BOMP/id/1936/rec/1.

trast, the Book of Mormon sees itself as a supplement to the Bible, and Latter-day Saints today continue to read the Bible alongside the Book of Mormon. Indeed, it might be useful to see Mormon as producing a sequel to the Deuteronomistic History (Joshua through 2 Kings).

All four of the new, canon-expanding scriptures I mentioned draw upon their predecessors: the Book of Mormon borrows chapters from the Old and New Testaments, just as the *Adi Granth* incorporates the songs of fifteen medieval sufi and bhakti poets who were not themselves Sikhs, as Baha'u'llah's *Kitab-i-Iqan* (The Book of Certitude) constantly quotes the Qur'an, and as the Qur'an itself retells stories from the Bible.[13] The last example would be challenged by many Muslims, who see the Qur'an as having an independent origin completely separate from the Bible, but faiths based on new revelations have to work out what this means with respect to earlier, inherited religious traditions.

The connection between old and new scriptures is often reinforced by structure and formatting. For instance, although Sikhism draws from both Hinduism and Islam, its notions of scripture are much more aligned with the latter, and indeed, the Sikh reverence for the *Adi Granth* even surpasses the devotion that Muslims show for the Qur'an, at least in terms of outward ritual. Gurinder Singh Mann has pointed out how early manuscripts of the *Adi Granth* incorporate design elements in the borders and geometrical flourishes that were borrowed from the Qur'an, and even the repeated invocations at the beginning of sections are reminiscent of the Muslim holy book.[14] Similarly, the division of the Book of Mormon into books named for prophets is similar to the Bible, and Paul Gutjahr noted how the first edition of the Book of Mormon echoed the binding of the ubiquitous American Bible Society Bibles of the time.[15] The connection between the two books was further emphasized when the Book of Mormon was published in verses in 1879 and then in double columns in 1920. At that point, it looked like "scripture" to most Americans (though with the rise of modern biblical translations, the current formatting of the standard LDS edition only looks like "scripture" to senior citizens).

---

13. For the Sikh example, see Pashaura Singh, *The Bhagats of the Guru Granth Sahib: Sikh Self-Definition and the Bhagat Bani* (New Delhi: Oxford University Press, 2003).

14. Gurinder Singh Mann, *The Making of Sikh Scripture* (New York: Oxford University Press, 2001), 100–101.

15. Paul C. Gutjahr, *An American Bible: A History of the Good Book in the United States, 1777–1880* (Stanford: Stanford University Press, 1999), 152–53.

Daniel Madigan has observed that "the Qur'an is both itself and *about* itself," that "it retains the freedom to comment upon itself and upon the vicissitudes of its encounter with those who are slow to accept it."[16] Stefen Wild echoes this perspective:

> Many verses of the collection of these recitations that we now call the Qur'an speak about the communicative process between God and man in general, about the communicative process between the Prophet and God in particular, and finally about the relation between Muhammad's revelation and earlier revelations. The prophetic voice in the Qur'an constantly reflects, hones, and explains what it is saying, to whom it speaks, and what the relation between this and other prophetic messages is.

He argues that this intense self-consciousness makes Muhammad's recitation different from the Old and New Testaments, and concludes that the Qur'an is "probably the most self-reflexive and self-referential foundational text of any world religion."[17]

The Book of Mormon's self-awareness may not surpass that of the Qur'an, but it is certainly in the same league. Throughout the Latter-day Saint scripture, the narrators reflect on their sources, editing, and communicative strategies, and they frequently address their readers directly.[18] In addition, they constantly talk about their scripture-writing project—its origins, its divine mandate, its function, and its destiny. A sample of such passages, with some overlapping of themes, would include the following:

- Statements of purpose and intention: 1 Nephi 6:1–6, 9:1–6; 2 Nephi 5:29–33; Words of Mormon 1:1–11; Alma 37:1–20; Mormon 5:1–19, 7:1–10, 8:13–22

---

16. Daniel A. Madigan, *The Qur'an's Self-Image: Writing and Authority in Islam's Scripture* (Princeton: Princeton University Press, 2001), 62, 76; emphasis in original.

17. Stefan Wild, "Why Self-referentiality?" in *Self-Referentiality in the Qur'an*, ed. Stefan Wild (Wiesbaden: Harrassowitz Verlag, 2006), 3; emphasis in original. Wild cites a few instances of self-reflection in the New Testament, including John 20:30–31, 21:24–25, 2 Peter 1:15–18, 3:15–16, and Revelation 22:18–19, but he notes that "these self-referential verses do not mark the whole text; they do occur, but they do not have any special emphasis," unlike what we see in the Qur'an or the Book of Mormon (pp. 17–18).

18. See Grant Hardy, *Understanding the Book of Mormon: A Reader's Guide* (New York: Oxford University Press, 2010), esp. 3–16, 89–120.

- Visions or prophecies of the production of the text: 1 Nephi 13:34–41; 2 Nephi 3:6–23, 25:17–23, 27:1–23; 3 Nephi 21:1–10; Mormon 8:23–35; Ether 4:4–19
- Predictions of the effects or reception of the book: 2 Nephi 29:1–14, 30:1–7; Enos 1:11–18; 3 Nephi 16:4–5, 23:4–5, 27:23–26, 29:1–9; Ether 12:22–28; Moroni 10:27–29
- Accounts of Christ telling narrators precisely what to include or exclude: 1 Nephi 14:18–30; 3 Nephi 26:6–12, 30:1–2, 33:10–11; Ether 4:4–5, 13:13
- Affirmations of the truth of the record: 1 Nephi 1:1–3; 2 Nephi 33:1–15; 3 Nephi 5:12–19, 8:1, 17:25; Mormon 9:30–37; Moroni 10:1–7
- Prophecies of, and advice to, the future translator (Joseph Smith): 3 Nephi 3:6–21; Mormon 8:13–21; Ether 5:1–6

Why does the Book of Mormon talk this way? Because it is post-canonical canon.

Another way in which the Book of Mormon differs from the Qur'an, as well as from several other self-conscious new revelations, is that it does not claim sufficiency, completeness, or finality; instead, it keeps the canon open with explicit promises of scripture yet to come. Although no biblical authors saw themselves as contributing to a fixed collection of sacred documents, the two most self-consciously literary, late books are Deuteronomy and Revelation, both of which famously called down curses on anyone who would add or delete from their pages (Deut. 4:2, 12:32; Rev. 22:18–19); after the Christian scriptures were canonized, with Revelation as the last book, believers applied the proscription of adding or taking away to the Bible as a whole. Similarly, the Qur'an speaks of Islam as having been perfected and completed (Q 5:3), of its words as being unalterable (Q 15:27), and of Muhammad as the "seal of the prophets," after which there would be no more additions to the canon (Q 33:40). And the tenth Sikh guru, Gobind Singh, fixed the contents of the *Adi Granth* for all time when he pronounced it as his successor, the eternal guru, in 1708.

Contrast this with the Book of Mormon, which prophesies that the Jewish scriptures and the Nephite scriptures will someday be augmented by holy records from the Lost Tribes of Israel and all the nations of the earth. To quote more fully a passage that was cited above:

> For behold, I shall speak unto the Jews and they shall write it; and I shall also speak unto the Nephites and they shall write it; and I shall also speak unto the other tribes of the house of Israel, which I have led away, and they

shall write it; and I shall so speak unto all nations of the earth and they shall write it. And it shall come to pass that the Jews shall have the words of the Nephites, and the Nephites shall have the words of the Jews; and the Nephites and the Jews shall have the words of the lost tribes of Israel; and the lost tribes of Israel shall have the words of the Nephites and the Jews. (2 Ne. 29:12–13)

Moreover, during Jesus's post-resurrection visit to the Americas he told the Nephites that he had other stops to make elsewhere in the world, and Latter-day Saints assume that people in those unknown locations would have been commanded to keep records of their experiences just as the Nephites were (3 Ne. 16:1–4). So according to the Book of Mormon, other sacred ancient documents are still forthcoming, which will someday have equal claim to canonical status.[19] In the meantime, there are modern revelations recorded in the Doctrine and Covenants and Pearl of Great Price (though Mormonism's commitment to an open canon may eventually become problematic since the canon has been virtually closed since Joseph Smith).[20]

To recap quickly, the Book of Mormon claims more direct access to truth than the Bible, counters common criticisms of the Old and New Testaments, incorporates or amends earlier scripture, adopts traditional structure and formatting, somewhat atypically does not attempt to reclose the canon, and exhibits a high degree of self-referentiality. These are just a few of many, many observations that could be made. What we see in the Book of Mormon depends, to some extent, on what we compare it to and on the questions that we bring to the text. In an era when Mormon Studies is a rising field, when Latter-day Saints are saying to outsiders in academia and elsewhere, "Look at us; we're interesting; we have rich

---

19. At Ether 4:4–7, Moroni promises that after the Gentiles repent, they will receive the full revelations given to the Brother of Jared. And Mormon at 3 Nephi 26:10, speaking of people in the last days, states: "And when they shall have received this [the Book of Mormon], which is expedient that they should have first, to try their faith, and if it shall so be that they shall believe these things, then shall the greater things [a more extensive history of the Nephites] be made manifest unto them."

20. The three sections of the Doctrine and Covenants that postdate the death of Joseph Smith in 1844 are an account of the martyrdom written shortly thereafter, a revelation to Brigham Young in 1847, and a vision of Joseph F. Smith's in 1918. The material in the Pearl of Great Price is all from Joseph Smith. In contrast to the LDS Church, the Community of Christ has continued to add new sections regularly to their version of the Doctrine and Covenants.

traditions of history, theology, and scripture," we (speaking of myself and other Latter-day Saints) should, at the same time, be reading more in the history, theology, and scriptures of other religions. It's only fair, but it's also engaging and even inspiring. The more we know about other people's scriptures, the better we will be able to understand and evaluate our own sacred texts.

6

READING FROM THE GOLD PLATES

Richard Lyman Bushman

I am under the impression that in recent years the Book of Mormon has become the primary devotional text of Latter-day Saints. Judging from references in talks and the stories told in Primary, it seems to have become the scripture of choice for many Mormons. We study the four standard works pretty evenly in Sunday School, but when it comes to Sacrament Meetings we hear most frequently about the sons of Helaman or Nephi's resolve to go and do. The Book of Mormon is the scripture we are told we should read every year.

This is true probably because the Book of Mormon is so much more intelligible than the King James Version of the Bible. If we are ever going to restore the Bible to its former position, we will have to supplement the King James Version with the New Standard Revised or some other modern translation.

In this paper, I want to comment on the way we approach the Book of Mormon as modern, educated Latter-day Saints, particularly as our reading is affected by the gold plates. How does the book's fabulous background influence Mormons as they read? We don't usually think of the plates as we open to 2 Nephi or Helaman, but they are always there as the backstory of the text, and their presence, in my opinion, does affect how we read.

In a sense, our situation parallels that of modern, educated Christians who read the Bible knowing that the text comes from codexes inscribed long after the fact by unknown scribes. In both cases, the source of the devotional reading—plates or parchments—raises questions about the nature of the scriptural texts. Do they deserve our devotion?

Believing Christians realize, when they stop to think, that perhaps the man Isaiah did not really inscribe the words found in the book named for him. The original seventh-century text, long since gone, was passed down, edited, revised, interpolated, expanded, and reshaped by historical circumstances long after the original Isaiah died. The text, in other words, is not exactly what it appears to be. Centuries later, well-meaning editors may have combined original manuscripts into a single writing, introduced phrasing more relevant to their time, and hid all their doings under a pretext that everything was the product of the original prophet. In other words, Bible readers cannot be completely sure that the text from which they draw comfort and understanding is actually what it appears to be.

Book of Mormon readers labor under similar but different uncertainties. The fabulous gold plates, so unlike anything else in recorded history, so unlikely an object to fall into the hands of Joseph Smith, cast doubt on the whole enterprise. No one says the Bible is not an ancient text; but that charge is constantly brought against the Book of Mormon. Scarcely anyone outside of the Latter-day Saint movement considers it anything but a modern production. For most people, the book is essentially a hoax like the writings of Ossian or Washington Irving's Knickerbocker's *A History of New York*.[1]

Modern Mormons read the Book of Mormon well aware of how critics think of the book. They may believe in it whole-heartedly and derive light and truth from its pages, but at the same time they know that skeptics doubt its inspiration. The unbelievers consider the book a production of Joseph Smith or a collaborator, not Nephi, Mormon, and Moroni. Charles Taylor says that one condition of belief in the Secular Age is that even believers know there is an unbelieving, godless account of the world constantly rivaling their religious explanation.[2] Disbelief is likewise an inescapable alternative for modern readers of the Book of Mormon. Perhaps the surest evidence of this condition is the frequently heard comment from educated Mormons that Joseph Smith could not have written the Book of Mormon. The affirmation implies that readers are constantly asking themselves: Did Joseph Smith write the book himself? The question is inescapable.

Thus it is that modern readers go through the text thinking with two minds: the religious teachings of the prophets are processed with one mind, and the question about Joseph Smith's authorship is entertained in another. Readers may consistently affirm that Joseph Smith could not have imagined the text—it must have come from God—but the question remains.

---

1. James McPherson, trans., *The Poems of Ossian*, trans (London: J. Mundell, 1796); Diedrich Knickerbocker [Washington Irving], *A History of New York from the Beginning of the World to the End of the Dutch Dynasty*, 2 vols. (New York: n.p., 1809).

2. Charles Taylor, *A Secular Age* (Cambridge: Harvard University Press, 2007).

Particular passages may raise doubts more than others. Some may look very much like an insertion by the nineteenth-century Joseph. Years ago Blake Ostler proposed that the book is a hybrid of ancient and modern material—some from the Nephite past, some from Joseph Smith's present. He came to this conclusion despite his fundamental belief in the book's historicity because of passages that were so markedly nineteenth-century in flavor and content.[3]

One such passage that for many points to a nineteenth-century creation is found in the Words of Mormon. I am thinking of the verses where Mormon says that while writing his history he found another set of plates which he described as a "small account of the prophets, from Jacob down to the reign of this King Benjamin, and also many of the words of Nephi" (W of M 1:3). This small account covered the same period he had just abridged from the plates of Nephi but dealt more with prophets than with kings. Mormon liked the "small account" so much that he decided to add it to his own abridgement, and presumably the two were spliced together, perhaps bound into the same set of rings, like adding pages to a loose-leaf notebook.

At this point, modern events thrust themselves into the story in a way that may unsettle believing readers. The small plates seem to come along all too conveniently to solve the problem of the so-called lost 116 pages. Through the winter and spring of 1828, Joseph Smith had dictated Mormon's abridgement of the plates of Nephi down to the reign of King Benjamin helped by his Palmyra friend Martin Harris. When Harris begged to borrow the manuscript to show to his doubting wife, the pages were lost, leaving Joseph in a quandary.

He was horrified and at a loss what to do. For months he stopped translating. He said he was afraid that if he retranslated the text, the conspirators would doctor the original which, varying from the new text, would be deemed a fraud. But of course modern skeptics see in his anxiety a fear that he would be unable to duplicate his previous work. If there were no plates to translate at all and the 116 pages were purely Smith's creation, of course he could not dictate a second version that would exactly match the first (D&C 10:14–33).

His solution to the problem was to retrofit the Book of Mormon. In this critical reading, Smith had the prophet Nephi inscribe a second smaller set of plates, parallel to the first, and conveniently pile them in

---

3. Blake T. Ostler, "The Book of Mormon as a Modern Expansion of an Ancient Source," *Dialogue: A Journal of Mormon Thought* 20, no. 1 (Spring 1987): 66–123.

with the first plates of Nephi where Mormon could stumble across them. In the text, Nephi admitted that he knew not why he was asked to double up on his history, only proposing that the Lord had his purposes (1 Ne. 19:3). For the doubters, the purpose, of course, was to help Joseph Smith out of a jam. These are thoughts that may occur even to believing readers as they entertain the question of whether Joseph Smith wrote this text. The small plates look like a somewhat awkward recovery from a disaster that blew Smith's cover.

Before we move to this conclusion, however, we need to consider how Nephi's small plates fit into the Book of Mormon story: If Smith was retrofitting the text to get out of a tight spot, how did he do it? What does the author of the book, whether Nephi or Joseph Smith, make of the second set of plates? As it turns out, inside the Book of Mormon, the plates have a significant part in the plot, virtually becoming an actor in the history. They seem more than a contrivance to replace the lost 116 pages.

Nephi began the large plates of Nephi—the ones Mormon abridged—soon after his father's party had reached the land of promise (ca. 589 BCE). Nephi reported that they found "all manner of ore, both of gold, and of silver, and of copper" (1 Ne. 18:25).

> Wherefore I did make plates of ore that I might engraven upon them the record of my father, and also our journeying in the wilderness, and the prophecies of my father; and also many of mine own prophecies have I engraven upon them. (1 Ne. 19:1)

At the time, Nephi thought these original plates were all he would write on (1 Ne. 19:2). He told his people that when he was gone, "these plates should be handed down from one generation to another, or from one prophet to another, until further commandments of the Lord" (v. 4).

Then about twenty years later, thirty years after Lehi had left Jerusalem, Nephi was commanded to make another set of plates: "The Lord God said unto me: Make other plates; and thou shalt engraven many things upon them which are good in my sight, for the profit of my people" (2 Ne. 5:30). To distinguish the two sets of plates, Nephi said that on the small plates he "engraved that which is pleasing unto God," while for "the more particular part of the history," the story of kings and wars, they must go to the other plates he had been working on since their arrival. The two sets of plates were characterized as roughly historical on the one hand and spiritual on the other (1 Ne. 19:3).

Within Nephi's narrative, however, the small plates served a far more serious purpose. They were not merely a collection of sermons, visions, and prophecies; they were a potent political document in Nephi's long-standing feud with his brothers. The timing of their creation has to be kept in mind. Nephi began the small account immediately after a violent split within the family. Until the death of their father, the six brothers fought and argued but remained one family. Lehi held them together despite his misgivings about his two oldest boys, Laman and Lemuel (2 Ne. 2:26).

Almost immediately after Lehi's death, the long-brewing animosity between Nephi and his two older brothers burst into the open. Nephi could not restrain himself from rebuking them, and they did not take it lying down (2 Ne. 4:13, 14). Finding it unbearable in this patriarchal society for their younger brother to rule over them, they determined to slay him (2 Ne. 5:3–4). Laman and Lemuel had sought Nephi's life before, but this time Lehi was no longer there to reconcile his sons' differences, and Nephi failed to keep the peace. Nephi was compelled to flee, taking with him three of his brothers, Sam, Jacob, and Joseph, and his sisters. The division that was to characterize Book of Mormon society until the end had been opened. Where there had been a single family, two nations in embryo came into being.

At this critical juncture in the history of Lehi's family, Nephi was instructed to "make other plates" (2 Ne. 5:30). They were begun at the exact moment when the tension in the family reached the breaking point. Unable to contain his anger, Nephi's animosity against the Lamanites boiled over onto the small plates. God, he said,

> had caused the cursing to come upon them, yea, even a sore cursing, because of their iniquity. . . . And thus saith the Lord God: I will cause that they shall be loathsome unto thy people, save they shall repent of their iniquities. . . . And because of their cursing which was upon them they did become an idle people, full of mischief and subtlety, and did seek in the wilderness for beasts of prey. (2 Ne. 5:21–22, 24)

Underlying his fury was the great issue that divided him and his brothers from the beginning. Nephi believed that God had said he "should be their ruler and their teacher," and the brothers would not yield to this fate (2 Ne. 5:19). They thought he was a usurper, not the chosen instrument of the Lord. The resulting break could be seen as the failure of Lehi's project.

The account on the small plates did contain the pleasing "things of God," as Nephi said it should, but it was driven by his break with his brothers (2 Ne. 5:32). The moral of story after story was that Nephi acted with the blessing of God and his father Lehi, while Laman and Lemuel had resisted both. The book of First Nephi and the first five chapters of Second Nephi were an extended apology for the split with Laman and Lemuel.

Perhaps Nephi feared that he had failed his father.[4] He certainly was driven to despair by the split in the family. Immediately after describing the divide and the Lamanites' base condition, he lamented his own failings as if he were at fault: "O wretched man that I am! Yea, my heart sorroweth because of my flesh; my soul grieveth because of mine iniquities" (2 Ne. 4:17). He had failed to maintain the unity his father had spent his life preserving. Depressed and perhaps conscience-stricken, Nephi had to explain to his posterity why he had failed. First Nephi, the first half of his small plates, was the justifying text.

Political aims drove the writing so long as Nephi was the chief historian, but as the small account passed to his brother Jacob and down through his lineage, its underlying purpose shifted. It became a different kind of book. As the Lamanites became a more distant threat rather than an ever-present reality, the immediate need for justification of Nephi's rule faded, and the small account assumed a different character. Instead of an indictment of Laman and Lemuel, it took the form of instruction to the Nephite people. Its aim was to keep the Nephites on the straight path and help them understand their place in the history of God's people. No longer was it necessary to discredit the wicked brothers. Jacob, Nephi's brother, even acknowledged that the Lamanites had become more righteous than the Nephites, an admission Nephi would have found hard to make (Jacob 3:5–9).

Where does this explication of the small plates leave the questioning reader who is troubled by their convenient injection into the story just as Joseph Smith is recovering from the loss of the 116 pages? The small plates could indeed have been an invention to rescue the floundering translator. But the plates were no Band-Aid to patch up a wounded narrative. They were deeply integrated into the plot and in some sense its cornerstone. The struggle between the brothers told so forcibly in Nephi's favor on the small plates motivates the rest of the narrative. The small plates were not just the physical carrier of the story but a major player in the entire Nephite drama.

So it is that the Book of Mormon frustrates easy judgments about the creator of the small plates. Yes, the hand of the nineteenth-century author may reveal itself in the Words of Mormon, but we cannot be so

---

4. For an elaboration of this possibility, see Grant Hardy, *Understanding the Book of Mormon: A Reader's Guide* (New York: Oxford University Press, 2010), 50–56.

sure when we look at the story more closely. The small plates seem like anything but an afterthought. Within the story they appear to be a necessary instrument of Nephi's campaign for dominance. The small plates may be Joseph's creation to bail him out of his difficulties, but Nephi also used them to bail himself out of his difficulties. They could be wholly Nephi's.

The facts of the matter do not allow a reader to come down decisively on either side. We must labor on through the text, perpetually asking who wrote these words. The gold plates prevent some readers from even considering the book to be authentic history. But for others, the tantalizing possibility that this marvelous artifact actually existed cannot be eliminated. While one part of the believing mind continues to question, the other finds guidance and inspiration in the book's pages.

7

HISTORY AND THE CLAIMS OF REVELATION: JOSEPH SMITH AND THE MATERIALIZATION OF THE GOLDEN PLATES[1]

Ann Taves

Introduction

Theologians and philosophers of religion have discussed the relationship between revelation and history at length in an effort to protect believers' claims from the corrosive effects of historical scrutiny.[2] Here I want to approach this relationship from the point of view of the secular historian in order to consider the questions that historians can bring to such claims, the kinds of data we can analyze, the sorts of explanations we might consider, and the responsibilities that we owe to our subjects *as historians* if we want to explain their claims in non-native terms. Using Mormonism, a relatively recent, well-documented, and still highly contentious instance of an alleged new revelation as a case study, I will seek to illustrate two points: (1) historical methods are well-positioned to bring

---

1. Versions of this paper were given at the conference on Researching Religion at Aarhus University in Denmark, the Mary Olive Woods Lecture at Western Illinois University in Macomb, the Alumna of the Year Lecture at the University of Chicago Divinity School, the Dickinson Distinguished Fellow Lecture at Dartmouth College, the Donald Benson Memorial Lecture at Iowa State University, and at the 2013 meeting of the Mormon History Association. I am grateful to conversation partners in all these contexts for helpful feedback and discussion. Thanks above all to Richard Bushman, Kathleen Flake, Stephen Fleming, Steven C. Harper, and Jan Shipps for reading drafts and providing feedback on my efforts to play fair with the Mormon sources. An earlier version of this essay was published in *Numen* 61 (2014): 182–207.

2. Van A. Harvey, *The Historian and the Believer: The Morality of Historical Knowledge and Christian Belief*, rev. ed. (Urbana: University of Illinois Press, 1996); see also Keith Ward, *Religion and Revelation* (Oxford: Clarendon Press, 1994).

well-documented "outliers"—unusual events, figures, and movements—into conversation with events, figures, and movements that are more amenable to study using ethnographic and experimental methods, and (2) Mormon claims regarding new revelation force non-Mormon scholars to struggle to make sense of seemingly implausible claims, a project that has long fascinated both anthropologists and historians of religion.

Neither of these aims requires us to draw upon unusual methods; we simply need to use familiar tools—historical critical, comparative, and explanatory—in an evenhanded and transparent way. First, we need to reconstruct the emergence of the newly claimed revelation in light of the full range of historical evidence offered by both believers and skeptics as the process unfolded. Second, if we seek to explain their claims, we need to articulate our presuppositions forthrightly in order to make the parameters within which we seek to explain explicit. Third, we need to use comparisons based on various stipulated points of analogy in order to illuminate aspects of the phenomenon and generate an explanation within the parameters specified.

The Mormon claim that Joseph Smith Jr. discovered ancient golden plates buried in a hillside in upstate New York provides an important test case since two leading Latter-day Saints (LDS) scholars of early Mormonism, Richard Bushman and Terryl Givens, argue that secular or non-Mormon historians have not taken the historical evidence for this claim seriously and that, as a consequence, historical scholarship on early Mormonism has remained highly polarized. Bushman has argued that it is this question of the plates that has led Mormon and non-Mormon historians to offer divergent characterizations of Smith. Non-Mormon historians, assuming there were no plates, presume there was something "fishy" going on, as Bushman puts it, and this then colors their entire assessment of Smith.[3]

To dismiss LDS claims, Bushman says, "unbelieving historians . . . repress material [evidence] coming from eyewitnesses close to Smith [who] consistently wrote and acted as if he had the Book of Mormon plates."[4] The crux of the problem, according to Givens, is that this evidence grounds the Book of Mormon "in artifactual reality."[5] If Smith only claimed to have spoken with an angel or seen the plates, Givens says,

---

3. Richard Bushman, *Believing History: Latter-day Saint Essays*, eds. Reid L. Neilson and Jed Woodworth (New York: Columbia University Press, 2004), 269.

4. Bushman, 93.

5. Terryl Givens, *By the Hand of Mormon: The American Scripture that Launched a New World Religion* (New York: Oxford University Press, 2002), 12.

we could explain his new revelation as a subjective experience for which there would be little objective evidence. Smith and his followers, however, claimed that that they not only saw but also held objectively real golden plates. "Dream-visions," Givens rightly insists, "may be in the mind of the beholder, but gold plates are not subject to such facile psychologizing."[6] From an LDS perspective, the materiality of the golden plates presents secular historians with a significant stumbling block. Givens was right, I think, to argue that we cannot just explain the golden plates in terms of "Joseph's psyche or religious unconscious."[7] For those of us interested in naturalistic explanations, this offers an intriguing challenge.

Explanations of the golden plates to date tend to presuppose an either/or choice: ancient golden plates either existed or they did not. If they existed, then Smith was who he claimed to be. If they did not and Smith knew it, then he must have consciously deceived his followers in order to convince them that they existed. Alternatively, if Smith believed there were plates when in fact there were not, then he was deluded. Although some non-believing historians have chosen to bracket the contentious issue of the golden plates, others—both non-Mormon and ex-Mormon—forthrightly acknowledge their belief that there were no actual golden plates; indeed, this is so obvious to some historians that they are taken aback when they discover that many Mormon intellectuals believe there were.[8]

In keeping with these either/or choices, non-believing contemporaries of Smith and non-believing historians in the present typically explain Smith's claims regarding the plates in terms of deception, fantasy, or a prank that got out of hand. Within two years of the alleged removal of the plates from the hill in 1827, Smith's neighbor, Peter Ingersoll, claimed that the box that supposedly contained the plates really contained only sand.[9] Historian Fawn Brodie, relying on this source, suggests that: "Perhaps in the beginning Joseph never intended his stories of the golden plates to be taken so seriously, but once the masquerade had begun, there was no point at which he could call a halt. Since his own family believed him . . . why

---

6. Givens, 42.

7. Givens, 42.

8. The latter includes Bushman and Givens, who wonder how well-trained, non-believing historians can dismiss so much evidence.

9. Dan Vogel, ed., *Early Mormon Documents*, 5 vols. (Salt Lake City: Signature Books, 1996–2003), 2:44–45.

should not the world?"[10] Historian Dan Vogel views the materiality of the plates as "the most compelling evidence" for "conscious misdirection" on Smith's part.[11] Speculating that Smith most likely made the plates himself out of tin, Vogel characterizes the recovery of the plates as a mix of deception and fantasy, the sort of "pious fraud" that he associates with shamans and magicians.[12]

Skeptics in my view have been too quick to jump from the assumption that there were no plates to the conclusion that Smith was either deluded or a fraud. In doing so, they sidestep the most interesting (and challenging) questions. For the sake of argument, I want to assume that there were no plates, or at least no ancient golden plates, and at the same time take seriously believers' claim that Smith was not a fraud. If we start with those premises, then we have to explain how the plates might have become *real* for Smith as well as his followers. The challenge, however, is not just to explain how they might have become real for Smith, but how they might have become real for him *in some non-delusory sense*.[13] This shift in premises forces us to consider a greater range of explanatory possibilities and has the potential to expand our understanding of the way that new religious movements emerge.

To open up some new options, I want to turn to a letter written by Jesse Smith, Joseph Smith's staunchly Calvinist uncle, to Joseph's older brother Hyrum in June 1829—two years after Joseph claimed to have recovered the golden plates, but before the translation was published in 1830.[14] In a scathing attack, Jesse Smith denounced "the whole pretended discovery" and compared Joseph to the Israelites in the desert bowing down before the golden calf. Joseph, Jesse wrote, was like a "man [who] . . . makes his own gods, [then] falls down and worships before it, and says this is my god

---

10. Fawn M Brodie, *No Man Knows My History: The Life of Joseph Smith* (New York: Vintage Books, 1995), 41.

11. Dan Vogel, *Joseph Smith: The Making of a Prophet* (Salt Lake City: Signature Books, 2004), xi.

12. Vogel, xi–xx, 44–45, 98–99. Characterizing shamans as "pious frauds" begs the question, as the literature on shamans and shamanistic practices is at least as complicated and contentious as the literature on Joseph Smith. For an overview, see Andrei A. Znamenski, ed., "General Introduction: Adventure of the Metaphor. Shamanism and Shamanism Studies," in *Shamanism: Critical Concepts in Sociology* (London: Routledge, 2004), xix–lxxxvi.

13. I am grateful to the philosophers at Western Illinois University for challenging me on this point.

14. Vogel, *Early Mormon Documents*, 1:552; for context, see 1:567.

which brought me out of the land of Vermont." In Joseph's case, though, it was not a golden calf but a "gold book discovered by the necromancy of infidelity, & dug from the mines of atheism." His Calvinist sensibilities outraged, Jesse summarized the letter he had received a year earlier, complaining, "[H]e writes that the angel of the Lord has revealed to him the hidden treasures of wisdom & knowledge, even divine revelation, which has lain in the bowels of the earth for thousands of years [and] is at last made known to him." To this very early account of the new revelation, Jesse then adds: "[H]e has eyes to see things that are not, and then has the audacity to say they are."[15]

This is an extraordinarily rich passage that opens up several lines of inquiry, two of which I want to consider here: first, the allusion to the golden calf, idolatry, and Joseph as the "maker of his own gods"; and second, Jesse's astute, albeit somewhat puzzling, observation that his nephew had "eyes to see things that are not, and then [had] the audacity to say they are." The first takes us into the complex relationships between materiality and sacrality, on the one hand, and between human creativity and divine manifestation, on the other. The second takes us into the problematics of perception. What exactly does it mean to say someone has eyes to see things that are not? Does it mean that the things do not exist, that they are imagined or made up, as Jesse believed? Does it mean that there are things that do exist that are not visible to those who do not have the eyes to see them, as Joseph's followers claimed? Or might it mean, as I will suggest, that he had eyes to see what *could be* and the audacity to give what he envisioned tangible form?

In making this argument, I am playing with the idea of discovery: turning away from discovery as a literal recovery of ancient golden plates buried in a hill in upstate New York to discovery as skillful seeing. If we view Smith as a skilled perceiver, we can view the appearance of the angel Moroni in 1823 as a dream-vision that opened up the possibilities present in a particular historical moment and the testimony to the materiality of the golden plates as evidence of Smith's ability to bring forth his dream-vision. Viewing Smith in this way takes his claim to seership seriously and allows us to consider the seer alongside the artist as the creator of things that, in Martin Heidegger's sense, open up new worlds.[16] Nonetheless, a seer, however perceptive, becomes a seer only with the support and collab-

---

15. Vogel, 1:552.
16. Martin Heidegger, *Poetry, Language, Thought* (New York: Harper and Row, 1971), 43–44.

oration of others who play a crucial role as co-creators of the new worlds their seers envision. In that sense, the seer is like the physician who cannot heal apart from his or her patients.

Building on a review of the evidence for the materiality of the plates, this essay uses a series of three comparisons—between the golden plates and sacred objects in other religious traditions, between Smith's claims and claims that psychiatrists define as delusional, and between Smith's role as a seer and the role of the artist and the physician as skilled perceivers—to generate a greater range of explanatory options. In light of these comparisons, I argue that the materialization of the golden plates might be better understood as an interactive process that involves a person with unusual abilities, intimate others who recognized and called forth those abilities, and objects that facilitated the creation of both the revelator and the revelation.

The Materiality of the Plates

Bushman is right to point out that those close to Smith did quite consistently act as if he had ancient plates. Although Jesse Smith died a fervent Calvinist, all of Smith's immediate family and many in his extended family were convinced that the gold book was real. Moreover, when it was published in 1830, the Book of Mormon contained the testimony of two sets of witnesses ("the three" and "the eight"), some of them family members and others closely involved with the translation process, who claimed they had seen or handled the plates. Stepping back, we can identify three types of evidence: first, accounts of feeling and "hefting" the plates while the plates were covered with a cloth or contained in a box; second, the accounts of the three and eight witnesses, who claim to have seen the plates directly; and third, relatively detailed visual descriptions, which characterize the plates in terms of size and appearance and have been used to create models of them.

Although Smith, his parents, and others, such as David Whitmer, provide detailed descriptions that have been used by believers to create models of the plates,[17] most of the sources agree that no one was allowed to look at the plates directly from the time they were recovered in September 1827 until they were shown to the witnesses in late June 1829, after which time they were no longer available. Most of the evidence offered by Smith's immediate family and those directly involved in the translation process is

---

17. Vogel, *Early Mormon Documents*, 1:171, 1:221, 1:462, 5:38.

of something material, which, though obscured by a cloth or kept hidden in a box, nonetheless could be felt and "hefted." Smith's younger siblings, William[18] and Catherine[19], both recount that they had hoped to see the plates when Smith brought them home, but that when he said they were not allowed to look at them directly, they obeyed. Smith's wife Emma provided a more detailed account that ran along similar lines.[20] Martin Harris, who helped with the translation, reported that "[t]hese plates were usually kept in a cherry box made for that purpose, in the possession of Joseph and myself. The plates were kept from the sight of the world, and no one, save Oliver Cowdrey, myself, Joseph Smith, jr., and David Whitmer [i.e., Smith and the three witnesses], ever saw them."[21] The signed testimony of the three and the eight witnesses provides relatively little physical detail. The three—Cowdery, Whitmer, and Harris—simply testified that "we beheld & saw the plates & the engraving thereon,[22] while the eight testified that the plates, which "we did handle with our hands & we also saw the engraving thereon," had "the appearance of gold."[23]

The more detailed descriptions of the plates seem not to reflect what people saw firsthand but the way Smith described the plates to them. Joseph Knight, who was staying with the Smiths the night Smith ostensibly recovered the plates, recounts that Smith described the plates to him the next morning, indicating "the Length and width and thickness of the plates[,] and[,] said he[,] they appear to be Gold." But according to Knight—and Smith's mother Lucy agrees on this point—Knight did not see the recovered plates, which were still not present in the house, but presumably hidden for safekeeping.[24] The later descriptions offered by Smith's parents and others are similar to the one that Smith offered to Joseph Knight, suggesting that the models of the plates are based on Smith's descriptions rather than what they actually saw.[25]

---

18. Vogel, 1:479, 497, 505, 508, 511
19. Vogel, 1:521, 524.
20. Vogel, 1:539–40.
21. Vogel, 2:306.
22. Vogel, 5:347.
23. Vogel, 3:471.
24. Vogel, 4:15.
25. Smith described the plates in an interview in 1842 (Vogel, 1:171), his mother in an interview in 1842 (Vogel, 1:221), and his father in a similar fashion in an interview in 1829 or 1830, published four decades later (Vogel, 1:462, 456). In 1878, David Whitmer, who aided in the translation and was one of the

If we look beyond this inner circle of believers, all of whom testified to the materiality of the plates, opinion as to the existence of the gold plates was sharply divided. There were many, mostly associates or former associates of Smith's in the local treasure-seeking network, who clearly believed the plates existed, viewed them as gold treasure rather than a gold bible, and went to great lengths to get them away from Smith, but without success. Then there were those who viewed Smith as a charlatan and a deceiver who fabricated plates in order to promote his revelatory claims, including Harris's wife Lucy,[26] Emma Smith's family,[27] and neighbors such as the Ingersolls.[28]

What I find most striking, though, is that the discussions of the materiality of the plates, whether by insiders or outsiders to the tradition, seem to presuppose that we are talking about materiality in the ordinary sense of the term.[29] If we examine key events in the material history of the plates, however, it appears that their material presence remains under the control of supernatural entities that have the power to manifest or withdraw them as they see fit. "The Testimony of the Three Witnesses" published with the Book of Mormon provides the most obvious example. Smith did not simply show the plates to the three witnesses; instead, they testified that they were shown the plates "by the power of God & not of man," and specifically that "an angel of God came down from Heaven & *he brought & laid before our eyes* that we beheld & saw the plates & the engraving thereon."[30] In contrast, the published "Testimony of the Eight Witnesses" indicates that Smith showed them the plates, not an angel.[31]

---

three witnesses, provided a similar description of what he saw when "an angel laid the plates before his eyes" in June 1829 (Vogel, 5:38).

26. Vogel, 1:382–86.
27. Vogel, 4:284–88.
28. Vogel, 1:385–86, 2:39–45.
29. Grant H. Palmer, *An Insider's View of Mormon Origins* (Salt Lake City: Signature Books, 2002) is the most notable exception.
30. Vogel, 5:347; emphasis added.
31. Vogel, 3:464–72. While there is general agreement that the testimony of the three witnesses could be read as describing a visionary experience, skeptics and believers tend to disagree with respect to the testimony of the eight, with believers arguing that the eight saw and handled the plates directly (see Givens, *By the Hand of Mormon*, 39–40; Richard L. Anderson, "Attempts to Redefine the Experience of the Eight Witnesses," *Journal of Book of Mormon Studies* 14, no. 1 (2005): 18–31, 125–27) and skeptics arguing that they did not (see Dan Vogel, "The Validity of the Witnesses' Testimony," in Dan Vogel and Brent Lee

Nonetheless, according to his mother Lucy, Smith did not bring the plates to the grove so that the eight could handle them. Rather, she indicates, the eight "repaired to a little grove where it was customary for the family to offer up their secret prayers[,] as Joseph had been instructed that *the plates would be carried there by one of the ancient Nephites*." Moreover, she adds, "[a]fter the witnesses returned to the house the Angel again made his appearance to Joseph and *received the plates* from his hands."[32]

Lucy Smith recounts other occasions in which an angel transported the plates from one place to another. Prior to traveling from Pennsylvania back to New York, the Lord told Smith to leave the plates in Pennsylvania and "he would receive the plates from the hand of an angel" after he arrived at the Whitmer's house in New York.[33] Smith also monitored the plates from a distance using his "interpreters." Thus, according to his mother, "Joseph kept the urim and thumim constantly about his person as he could by this means ascertain at any moment <if> the plates were in danger."[34] In addition, both Joseph's record[35] and Lucy's record[36] indicate that an angel took the plates back after Harris reported that the first part of the manuscript had disappeared.

In short, insider accounts do not depict the plates as an ordinary material object, but rather as an object that angels, "ancient Nephites," and, in particular, the angel Moroni, who was himself "an ancient Nephite," could display, deliver, and take away as appropriate. Even though the inner circle that saw and touched the plates generally acknowledged that they had either seen the plates in vision or obscured by a covering, believers and non-believers found the "magical realism" of the plates hard to grasp. In 1837–38 a number of well-placed believers left the church when

---

Metcalfe, eds., *American Apocrypha: Essays on the Book of Mormon* (Salt Lake City: Signature Books, 2002), 79–121; Palmer, *An Insider's View*; Dan Vogel, "Book of Mormon Witnesses Revisited: A Response to Richard L. Anderson, Stephen C. Harper, Daniel C. Peterson, Richard L. Bushman, and Alan Goff," accessed May 15, 2018, http://www.mormonthink.com/vogelwitnesses.htm). Although Richard L. Anderson quotes Lucy Smith's account (see Anderson, "Attempts to Redefine," 21–22), both he and his interlocutors focus on what the witnesses saw in the grove without commenting on how Lucy indicates the plates got there. Thanks to Mark Ashurst-McGee for bringing this discussion to my attention.

32. Vogel, *Early Mormon Documents*, 1:395–96; emphasis added.
33. Vogel, 1:391.
34. Vogel, 1:334, 338.
35. Vogel, 1:73.
36. Vogel, 1:370–71.

Harris allegedly testified, according to Warren Parish, that "he never saw the plates except in vision, and . . . that any man who says he has seen them in any other way is a liar, Joseph [Smith] not excepted"[37] and, according to Stephen Burnett, that neither the three nor the eight witnesses had seen "the plates with his natural eyes only in vision or imagination."[38] Although Harris's testimony apparently caused considerable consternation, Parrish noted that it was supported by the revelation Smith received in June 1829, preserved in the canonized Doctrine and Covenants (D&C 17:5), which indicated that the three witnesses would see the plates, "as my servant Joseph Smith, Jun., has seen them; *for it is by my* [God's] *power that he has seen them*, and it is because he had faith."[39] In other words, God (or Smith in revelatory mode, depending on how you look at it) conceded that Smith himself only saw the plates through the power of God in faith.

The fact that insiders do not describe the golden plates as an ordinary material object, but rather as one that ancient Nephites display, deliver, and take away as appropriate; the fact that Lucy Smith says that ancient

---

37. Vogel, 2:289.

38. Vogel, 2:291.

39. Vogel, 2:289n2; emphasis added. It is not clear what was so disturbing about Harris's testimony, partly because we do not know exactly what Harris said (for text and commentary, see Vogel, 2:288–93). Although he may have said that the testimony of the eight was false, he most likely said, under some duress, that the eight—like the three—saw the plates in vision, which then, as now, is not how believers typically interpret the witness of the eight. Whether or not he said "Joseph Smith not excepted" is not clear either, as it appears in Parrish's but not Burnett's account. There is no indication that Harris considered his testimony as a repudiation of the Book of Mormon; indeed Burnett reports him as saying "he knew it was true." Most likely, then, Harris simply reiterated his long-standing testimony to have seen the plates "with the eye of faith [although covered with a cloth] . . . just as distinctly as I see any thing around me" (Vogel, 2:292n11), and when pressed on the matter in the heat of an emotional meeting, claimed that the same was true for the eight as well. Since he allegedly said that "he would have let it pass as it was . . . if it had not been picked out of him" (Vogel, 2:292), I suspect that Harris typically allowed people to believe what they wished about the testimony of the eight because he knew some people had difficulty with the idea that all the witnesses had seen through the eyes of faith. Given the evidence already presented that people, including Smith, either saw ancient plates directly in vision or through the eyes of faith when the plates were covered or in a box, I take the consternation surrounding Harris's testimony as evidence of believers' difficulty grasping the "magical realism" of the plates.

Nephites—not Joseph—brought the plates to the grove where some argue the eight saw them with their natural eyes; and the fact that most believers testified to seeing the ancient plates either directly in vision or indirectly while hidden in a box or covered by a cloth suggests to me that there was a material artifact, but that it was most likely neither ancient nor gold. I think Vogel is probably correct in speculating that Smith made the plates himself, but, and this is the crucial question, is there any way he could have done this and still viewed them—in some non-delusory sense—as ancient golden plates?[40]

Idol Anxiety and the Making of the Golden Plates

As Givens acknowledges, it is not that hard to explain how Smith might have seen the plates. As a highly imaginative individual, prone to visionary experiences, Smith may well have believed he saw the plates in his visits to the hill.[41] While his ability to recover the plates is usually depicted in terms of having the right mindset and the right companion, I think there may have been another factor at work as well. Recovery of the plates may have depended on Smith realizing that he had to actively

---

40. Vogel, *Joseph Smith*, 98–99. I think it is possible, as Vogel argues, that Smith made the plates himself out of tin or other metal as an act of "conscious misdirection," but I also think it is possible, as Michael Quinn and Bushman argue, that Smith really believed in the power of his seer stone and used it to develop his revelatory abilities over time. Vogel believes their argument is premised on Smith seeing "objectively real treasures in his stone," an assumption precluded, he argues, by "the failure of present-day adepts to prove the efficacy of divination under scientific conditions" (Vogel, xvi). Assuming (as I would) that human psychological processes have not changed since Smith's day, he asks: "[I]n what way could Smith possibly train himself to be a prophet using such delusive methods?" Vogel, however, has not exhausted the range of psychological possibilities. Thus, for example, Brant Gardner has drawn from the scientific literature to offer a plausible naturalistic account of how seers "see" and how Smith might have "translated" based on unusual abilities rather than deception. In a similar vein, treasure-seeking might have involved visualization practices that later enhanced his ability to visualize spiritual treasure and visualize text while staring at a stone in his hat. See Brant A. Gardner, *The Gift and Power: Translating the Book of Mormon* (Salt Lake City: Greg Kofford Books, 2011), 259–77.

41. B. H. Roberts, *Studies of the Book of Mormon*, ed. Brigham D. Madsen, 2nd ed. (Salt Lake City: Signature Books, 1992), 243–50.

materialize the plates "in faith," rather than passively waiting for them to be "given" to him ready-made, as it were.

The historical evidence for this interpretation is speculative and derives primarily from Lucy Smith's description of the way Joseph told his family that the time had come to recover the plates.[42] Arriving home late one evening shortly before his last visit to the hill, Joseph reported to his anxious parents that he had just received "the severest chastisement that [he] had ever had in his life . . . [from] the angel of the Lord." The angel told him he had been "negligent [and] that the time has now come when the record should be brought forth." But, he added confidently, "Father give yourself no uneasiness as to this reprimand <for> I know what course I am to pursue an[d] all will be well."[43] I am hypothesizing that up until this time, insofar as Smith was thinking about recovering the plates, he knew that someone else had to be involved, but still was not clear how he was actually going to recover them. If, as I am assuming, he did in fact "materialize" the plates, the "chastisement from the angel" evidently convinced him that he needed to take a more active course.[44]

This more active course, I am hypothesizing, involved creating what was in effect a representation of the plates, perhaps using sand and later tin or lead, as detractors claimed, in the knowledge that they would become the sacred reality that the Smith family believed them to be only insofar as the angel made them so.[45] As such, his representation of the plates,

---

42. Vogel, *Early Mormon Documents*, 1:325.

43. Vogel, 1:325.

44. I am assuming that "chastisement from an angel" could be construed in naturalistic terms as a mental dialogue between two inner voices, one of which Smith attributed to an angel.

45. Disparate descriptions make it difficult to be more specific than this about how they might have been made. In an interview in 1859, Martin Harris said: "I hefted the plates, and I knew from the heft that they were lead or gold, and I knew that Joseph had not credit enough to buy so much lead." He says they were "usually kept in a cherry wood box . . . [and] weighed forty or fifty pounds" (Vogel 2:306–9). Harris's estimate of the weight needs to be reconciled with his description of Smith running with this object through the woods, striking a man who tried to attack him, and then handing it to Lucy through a window, whereupon she hid it under the hearth (Vogel, 2:306–7). In contrast to Harris who hefts (but does not claim to see or touch) the object, Emma Smith recounts feeling the pages or leaves under a cloth (Vogel, 1:539). She gives no indication of weight or hefting in her account, but rather describes tracing the outline and feeling edges that move. In recently discovered minutes of a court case where

placed under the cloth or in the box, can be understood as representing or even co-creating the reality of the plates along a continuum of possibilities, ranging from the way a crucifix represents the crucifixion, an Eastern Orthodox icon is said to manifest the reality of the saint it depicts, the way Eucharistic wafers are thought to be transformed into the literal body of Christ, or the way that Mary "created" Jesus in her womb.[46] As such, what I am construing as Smith's actions in creating plates would have analogues in other Christian "materializations" of the sacred.

I am not arguing that Smith necessarily thought about what he was doing in these terms. The logic of the insider stories nonetheless points in this direction. A similar logic is evident in key chapters in the Book of Mormon, which suggests that such a process also would have been in keeping with the new revelation.[47] Thus, in Ether 4, Moroni (the ancient Nephite who appeared to Smith as an "angel") describes how the plates came to be in the first place. According to Moroni, the Lord instructed him to write on "these plates the very things which the brother of Jared saw" and to "seal up the interpretation thereof" along with "the interpreters," hiding them in the earth until the day "that they shall exercise faith in me [the Lord] . . . even as the brother of Jared did." At this time, the Lord

---

Smith was tried for breaching the peace on June 30, 1830, Josiah Stowell said that he had seen "a corner of it [the golden Bible]; it resembled a stone of greenish caste; should judge it to have been about one foot square and six inches thick; he [Smith] would not let it be seen by any one; the Lord had commanded him not; it was unknown to Smith that witness saw a corner of the Bible, so called by Smith; [Smith] told the witness the leaves were of gold, there were written characters on the leaves" ("Mormonism," *New England Christian Herald*, November 7, 1832). A greenish cast would suggest copper rather than lead or gold, and pages could be made out of copper more easily than lead. Although believers tend to conflate the various descriptions, I think it is more likely that Smith saw the plates in vision, described what he saw to those close to him, and then made one or more objects to represent what he saw: initially, perhaps, a box containing something heavy, and then later, an object with metallic leaves.

46. Josh Ellenbogen and Aaron Tugendhaft offer a theoretically illuminating set of essays on the relationship between idols, icons, and divine presence. See Josh Ellenbogen and Aaron Tugendhaft, eds., *Idol Anxiety* (Stanford: Stanford University Press, 2011).

47. I am grateful to Loyd Isao Ericson at Greg Kofford Books for bringing Jared's brother to my attention.

said, "will I manifest unto them the things which the brother of Jared saw, even to the unfolding upon them all my revelations" (Ether 4:3–7).[48]

What Jared's brother saw, due to his "exceeding faith," was the bodily form of the Lord Jesus Christ, initially just the Lord's finger and then the whole "body of [his] spirit" (Ether 3:6–3:9, 15–16). Jared's brother demonstrated his exceeding faith—and this is the key point—by *preparing sixteen small stones*, carrying them "to the top of the mount," and *imploring the Lord*, who "hast all power," *to make them shine* (vv. 1–4). In response to his plea, "the Lord stretched forth his hand and touched the stones [that Jared's brother had made] one by one with his finger" (v. 6) and "caused them to shine in darkness" (6:1). Jared's brother "molten[ed]" the stones from a rock,[49] because the Lord had commanded him to do something (construct waterproof vessels to save his people from impending floods)

---

48. For a discussion of the place of this passage in the Book of Mormon, see Richard Bushman, *Joseph Smith and the Beginnings of Mormonism* (Urbana: University of Illinois Press, 1984), 118. For general background on the book of Ether, see Grant Hardy, *Understanding the Book of Mormon: A Reader's Guide* (New York: Oxford University Press, 2010), 227–40; on the story of Jared's brother specifically, see Grant Hardy, *Understanding the Book of Mormon: A Reader's Guide* (New York: Oxford University Press, 2010), 241–47. The book of Ether claims to be Moroni's abridgment of the twenty-four golden plates that recorded the history of the Jaredites, one of several ancient peoples who, according to the Book of Mormon, came to the Americas from the ancient Near East.

49. The text reads: "And it came to pass that the brother of Jared . . . did molten out of a rock sixteen small stones; and they were white and clear, even as transparent glass." As John L. Brooke indicates, the verb "molten" appears in other contexts (1 Ne. 17:9, 16) where it suggests metalworking. John L. Brooke, *The Refiner's Fire: The Making of Mormon Cosmology, 1644–1844* (Cambridge: Cambridge University Press, 1994), 159–60. The smelting of transparent stones from a rock suggests something more complex than ordinary metalworking, perhaps even some kind of transmutation of an esoteric variety in keeping with Brooke's general reading of early Mormonism. In any case, this passage is redolent with symbolism that is elaborated later. Thus, Doctrine and Covenants 130 explicitly links the white stone to the cosmic Urim and Thummim, the new name bestowed on each person who enters the celestial kingdom, and the white stone in Revelation 2:17. But as Brooke points out, the Masonic tradition associates the white stone of Revelation 2:17 with the alchemical philosopher's stone and the alchemical work of transmutation, which suggests esoteric possibilities that Smith might have had in mind if, as I am suggesting, he made plates and asked the angel to transform them (Brooke, 258–59). Thanks to Sally Gordon for urging me to consider possible esoteric interpretations.

but had not provided all that was needed to complete the task (a means of getting light into the sealed vessels). Smith, too, believed he had been commanded to do something (bring forth the golden plates from the hill), but after numerous attempts had not been able to complete the task. In the same way that the Book of Mormon depicts Jared's brother's solution to the lighting problem as a demonstration of his faith, so too Smith may have understood himself as demonstrating *his* faith by figuring out how to recover the ancient plates—that is, by taking homemade plates "to the top of the mount" (the Hill Cumorah) and imploring the Lord to transform them into the ancient golden plates he saw in his 1823 dream-vision.

Although we can only speculate on the course Smith pursued to recover the plates, there is a final parallel worth noting between Smith and the brother of Jared, this one explicit: both stories begin with severe chastisement and end in revelation. It turns out that after a period of four years, the Lord came to the brother of Jared and for three hours "chastened him because he remembered not to call upon the name of the Lord" (Ether 2:14). Jared's brother repents; the Lord forgives him and instructs him to build the vessels, which then leads to the events just described. In 1827, four years after the angel's first visit, Smith receives "the severest chastisement that [he] had ever had his life . . . [from] the angel of the Lord" for his negligence in recovering the plates.[50] Regardless of how we conceive the relationship between Smith and the text, "active materialization" does seem to be compatible with the Jaredite tradition.[51]

---

50. According to Terryl Givens, the story of Jared's brother opens in Ether 2:14 with "what must surely be the longest dressing-down in sacred history" and ends with "the most spectacular epiphany in the Book of Mormon." In using this story to illustrate the Book of Mormon's dialogic understanding of revelation, Givens notes that "the brother of Jared asks the Lord to touch and illuminate 16 molten stones," but he does not reflect on the fact that Jared's brother crafted the stones or on the parallels between Smith and Jared's brother. See Givens, *The Hand of Mormon*, 220.

51. The plausibility of this reading is strengthened by the explicit reference to Jared's brother in the June 1829 revelation (D&C 17) given through Smith to Cowdery, Whitmer, and Harris, who had just learned from the "translating" of Ether 5:2–4 that "three [who had assisted in bringing forth the work] shall be shewn [the plates] by the power of God." The revelation indicates that Cowdery, Whitmer, and Harris will not only see the plates through the power of God and their faith, just as Smith had seen them, but also "the brestplate [*sic*], the sword of Laban, the Urim and Thumim which was given to the brother of Jared upon the mount, when he talked to the Lord face to face." See Robin Scott Jensen,

Jared's brother notwithstanding, it is the idea of "active materialization" that gives rise to charges of fraud and deception, and if not fraud and deception, then idolatry and delusion. As already noted, Vogel considers the materiality of the plates "the most compelling evidence" that Smith consciously misdirected his followers and compares the making of the plates with the practices of adepts who comingle trickery and sincere belief. Smith's logic, however, may have been less like an adept deceiving his subjects and more like a Catholic priest making Christ present in the Eucharistic wafer. In the first case, the adept knowingly misleads his viewers, albeit for their own good. In the second, a priest calls upon the Holy Spirit to transform the bread and wine into the body and blood of Christ.[52]

Comparison of the golden plates and the Eucharist allows us to consider the possibility that Smith viewed something that he made—metal plates—as a vehicle through which something sacred—the ancient golden plates—could be made (really) present. In both cases, the sacred character is visible only to those who believe. In both cases, the materialization unfolds in accord with a story: in the case of the Eucharist, the story of the last supper; in the case of the Mormon Prophet, the story of the angel and the buried plates. Moreover, in both cases, believers claim that this is not just an enactment. The priest does not just pretend that the wafer is the body of Christ. Standing in for Christ, he says, referring to the wafer, "This is my body." Nor did Smith claim that the plates were a representation of ancient golden plates; he claimed that they really were. In much the way that Jesus is said to have held up human-made bread and said to his disciples, "This is my body," Smith may have made plates, placed them

---

Robert J. Woodford, and Steven C. Harper, eds., *Revelations and Translations, Volume 1: Manuscript Revelation Books*, in *The Joseph Smith Papers [Revelations and Translations]*, ed. Dean C. Jessee, Ronald K. Esplin, and Richard Lyman Bushman (Salt Lake City: Church Historian's Press, 2011), 654–55.

52. The Tibetan Treasure tradition also presents a suggestive opportunity for comparison beyond the scope of this paper. This tradition maintains that these Treasures (*gter-ma*) are special teachings, originally preached by a buddha and later hidden (in most cases) by the Indian master who introduced tantric Buddhism to Tibet. The master is "said to have concealed these teachings in such a way that they would be discovered at a later date by various predetermined Tibetan Treasure discoverers (*gter-ston*), who would then 'translate' their revelation into a form comprehensible to their contemporaries." Janet Gyatso, "The Logic of Legitimation in the Tibetan Treasure Tradition," *History of Religions* 33, no. 2 (1993): 98. I am grateful to Jesper Oestergaard of Aarhus University for directing me to this literature.

in a box, and said to his family: These are the golden plates. While some in each tradition may view these statements as figurative, others—orthodox Catholics and orthodox Latter-day Saints—might view them as more literally true in light of their belief in the power of divinity to manifest itself in material bodies and objects.

Delusions and the Emergence of New Religious Movements

If, as I am suggesting, Smith might have made something through which he believed other worldly powers would manifest the ancient plates, then we would not have to view Smith as making something in order to convince others of something *he* did not believe. But if he believed this, was he deluded? Strictly speaking, from a psychiatric perspective, we cannot call Smith delusional. Technically, according to the DSM-IV (*Diagnostic and Statistical Manual of Mental Disorders*), a delusion is

> a false belief based on [an] incorrect inference about external reality that is firmly sustained despite what almost everyone else believes and despite what constitutes incontrovertible and obvious proof or evidence to the contrary. The belief is not one ordinarily accepted by other members of the person's culture or subculture (e.g. it is not an article of religious faith).[53]

Although philosophers find the religious exception unsatisfying in that it fails to distinguish between delusions and ordinary religious beliefs, they concede that their efforts to distinguish between them on intrinsic grounds have failed.[54] In a recent effort, philosopher Jennifer Radden concludes, "to differentiate spiritual delusions from more ordinary spiritual convictions, it seems we must rely on aspects of context or accompanying symptoms rather than [features] of the delusions themselves."[55]

In the absence of accompanying symptoms, the distinction between ordinary belief and delusion turns on context—that is, on whether the beliefs make sense within the context of a culture or subculture. From this perspective, the key issue with respect to Smith's claims is what others thought of them. Notice, though, how the definition of delusions with its exception for articles of religious faith is premised on preexisting claims already accepted by people. There is little room in this definition for novelty,

---

53. American Psychiatric Association, *Diagnostic and Statistical Manual of Mental Disorders [DSM]*, 4th ed. (Washington, DC: American Psychiatric Association, 1994), 765.

54. Jennifer Radden, *On Delusion* (London: Routledge Taylor and Francis, 2011).

55. Radden, 108.

for the possibility of new revelation. At the same time, once new beliefs are accepted by others—once the individual is no longer alone in his or her beliefs—then he or she can no longer be considered deluded in the psychiatric sense. From this vantage point, whether or not an individual is deluded or the founder of a new religious movement rests on whether or not they can get others to share their novel beliefs.

This process of sharing novel beliefs took place initially within Smith's family, which, as historians such as Michael Quinn have demonstrated, embraced a range of folk beliefs and practices that they probably considered Christian, including recounting significant dreams, treasure-seeking by means of seer-stones, and divinatory practices.[56] Smith's claim to have recovered actual ancient golden plates is premised on his belief that such things existed, a belief that we can trace back to the morning after the mysterious personage appeared to Smith three times during the night of September 21, 1823. I stress the morning after because Smith went to work in the fields as scheduled the next morning. He did not go the hill until after the personage appeared again, instructed him to tell his father what had transpired during the night, and his father pronounced his dream-visions "of God." Without his father's firm belief that the appearances of the "personage" were real, that the knowledge being conveyed was authentic, and that its instructions were to be obeyed, the evidence suggests that Smith may not have acted on it on his own.[57] Moreover, when he saw but was unable to remove the plates, his account of his failure, as recounted to his family, paralleled the stories he and others told of buried treasure spirited away by mysterious treasure guardians.[58] Most crucially, his inability to recover the plates for four years did not preclude the ancient personage from telling him what was written on the plates nor prevent Smith from recounting what he had learned about the ancient inhabitants of the continent to his enthralled family "as though," his mother

---

56. Michael Quinn, *Early Mormonism and the Magic World View*, rev. ed. (Salt Lake City: Signature Books, 1996).

57. I am basing this conclusion on a comparison of the various accounts of the events in September 1823 as recounted by Smith and members of his family. For a fuller discussion, see Ann Taves, *Revelatory Events: Three Case Studies of the Emergence of New Spiritual Paths* (Princeton, NJ: Princeton University Press, 2016), 55–58, 311–14.

58. Vogel, *Joseph Smith*, 47–50; Mark Ashurst-McGee, "Moroni as Angel and Treasure Guardian," *FARMS Review* 18, no. 1 (2006): 34–100.

recalled, "he had spent his life with them".[59] His family, in short, shared Smith's belief in ancient Nephites, the angel Moroni, and ancient buried plates long before Smith claimed to recover them.

It is because his family already believed in the reality of the golden plates that they did not challenge Smith's statement that God had commanded them not to look at them directly, a response that outsiders found rather puzzling.[60] Insiders also protected the plates from those who doubted their existence. Suspicious that her husband Martin was being duped by Smith and putting their property at risk in the process, Lucy Harris went to extraordinary lengths to investigate believers' claims, and Lucy Smith provides a detailed account of the family's efforts to thwart her.[61] Ultimately convinced that there were no actual ancient plates, Lucy Harris found three neighbors willing to testify to that effect in court; the judge, however, dismissed the case in response to her husband Martin's positive testimony.[62]

If we consider Joseph's directive, the obedient response of insiders, and their willingness to protect the plates from skeptical outsiders, we can envision an alternative way to view the materialization of the plates that involved neither recovery and translation in any usual sense nor necessarily deception or fraud, but rather a process through which a small group—who believed in the power of revelatory dream-visions, in ancient inhabitants of the Americas, and in golden records buried in a hillside—

---

59. Vogel, *Early Mormon Documents*, 1:295–96.

60. When Smith's brother William told an interviewer that, while disappointed that they could not view the plates directly, they obeyed, the interviewer commented to the elderly William that "most people would ha[v]e examined them any way." At that, the interviewer recounted, "[T]he old man suddenly straightened [sic] up and looked intently at him and said. The Lord knew he could trust Joseph and as for the rest of the family we had no desire to transgress the commandment of the Lord but on the other hand was exceeding anxious to do al[l] we were commanded to do" (Vogel, 1:508). Smith's wife Emma made much the same point, though less emphatically, saying: "I did not attempt to handle the plates nor, uncover them to look at them. I was satisfied that it was the work of God, and therefore did not feel it to be necessary to do so" (Vogel, 1:540). Smith's directive, understood by insiders as a divine injunction, functioned to set the plates apart in the Durkheimian sense. Although Smith could supply the directive, others had to observe it in order for it to have any effect, and insofar as they did, they participated in the materialization of ancient plates.

61. Vogel, 1:382–87.

62. Vogel, 1:387.

came to believe that a material object covered by a cloth or hidden in a box were the ancient plates revealed to Smith by the ancient Nephite Moroni. Either/or views of the plates rest on a narrow conception of the materialization process, such that he either dug them up or he did not. Highlighting the crucial role played by those who believed in the reality of the ancient plates suggests a broader view that embeds the recovery of the plates in a process of materialization that stretched (at least) from Smith's dream vision in 1823 to the publication of the Book of Mormon in 1830.

Recognizing the importance of the small group interactions in the materialization of the plates, however, does not adequately account for Smith's role in the process. He was the one who had the dream visions in 1823; he was the one who returned to the hill each year, conversed with the ancient personage, learned more about what was contained in the golden plates, and recounted what he learned to his appreciative family; and he was the one who figured out what he had to do in order to "recover" the plates. Here we return to the problem of seeing things that are not and saying that they are. We enter into the realm of hallucination and hypnotism, but also of creative inspiration, skilled craftsmanship, and the arts. The concepts of hallucination and hypnosis, like delusion, are premised on a stable, shared understanding of reality. Like the idea of delusions, these concepts leave little room for the emergence of something new or for those with the ability to see what might emerge, what might manifest or be revealed—little room, in other words, for artists, designers, or seers.

Skilled Perception and the Discovery of the Plates

Although Smith is most commonly described today as simply a prophet, he is depicted in early accounts as a seer, translator, and prophet, as are key figures in the Book of Mormon itself.[63] The Book of Mormon's copyright, recorded by Smith in 1829, encapsulates what Susan Staker has described as its central narrative thread—that is, an account of seers, who are also revelators and prophets, who hand down records from one generation to the next in order to ensure that through them—to quote the Book of Mormon—"shall all things be revealed, or, rather, shall secret things be made manifest, and hidden things come to light . . . which otherwise could not be known" (Mosiah 8:17).[64] According to the Book of

---

63. Jensen, Woodford, and Harper, *Revelations and Translations*, xix-xx.
64. Susan Staker, "Secret Things, Hidden Things: The Seer Story in the Imaginative Economy of Joseph Smith," in *American Apocrypha: Essays on the*

Mormon, the role of the seer supersedes that of the revelator and prophet because the seer has additionally been commanded by God to translate ancient records using "interpreters" (vv. 16). A seer is thus one whom God has commanded to see things—secret things—that are not visible to those who do not have the gift of seeing or the means to do so. There is a sense, then, in which the revelation reflexively depicts Smith as a skilled perceiver in a long line of skilled perceivers, who perceive at the command of God, using abilities and tools given to them by God.

The characterization of Smith as a seer in a long line of seers tends to be read—for good or ill—against the backdrop of his local renown as a seer of buried treasure, called upon, as his mother put it, because people believed "he [Smith] possessed certain keys, by which he could discern things invisible to the natural eye."[65] The keys in question were seer stones, which he not only used to seek buried treasure and most likely to locate the golden plates but also to translate the plates and to obtain some of the early revelations recorded in the Doctrine and Covenants.[66] When Smith was brought up on charges related to treasure seeking in 1826, the witnesses, like his extended family, disagreed sharply over whether Smith could actually see things that others could not. Those who brought the charges testified that they had investigated Smith's abilities to "discern objects at a distance" by means of a stone and "came away disgusted, finding the deception so palpable."[67] The man who hired him, however, testified to his "faith in Prisoner[']s skill," as did another treasure seeker who expressed his confidence in Smith's abilities to "divine things by means of said Stone and Hat."[68]

Although I doubt that his seer stones had powers apart from those that Smith imputed to them, I do not think that this requires us to conclude either that they were unnecessary (at least initially) or that he saw nothing when looking at the stone in the hat. I think it is possible that a stone perceived as special could afford "seeing" or "visualizing" in much the same way that a placebo perceived as a drug can afford healing. In

---

Book of Mormon, ed. Dan Vogel and Brent Lee Metcalfe (Salt Lake City: Signature Books, 2002), 235–74.

65. Vogel, *Early Mormon Documents*, 4:130n5.

66. Richard Van Waggoner and Steven Walker, "Joseph Smith: The Gift of Seeing," *Dialogue: A Journal of Mormon Thought* 15, no. 2 (1982): 48–68; see also Jensen, Woodford, and Harper, *Revelations and Translations*, xxi.

67. Vogel, *Early Mormon Documents*, 4:253.

68. Vogel, 4:250–53, 255–56.

both cases, I would argue that the believed-in powers of an object might enable some but not all to activate latent abilities (to visualize text or to heal themselves) that they cannot access consciously.[69] Here, however, I am concerned with seeing in a wider context, not just in relation to buried treasure or translating the plates but in relation to the entire process of materialization beginning with his dream visions through the publication of the Book of Mormon. Viewed in the context of this longer process, the focus on whether he could see and recover actual buried treasure, including golden plates, has obscured his patent ability to see and create a new reality for himself and others. In this process, we can consider the seer alongside the artist as a skilled perceiver of new possibilities and the skilled healer who knowingly prescribes a placebo.

Hubert Dreyfus and Sean Kelly, drawing on Heidegger, highlight the role of ability and training in perceiving things that are not apparent to others.[70] Quoting a nineteenth-century wheelwright, they highlight differences that a skilled craftsperson can feel under the plane or the axe and teach to an apprentice learning the craft but cannot explain to outsiders in a way they can understand. With this example, Dreyfus and Kelly try to capture the extent to which meaning or possibility inheres in an object or situation as potential that can be discerned by a skilled perceiver and revealed through creative interaction.[71] The ability could be innate, evoked by circumstances, or deliberately cultivated. However it is acquired, I think it allows some people to see possibilities that are not apparent to others not only in materials but also in situations. Highlighting the role of skillful perception allows us to recognize that possibilities may inhere in objects or situations without having to think of possibilities as essences and to acknowledge that some people may perceive these possibilities through insights or inspirations that seem to come from beyond the self without dismissing them as delusions or hallucinations.

The scholarly discussion of so-called "fetishes"—a dismissive term for human-made objects to which people attribute supernatural qualities—can help us to see the additional complexities that surround the skilled perception of sacred possibilities. David Graeber, building on the work of William Pietz, lifts the discussion of fetishism outside the realm of so-called primitive superstition and relocates it in the realm of the creative

---

69. This possibility is in keeping with Gardner, *The Gift and Power*.
70. Hubert Dreyfus and Sean Kelly, *All Things Shining: Reading the Western Classics to Find Meaning in a Secular Age* (New York: Free Press, 2011), 207–8.
71. Dreyfus and Kelly, 209.

process more generally, where, as he notes, the ascription of powers to things with unclear origins abound. Thus, he notes,

> when artists, musicians, poets, or authors describe their own experience of creativity, they . . . almost never . . . see themselves as anything like an architect rationally calculating dimensions and imposing their will on the world. Instead one almost invariably hears how they feel they are vehicles for some kind of inspiration coming from outside, how they lose themselves, fragment themselves, leave portions of themselves in their products.[72]

Evoking a kind of double consciousness, he observes: "[E]ven when the [social] actors seem perfectly aware that they were constructing an illusion, they also seemed aware that the illusion was still required."[73] I would suggest that Smith, like most purveyors of something new, enacted the role of seer on just this sort of cusp between fetish and deity, idol and icon, magic and religion, fabrication and manifestation.

Physicians who prescribe placebos position themselves on a similar sort of cusp. Researchers have typically defined placebos as inert treatments that nonetheless produce an effect, that is, as a "fake pill." Fakes have long been used to prove that something people claim is real is actually imaginary, from demonic possessions in the sixteenth century to mesmerism in the eighteenth century to present-day drug trials.[74] As a control used to debunk claims, the placebo has a negative connotation. Placebos are often referred to as "fake pills" and "sham procedures." Conceived as fakes, they are conceptually similar to allegedly "fake deities," such as fetishes and idols. Conceived in this way, physicians often hesitate to prescribe placebos even though they know they may have beneficial effects, because doing so typically involves deceiving the patient, suggesting to them that the placebo is a real drug, when the physician knows it is not. Viewed as fakes, a comparison between the plates and placebos is another way to say that the plates were fakes and that Smith deceived his followers.

But research on placebos, like Graeber's work on fetishes, is starting to paint a more complex picture, and doing so has meant letting go of the language of real and fake. Researchers have realized for some time that defining a placebo as an inert treatment that causes an effect makes little sense since a treatment that causes an effect is not technically inert.

---

72. David Graeber, "Fetishism and Social Creativity, or Fetishes Are Gods in Process of Construction," *Anthropological Theory* 5, no. 4 (2005): 430.

73. Graeber, 432.

74. Ted J. Kaptchu, Catherine E. Kerr, and Abby Zanger, "Placebo Controls, Exorcisms, and the Devil," *Lancet* 374 (2009): 1234–39.

In an effort to be more precise, some researchers are focusing instead on the placebo as "a *simulation* of an active therapy within a psychosocial context" such that the "capacity of simulation empowers the influence of the placebo."⁷⁵ Placebo effects, thus, are effects that patients attribute to placebo itself, when in fact they are responses to the simulation as a whole. While clinical trials are designed to test the effects of pharmacologically active ingredients, the emerging interest in placebos (or simulated drugs) *as such* is allowing researchers to examine the measurable effect of "words and rituals, symbols, and meanings . . . in shaping the patient's brain."⁷⁶

If we shift from viewing postulated created plates not as fake plates but as a simulation or enactment of ancient golden plates, we can compare Smith to a physician who prescribes a placebo knowing that it contains no pharmacologically active ingredients not to deceive his patient but because the physician knows that placebos can have a healing effect. We can characterize the physician who prescribes a placebo—like Smith—as one who has "eyes to see things that are not, and the audacity to say they are." As in the case of Smith, this can mean different things. In keeping with the older research, it could mean the physician sees a "fake drug" and has the audacity to say or imply that it is real. In keeping with the more recent research, it could mean that the physician has eyes to see what could be (a non-pharmacologically induced healing process) and the audacity to initiate it. In the first formulation, the focus is on what the physician believes about the drug; in the second, the focus is on what the physician believes about the role of simulations in the healing process.

For this comparison to make sense, we have to assume that Smith sincerely believed that he had access to new revelation. We need to further assume that in simulating plates and expressing his confidence in them, he was in effect expressing his confidence in the reality of a supernatural world populated with persons and powers that made their presence felt in this world. In this simulation, the created plates played a necessary, if not fully understood, role, just as the wafer does in the Eucharist and the pills do in simulated treatments. But like the wafer and the pills, *powers* had to act through the created plates to transform them into an ancient golden

---

75. Donald D. Price, Damien G. Finniss, and Fabrizio Benedetti, "A Comprehensive Review of the Placebo Effect: Recent Advances and Current Thought," *Annual Review of Psychology* 59 (2008): 567; Fabrizio Benedetti, Elisa Carlino, and Antonella Pollo, "How Placebos Change the Patient's Brain," *Neuropsychopharmacology* 36, no. 1 (2011): 32–35.

76. Benedetti et al., 339–54.

record. For Smith and his followers, I am assuming, those powers were supernatural ones. From a naturalistic perspective, the powers were those of the human mind.

Conclusion

We can view the materialization of the plates as a process that unfolded over a period of years beginning with the dream-visions of September 1823 and culminating in the publication of the Book of Mormon. Within that time span, believers claim that the plates were materially present for approximately two years. In that two-year window, I am proposing that believers materialized the plates in two steps. The first step involved the creation of one (or more) representation(s) of the plates that could be hefted in a box, touched through a cloth, and translated by means of "interpreters," but not viewed directly. The second step involved the direct seeing of the plates in vision by those already deeply invested in the translation process and strongly disposed to believe. While many Mormons take the witness of the three and the eight as testimony to the materiality of the plates, the plates in question—by believers' own descriptions—were not material in the usual sense of the term. Their testimony, thus, should not be taken as testimony to the ordinary materiality of the plates, but rather as testimony to the witnesses' ability to see reality in the way Smith did—that is, as a supernaturally charged reality in which angels produced, transported, and ultimately withdrew a believed-in simulation. In naturalistic terms the witnesses testified to the powers of the human mind not only to see things others could not see, but also to the power of human minds to see things together in faith.

If we return to the historical data, I think that this line of interpretation has certain advantages. Not only does it provide a way to understand what Smith, his closest followers, and outsiders said about the materiality of the plates that has analogues in other Christian claims to have materialized the sacred, it also allows us to make sense of a series of events that have more to do with *seeing* than with materiality and takes us back to Jesse Smith's observation that Joseph had "eyes to see things that are not, and the audacity to say they are." Three events stand out in this regard: the way Smith translated the plates, his characterization of the Urim and Thummim as the key the morning after he claimed to have recovered the plates, and his intense happiness when the three witnesses saw the angel and the plates.

Although modern LDS depictions of Smith translating the revelation often depict him looking at the plates, there is extensive insider testimony to the effect that he actually dictated his translation of the plates to scribes while looking at the "interpreters"—the Urim and Thummim or his seer stone—positioned in a hat to block out the light.[77] Just as he could use his seer stone to see if the plates were safe in their hiding place, so too he could see the characters inscribed on the plates (and understand what they meant) without having to look at them directly. The importance of seeing also makes sense of the fact that the morning after he claimed to have recovered the plates, Smith described the "interpreters" to his mother as the "key," and according to Joseph Knight, seemed more excited about recovering them than he was about recovering the plates.[78] This suggests that the interpreters were not only the key to "translating" the plates, but also and more deeply the key to seeing what was written on the plates without anyone having to actually look at them. The unusual mode of translation, in other words, was part and parcel of the "magical realism" of the plates.

Above all, this line of interpretation makes sense of Smith's intense happiness when the three witnesses saw what he claimed to see: an angel laying the plates before their eyes. As Lucy recounts, he exclaimed afterwards:

> Father! — Mother! . . . you do not know how happy I am[.] The Lord has caused the plates to be shown to 3 more besides me who have also seen an angel and will have to testify to the truth of what I have said for they know for themselves that I do not go about to deceive the people. . . . I do feel as though I was relieved of a dreadful burden which was almost too much for me to endure but they will now have to bear a part and it does rejoice my soul that I am not any longer to be entirely alone in the world.[79]

Up until that point, he was alone in the world in "seeing things that are not" and having "the audacity to say that they are." If we do not assume that Smith was being deceptive, *the burden he refers to here is that of being alone in his perceptions, or in other words, alone in what he was able to see.* The burden was not one of deception but of being *accused* of deception.

If, as I have suggested, the plates were real for Smith and his family long before he claimed to have recovered them, then we need to view the process of materialization as extending from at least 1823 to 1830. If we

---

77. Richard Van Waggoner and Steven Walker, "Joseph Smith: The Gift of Seeing," *Dialogue: A Journal of Mormon Thought* 15, no. 2 (1982): 48–68; Jensen, Woodford, and Harper, *Revelations and Translations*, xx–xxi.

78. Vogel, *Early Mormon Documents*, 1:328–29, 338; 4:15.

79. Vogel, 1:394.

view Smith as a skilled perceiver, we can view his dream-visions the night of September 21, 1823, as revealing a course of action—the recovery of an ancient book—with the potential to resolve tensions and longings not only in that particular historical moment but also, so his followers claim, down to the present day. In highlighting Smith's ability to perceive this course of action, we need not ignore the way his abilities may have been honed within his family and through his practical work as a village seer. Nor should we ignore the way the tensions and dispositions within his family and community prepared some, but not all, to respond to what he perceived. Above all, I am suggesting we cannot ignore the active role that Smith and those closest to him played in the process of materializing his visions. Viewing Smith in this way takes seriously his claim to have been a seer and allows us to consider the seer alongside the artist as the creator of things that, in Heidegger's sense, open up new worlds.[80]

---

80. Heidegger, *Poetry, Language, Thought*, 43–44.

8

"THE BOOK WHICH THOU SHALT WRITE": THE BOOK OF MOSES AS PROPHETIC MIDRASH

David Bokovoy

One of the unique and fascinating features of Latter-day Saint Christianity is its reverence for sacred religious texts in addition to the Bible. For nearly two thousand years, the mainstream Christian tradition has defined its religious canon almost exclusively in terms of the books of the Old and New Testaments, with, of course, an occasional dose of the Apocrypha. Mormons certainly share this long-held Christian reverence for the Bible, yet at the same time, Latter-day Saints accept books produced primarily by the Mormon prophet Joseph Smith as part of an expanded religious canon. For Latter-day Saints, these scriptural texts include the Book of Mormon, the Doctrine and Covenants, and the Pearl of Great Price. This final example of unique LDS scripture includes two captivating texts purporting to present original writings from key biblical patriarchs including Adam, Enoch, Abraham, and the prophet Moses. The words of Moses appear in the pages of the Pearl of Great Price under the title "the Book of Moses." As a segment of Joseph Smith's revision of the King James Bible known by Latter-day Saints as the "Inspired Translation," the Book of Moses represents a highly modified version of the opening chapters of Genesis.

Since the Mormon prophet Joseph Smith began production of his scriptural Book of Moses in 1830, major advancements in the academic sphere of biblical scholarship have provided significant insights into ancient Israelite textual and religious history. These discoveries carry ramifications for a critical assessment of this intriguing example of Mormon scripture. In this essay, I will present a basic summary of this approach. I will then illustrate that when read from a historical perspective, the Book of Moses follows an ancient venerable tradition of adopting and revising preexistent scripture into the formation of a new religious text. Finally, I suggest that Latter-day Saints who accept the observations of mainstream biblical scholarship concerning the authorship of Genesis can define the Book of Moses as a scriptural example of inspired prophetic midrash.

In terms of his approach to biblical analysis, Joseph Smith was what we might refer to today as a "critical" reader of the text, paying close attention to both narrative and theological inconsistencies. He taught that in the production of the Bible, "ignorant translators, careless transcribers, or designing and corrupt priests . . . committed many errors."[1] Throughout his efforts to explicate the Bible, we find in Smith's sermons a variety of references to alternate translations from the King James Bible (including the German), as well as allusions to the original Hebrew of the Old Testament.[2] "There are many things in the Bible," he declared, "which do not, as they now stand, accord with the revelations of the Holy Ghost to me."[3] And the Mormon prophet was not afraid to point them out.

Shortly after the organization of the Church and the publication of the Book of Mormon, Smith began his next scriptural project of adding to and correcting the Bible. "It is hard to imagine now how this twenty-four-year-old came to believe that he could revise the Bible," writes historian Richard Bushman. "[I]t was a striking demonstration of his outrageous confidence; to take on this hallowed book, he had to think of himself as a prophet among prophets."[4] The Bible used for this project was a King James Version purchased on October 8, 1829, at the E.B. Grandin bookstore in Palmyra, New York, where the Book of Mormon was then being typeset.

Though there is no evidence of Smith taking into consideration the original languages of the Bible during his efforts to revise the Bible, Mormon scripture specifically refers to this project as a "translation." In terms of its production, the translation tools Smith referred to as an important part of the production of the Book of Mormon—the Urim and Thummim—were not used in his translation of the Bible; instead, Smith

---

1. Joseph Smith, *Teachings of the Prophet Joseph Smith*, ed. Joseph Fielding Smith (Salt Lake City: Deseret Book, 1977), 327.

2. "I am going to take exceptions to the present translation of the Bible in relation to these matters [interpreting prophecy]. Our latitude and longitude can be determined in the original Hebrew with far greater accuracy than in the English version. There is a grand distinction between the actual meaning of the prophets and the present translations." Smith, 290–91.

3. Smith, 310.

4. Richard Bushman, *Joseph Smith: Rough Stone Rolling* (New York: Alfred A. Knopf, 2005), 132.

and his scribe would simply sit at a table while the Prophet would verbally dictate his revisions.[5] In June of 1830, Smith's scribe Oliver Cowdery first set to writing these significant changes that would eventually create a new opening text for the King James Bible.

Known today by Latter-day Saints as Moses 1, Smith's revelatory introduction provides a new *Sitz im Leben* (setting in life) for the opening chapters of Genesis. The revelation includes a statement from God directly to Moses concerning his role as author: "And in a day when the children of Men shall esteem my words as naught and take many of them from the book which thou shalt write, behold, I will raise up another like unto thee; and they shall be had again among the children of men—among as many as shall believe" (Moses 1:41). With this statement, the Bible's stories of human prehistory, including the creation, the Fall, and the flood, are identified as narratives literally written by the prophet Moses himself as part of a visionary encounter he experienced on an "exceedingly high mountain" (v. 1). Smith would be the one like unto Moses who would restore Moses's lost words for the faithful. The book of Genesis is thus transformed into a book written by Moses—something that the biblical text itself never claims.

Smith's revelation of Moses 1 was originally an independent literary unit—a stand-alone revelation meant to provide a new beginning to the book of Genesis, not a revision of it. The original editorial introduction to the text read, "A Revelation given to Joseph the Revelator June 1830." However, Smith's independent revelation of the "words of Moses" set the stage for his subsequent revisionary efforts of the Bible.

From a literary perspective, the revelation features a biblical-like *inclusio* bracketing the revelation through a repetition of key words in the text's introduction and conclusion. The revelation begins with the superscription:

---

5. "The original documents behind this publication are an 1828 KJV Bible (with Apocrypha) having various markings in pencil and ink, purchased by Smith and Oliver Cowdery in October 1829, and hundreds of sheets of paper with writing on both sides by various scribes. These documents reveal that Smith's revision progressed in stages; many passages contain not only revisions of the KJV but revisions of revisions of still earlier revisions. Other passages show evidence of revisions that were later discarded in favor of the original KJV reading. Some show later revisions of biblical chapters previously marked 'correct.' Joseph Smith clearly experimented with the Bible as he sought to bring its text in line with the insights of his revelations and understanding." Philip Barlow, *Mormons and the Bible: The Place of Latter-day Saints in American Religion* (Oxford: Oxford University Press, 2013), 50.

> The Words of God, which he spake unto Moses at a time when Moses was caught up into an exceedingly high mountain. (Moses 1:1)

The document then concludes forty-one verses later with an editorial colophon that repeats key thematic elements from the beginning of the text:

> These words were spoken unto Moses in the mount, the name of which shall not be known among the children of men. And now they are spoken unto you. Show them not unto any except them that believe, Even so. Amen. (Moses 1:42)

Interestingly, this editorial technique parallels the envelope structure that brackets the Bible's opening story of creation as a distinct literary unit:

> In the beginning God created the heaven and the earth. (Gen. 1:1)

> These are the generations of the heavens and of the earth when they were created. (Gen. 2:4a)

For both Moses 1 and Genesis 1–2:4a, the *inclusio* creates a dramatic sense of closure to the accounts, marking out a clear beginning and conclusion to the two units.

Though the original revelation ended with *inclusio*, creating a clear sense of closure, Smith's revelation was truly a new beginning to a project that was both shocking and bold—especially for Smith's nineteenth-century Christianity. For centuries, readers of the Bible interpreted the book as a "privileged" text, not to be read or critiqued like normal books.[6] Scholar James Kugel explains this traditional interpretive approach:

> Scripture is perfect and perfectly harmonious. By this I mean, first of all, that there is no mistake in the Bible, and anything that might look like a mistake—the fact that, for example, Gen. 15:13 asserts that the Israelites 'will be oppressed for four hundred years' in Egypt, while Exod. 12:41 speaks of 430 years, whereas a calculation based on biblical genealogies yielded a figure of 210 years—must therefore be an illusion to be clarified by proper interpretation.[7]

This method to interpreting the Bible sees the entire record as perfectly harmonious and, by extension, without error. It assumes that since some (if not all) of the Bible came directly from God, it should be interpreted according to its own unique rules that either harmonize or simply ignore inconsistencies. Throughout the centuries prior to Joseph Smith, when biblical texts appeared to contradict each other, qualified "professional" interpreters (such

---

6. Adopting the term from Marc Zvi Brettler, *How to Read the Bible* (Philadelphia: Jewish Publication Society, 2005), 1.

7. James Kugel, *The Bible As It Was* (Cambridge: Belknap Press, 1999), 20.

as scribes, rabbis, or priests) would reinterpret the plain meaning of words for their respective communities in a way that made the Bible conform both with itself and with later religious preferences. In some ways, Smith's project was an effort to harmonize the Bible and smooth out the difficulties in the text (thus making his effort similar to those of earlier Jewish and Christian commentators that preceded him). Smith, however, differed from these earlier efforts by harmonizing the text with his own doctrinal, historical, and theological convictions—his own revelations. Smith saw problems in the Bible, and these problems needed to be addressed.

Even still, Smith was not the first critical reader of the Bible to take seriously its various textual, narrative, and theological difficulties. The Western world that Smith inherited experienced a serious intellectual transformation in the seventeenth century that would ultimately impact the way many Americans would come to read the Bible, including the Mormon prophet. The long-held traditional approach of interpreting the Bible as a "privileged" text began to change with the rise of European rationalism. During this transformative era, European philosophers started to question many long-held assumptions regarding the Bible, including the very concept of biblical inerrancy. In sum, the Bible began to be read during this era as a "real" book (not just perfectly-harmonious scripture) that could be interpreted by the standard rules of logic.[8]

During the life of Joseph Smith, this new "enlightened" approach to reading the Bible produced a German school of interpretation in the theology departments of Protestant universities. The most influential member of this intellectual "school" was the German scholar Julius Wellhausen. In 1878 (thirty-four years after the death of the Prophet) Wellhausen synthesized previous scholarly discoveries in higher criticism

---

8. New Testament scholar Bart Ehrman expresses this notion of the Bible as a "real book" rather than inerrant scripture: "Since the Bible is a book, it makes better sense to approach it the way one approaches books. There are certainly books in the world that don't have any mistakes in them. But no one would insist that a particular phone book, chemistry textbook, or car instruction manual has absolutely no mistakes in it before reading it to see whether it does or not. Rather than thinking that the Bible cannot have mistakes, before looking to see if it does, why not see if it does, and only then decide whether it could. . . . If God created an error free book then it should be without errors. If what we have is not an error-free book, then it is not a book that God has delivered to us without errors." Bart D. Ehrman, *Forged: Writing in the Name of God—Why the Bible's Authors Are Not Who We Think They Are* (New York: HarperOne, 2011), 117.

through the publication of his highly influential *Prolegomena to the History of Ancient Israel*.[9] Ultimately, Wellhausen's work did for biblical scholarship what Darwin's *Origin of the Species* accomplished for natural science. As Darwin's concept of evolutionary adaptation through natural selection has become central to modern evolutionary theory, so Wellhausen's work on historical criticism provides the foundation for modern scholarly assessments of the Bible.

In order to take seriously the types of textual and theological problems that Joseph Smith and others observed, *Prolegomena* separated the Bible, especially its first five books, into individual sources that Wellhausen dated to specific times in Israelite history. Wellhausen then put those sources back together again according to his own theory regarding the evolution of Israelite religion. Though in the years that followed not all of Wellhausen's interpretations of the development of various biblical sources were accepted by subsequent scholars, as of today almost all contemporary Biblicists recognize that the first five books of the Hebrew Bible were not written by a single author and that they are in fact a compilation of separate sources composed by different scribal schools of thought long after the time period associated with Moses.[10]

---

9. Historically, the identification of textual duplicates led to the view of the Pentateuch as an amalgamation of separate sources. An early advocate of this position was Richard Simon (1603–1712). Simon maintained that the Pentateuch consisted of various documents, some of which derived from Moses, but he attributed most to Ezra in the post-exilic period. Following Simon, Jean Astruc (1684–1766) expressed the view that two separate sources appear in the book of Genesis, one that used Elohim (God) and the other the divine name Yahweh (LORD). In his articulation of source criticism, Astruc argued against the traditional view that Moses complied the Pentateuch. Astruc's analysis prepared the way for further discussion concerning whether these sources were documents or simply fragments combined from other sources. These studies prepared the way for Wellhausen's groundbreaking synthesis of the Documentary Hypothesis. For a basic history, see Anthony F. Campbell and Mark A. O'Brien, *Sources of the Pentateuch: Texts, Introductions, Annotations* (Augsburg Fortress Press, 2000), 1–9.

10. In recent years, some continental scholars have abandoned the traditional theory of documentary sources in the Pentateuch as a relevant model for explaining its development, and in its place adopted a "Fragmentary" or "Supplementary" Hypothesis. The so-called Fragmentary Hypothesis was inaugurated by Johann Severin Vater in his work *Commentar über den Pentateuch: Mit Einleitungen zu den einzelnen Abschnitten, der eingeschalteten Übersetzung von Dr. Alexander Geddes's merkwurdigeren critischen und exegetischen Anmerkungen, und einer Abhandlung*

This perspective brought into question the traditional Jewish and Christian belief that the prophet Moses wrote the Bible's first five books. Though never stated anywhere in the books themselves, this tradition regarding Mosaic authorship developed early in Jewish history.[11] The Bible indicates that Moses stayed on Mount Sinai in the presence of God for forty days and forty nights (Ex. 24:18, 34:28; Deut. 9:9, 10:10). Jewish interpreters eventually came to the conclusion that this was too long of a period for Moses to have only received the laws that the Bible itself identifies as the revelation Moses received.[12] Surely, they reasoned, in forty days, Moses must have received more. Traditions therefore developed of Moses receiving the entire written Pentateuch (Genesis through Deuteronomy) at this time. Eventually, Jewish rabbis even expanded this view to include the entire oral tradition that provided an authoritative interpretation of the written law. Historically speaking, Smith's Book of Moses revelation is an heir to this expansive interpretive tradition.

In contrast to this tradition concerning Moses, most contemporary scholars believe that the Pentateuch began to take its preliminary shape in Jerusalem sometime during the late eighth century BCE.[13] This was the time period of the prophet Isaiah and the Judean king Hezekiah. With the emergence of Jerusalem as an important political center, together with the

---

über Moses und Verfasser des Pentateuchs (Halle: Waisenhaus-Buchhandlung, 1802–5), see especially 393–94. This assessment does not mean to suggest that continental studies have rejected the basic premise of separate sources within the Pentateuch. As Konrad Schmid notes regarding this recent European trend, "The newer contributions to Pentateuchal research from Europe do not aim at overthrowing the Documentary Hypothesis, rather, they strive to understand the composition of the Pentateuch in the most appropriate terms, which . . . includes 'documentary' elements as well." Konard Schmid, "Has European Scholarship Abandoned the Documentary Hypothesis?" in *The Pentateuch: International Perspectives on Current Research*, ed. Thomas B. Dozeman, Konrad Schmid, and Brauch J. Schwartz (Tubingen: Mohr Siebeck, 2011), 17–18.

11. For the evolution of the term *torah* (law) in the Hebrew Bible from laws Moses gave to eventually the Law (meaning first five books), see Marc Zvi Brettler, "My Bible: A Jew's Perspective," in *The Bible and the Believer: How to Read the Bible Critically and Religiously*, eds. Marc Z. Brettler, Peter Enns, and Daniel J. Harrington (Oxford: Oxford University Press, 2012), 26–31.

12. Marc Zvi Brettler, "Torah," in *Jewish Study Bible* (Oxford: Oxford University Press, 2004), 2.

13. William M. Schniedewind, *How the Bible Became a Book: The Textualization of Ancient Israel* (New Haven: Yale University Press, 2005), 5.

rise of the Assyrian empire, we encounter Judean scribes beginning to collect and record Israelite oral traditions, as well as composing new religious literature that eventually made its way into the pages of the Hebrew Bible.[14] The rise of the Assyrian empire to political power led to the development of what historians refer to as "scribalization" in the ancient Near East, and this movement greatly affected the kingdoms of both Israel and Judah.

Israelite and Judean scribes trained and influenced by their Assyrian conquerors were the authors who produced the written sources used to create the Pentateuch. When we consider the issue of dating these various texts, relative dating is possible with quite a bit of confidence; it is simply in the specifics that this effort admittedly gets a bit challenging.[15] On this topic, there exists considerable academic debate. Scholars will probably never know with any degree of certainly how to precisely date all of this material. New theories are constantly being presented; so conceptually, readers need to allow for a bit of flexibility. However, there are some important issues concerning which scholars do have quite a bit of confidence that carry significant ramifications for a critical assessment of the LDS Book of Moses. To quote David Carr, many scholars are "agnostic on whether there was any writing of biblical materials in tenth-century Judah, given the uncertainties surrounding it."[16]

Archeological evidence suggests that writing itself was probably only beginning to take place in Israel and Judah during this time period.[17] This

---

14. See the summary provided by Michael L. Satlow, *How the Bible Became Holy* (New Haven: Yale University Press, 2014), 73–74. David Carr writes in his most recent assessment, "Though there were potential early cores behind separate Pentateuchal traditions, such as the ancestral or Exodus-Moses traditions, most specialists in the study of the Pentateuch now think that the first proto-Pentateuchal narrative, one extending from creation to Moses, dated to the exile at the earliest." David M. Carr, *The Formation of the Hebrew Bible: A New Reconstruction* (New York: Oxford University Press, 2011), 359.

15. To reveal my own feeling on the matter, I currently hold that the documentary sources identified by Wellhausen were developed in the following sequential order: E, J, P, D; see David Bokovoy, *Authoring the Old Testament: Genesis–Deuteronomy* (Salt Lake City: Kofford Books, 2013).

16. Carr, *Formation*, 359.

17. Here is how biblical scholar Seth Sanders presents what we know to be true via the archeological evidence: "In the tenth-century the first records of an inland script appear in Israel, but they are in an unstandardized Canaanite. We have alphabetic writing and official seals from the probable period of the United Monarchy in the tenth century but the writing is not yet Hebrew and

means that during the era of Saul, David, and Solomon, a written form of Hebrew was only beginning to develop, and when it finally did the written form of Hebrew derived from the earlier Phoenician script. Historians actually see this happening in terms of Hebrew/Canaanite inscriptions.[18] The archeological evidence indicates that biblical figures such as Abraham, Isaac, Jacob, Moses, and any other individuals prior to the time of the divided monarchy most likely did not possess an actual written language. If they did, it certainly would not have been Hebrew, and we would have no idea what that script possibly could have been. One could make an argument that Moses might have possibly known how to write in an Egyptian hieroglyphic script and that Abraham could have written in some type of early cuneiform, but given the complexity of these systems and the fact that such knowledge was highly restricted to those devoted to years and years of highly technical scribal education, this hypothesis seems highly unlikely. More importantly, there is simply no historical evidence to support the idea that these men actually wrote records.

Our current society places so much emphasis upon literacy that we tend to look back at human history and assume that everyone in the past was just like us, but this is simply not the case. Prior to the modern era, most people did not have the time or opportunity to go to school in order to learn to read and write complicated ancient scripts. After the alphabet

---

the seals are wordless. Standardized local script-languages appear in monumental form hand in hand with local states in the Levant by the late ninth century. The first deliberate vernaculars are royal tools. Hebrew arose alongside these written language and was produced in both the north and south of Israel by the beginning of the eighth century B.C.E. through the sixth century B.C.E." Seth L. Sanders, *The Invention of Hebrew (Traditions)* (University of Illinois Press, 2011), 106. See also the recent historical assessment provided by William M. Schniedewind, *A Social History of Hebrew: Its Origins Through the Rabbinic Period* (New Haven: Yale University Press, 2013).

18. Biblical scholar David Carr has made this clear in his most recent analysis of the Pentateuchal sources: "It is plausible to suggest that these early kingdoms [Judah and Israel] developed a preliminary literary system. . . . A combination of archaeological and biblical evidence, critically read, suggests the emergence of a new kind of textual system in the tenth and ninth centuries, one built on the Phoenician script (and potentially depending on other elements of the Phoenician system), one influenced in some ways by Egyptian educational-literary prototypes, and one shared between the Southern and Northern highlands, along with some areas of the Transjordan that were dominated at times by Israel-Judah (e.g., Moab)." Carr, *Formation*, 385.

had been developed, and prior to the days of the printing press, we still find that by the end of the Middle Ages in Europe, the literacy rate was approximately only 25 percent of the population. Going back further into the world of the Bible, as expected, this percentage drops dramatically:

> Though the figures differ depending on place and period, literacy was always restricted to a small segment of society. The Mesopotamians were the first humans to write, but less than 5 percent of the populations were actually literate. In Egypt the rate of literacy was slightly higher than in Mesopotamia, but even the most generous estimates put it as no more than 7 percent of the population. In the classical world the situation was not much different. Greece had an overall literacy rate of about 10 percent, yet it was still predominately an oral culture, rhetoric being the foundation, and eloquence the aim, of education.[19]

This archeological assessment reflects the fact that neither the act of writing itself nor references to actual written texts holds an important place in the books of Genesis, Exodus, Leviticus, and Numbers. Writing and the production of written scriptural texts was simply not an important issue in early Israelite history.[20] The authors of the Bible's first three books did not conceptualize a time period when inspired prophets such as Moses would sit down and actually *write* scriptural texts. Instead, even in Exodus, the focus of transmitting revelation from God is on orality rather than textuality. Therefore, the evidence of historical criticism in relationship to the Book of Moses indicates that the sources that Smith revised to read as texts written by Moses himself are in fact Judean and Israelite scribal production that were beginning to take shape as written material during the Neo-Assyrian time period when Judea was an occupied vassal state.

---

19. Karel van der Toorn, *Scribal Culture and the Making of the Hebrew Bible* (Cambridge: Harvard University Press, 2009), 10.

20. Schniedewind writes: "During the early Iron Age, the term Hebrew writing is problematic. It is better to employ a local geographical term like Israelite writing or a more general term like Levantine or Canaanite writing. Though the ancient Israelites undoubtedly had their own local dialects and speech communities, there is little evidence to suggest that they developed an independent writing system or scribal community." Schniedewind, *A Social History of Hebrew*, 62. It's really during the eighth century BCE that we begin to see the emergence of serious scribalization in ancient Israel and Judah, though the epigraphic evidence of "Canaanite" writing suggests some form of Israelite literacy existed in the 9th century; see, for example, Christopher A. Rollston, *Writing and Literacy in the World of Ancient Israel: Epigraphic Evidence from the Iron Age* (Society of Biblical Literature, 2010), 134–35.

Yet even without the insights gained into Israelite textual and religious history through historical criticism, this assertion really should be apparent to all careful readers of Smith's revelation. Moses 1 constantly invokes the voice of an omniscient narrator speaking about Moses in third person. Statements such as "And *he* saw God face to face, and *he* talked with him, and the glory of God was upon *Moses*; therefore *Moses* could endure his presence. And God spake unto *Moses*" (Moses 1:2–3; emphasis added), appear all throughout the course of Smith's entire revelation. This pattern stands in stark contrast to the first person biographical formulation of Smith's subsequent scriptural text, the Book of Abraham.

Moreover, later in his prophetic ministry, Smith gave a sermon in which he claimed to recreate the original form of Genesis 1:1 as written by the original inspired author: "'In the beginning the head of the Gods brought forth the Gods,' or, as others have translated it, 'The head of the Gods called the Gods together.'"[21] Thus putting the three texts (Genesis 1:1, Moses 2:1, and Joseph Smith urtext) together for comparative purposes, we can see that from Smith's own perspective the Book of Moses was not the original form of the Priestly creation narrative:

In the beginning God created the heaven and the earth. (Gen. 1:1 KJV)

In the beginning I created the heaven, and the earth upon which thou standest. (Moses 2:1–2)

In the beginning the head of the Gods brought forth the Gods. (Joseph Smith urtext)

Therefore, if Smith's Book of Moses does not recreate what the biblical prophet himself actually wrote, how might a believing Latter-day Saint assess this important component of the LDS canon?

In presenting itself as words once literally written by the prophet Moses himself, the Book of Moses follows an ancient literary pattern for revelatory texts. This same type of genre is seen in later Jewish pseudepigrapha and Rabbinic midrash, as well as within the Bible itself. The term "midrash" refers to a method of interpreting biblical material that fills in literary and legal gaps featured in the biblical sources. This process, which eventually becomes a highly sophisticated rabbinic activity, has its origins in the Hebrew Bible.

---

21. Joseph Smith et al., *History of the Church of Jesus Christ of Latter-day Saints*, ed. B. H. Roberts, 7 vols., 2nd ed. rev. (Salt Lake City: Deseret Book, 1948 printing), 6:475.

The biblical books of Jeremiah and Isaiah, for example, adopt and reconfigure earlier religious texts. This process of creating new scriptural material through preexistent source material can be seen within a critical assessment of the book of Isaiah itself. Scholars typically divide the book of Isaiah into three historical sections: First Isaiah, written mainly in the eighth century BCE (more or less the initial thirty-nine chapters); Deutero-Isaiah, written during the mid-sixth century BCE (chapters 40–55); and Third Isaiah, written during the late sixth or early fifth century BCE (chapters 56–66). The later contributors to the Isaiah corpus intentionally adapt the words and themes that appear in First Isaiah. A similar process occurs in the books of Chronicles, which include a creative rewriting of the material in Samuel and Kings. Many of the biblical Psalms include texts that reinterpret earlier biblical passages. And the attributes of God in Exodus 34:6–7 appear reworked into several later biblical sources, including Jonah 4:2 and Psalm 86:15.

Later Jewish theologians continued this tradition through the production of scriptural texts that adapted and added onto preexisting "biblical" material. The Dead Sea Scroll community at Qumran produced a type of biblical commentary known as *Pesharim* that interpreted earlier material in light of the community's history. This is the same process that we encounter in the New Testament, particularly the book of Matthew, which adopts and recontextualizes scriptural material from the Hebrew Bible as messianic prophecies pointing to Jesus. We find this process at work in the writings of the first century Jewish historian Josephus as well. In his twenty-volume history, *Jewish Antiquities*, Josephus created a new rewritten Bible of sorts by quoting portions of the Septuagint verbatim and then adding both new material and his own commentary directly to the narrative. From this same time period, the Hellenized Jew, Philo of Alexandria, combined Jewish texts with concepts of Platonic philosophy, thus creating new religious material based upon the Bible. Smith's Book of Moses, therefore, follows a long history of reformulating and adding onto biblical material in the creation of a new religious text.

When we survey this material, we find that pseudonymous authors from antiquity often appear identified as authors of many of these texts, including much of what appears in the Bible. In fact, we must keep in mind that from a mainstream scholarly perspective, despite their scriptural status, even the laws that Moses declares in the Pentateuch were actually written by later Israel and Judean scribes and subsequently attributed to Moses. Later Jewish books (held as "scripture" by various communities) appear attributed to Adam, Enoch, Noah, Melchizedek, Abraham, Jacob, Moses, Elijah, and Ezekiel (just to name a few). In reality, these religious texts that attribute the scriptural account to an ancient figure do not recreate words he or she once literally wrote. Instead, as one scholar has observed, "[a]ttribution (attaching names to Biblical books) belongs to the realm of literary scholarship, and has little to do with the intentions of the composers of works. It isn't so much about what an author did write, but rather it is about what he would have written (or; from the perspective of ancient literary interpreters, what he must have written)."[22] Taking into consideration the observations scholars have made concerning the historical origins of the book of Genesis, the Book of Moses can be seen as an account of what Moses, Israel's great lawgiver, would have written; or, from the perspective of Smith's revelatory text, what Moses *must* have written.

The Book of Moses, in a sense, is similar, therefore, to other ancient scriptural texts, including the second-century BCE book of Jubilees. This ancient account reports that during the first year of the Exodus, Moses experienced a forty-day epiphany on a sacred mountain. On this occasion, God shared with his prophet a panoramic vision concerning the history of the world (see Jubilees 1:1–4). According to the account, God intended this vision and the subsequent testimony Moses would record to provide a witness to the descendants of Israel concerning the covenants of the Lord. The account presents God's words to Moses:

> Set your mind on every thing which I shall tell you on this mountain, and write it in a book so that [Israel's] descendants might see that I have not abandoned them on account of all of the evil which they have done to instigate transgression of the covenant which I am establishing between me and you today on Mount Sinai for their descendants. (Jubilees 1:5–6)

The account then moves into a citation and reformulation of the early chapters of Genesis, depicting this material as the revelation concerning creation God gave to Moses and that Moses, in turn, put to writing. This shows that Smith's Book of Moses follows a significant trend in ancient Jewish traditions. The Book of Moses not only defends the inspired nature of Genesis's prehistory, it elevates the text to a revelatory status by using the biblical prophet Moses as a conduit for Smith's own revelations that corrected the Bible.

---

22. Jed Wyrick, *The Ascension of Authorship: Attribution and Canon Formation in Jewish, Hellenistic, and Christian Traditions* (Cambridge: Department of Comparative Literature, 2004), 80.

Like the Book of Jubilees, Smith's revelation follows a pattern first witnessed in ancient Judean history as a response to Hellenistic concerns. Greek philosophical traditions that influenced later Jewish thought held a text like Genesis with suspicion because it features accounts that many Greek philosophers would associate with the category of myth rather than history. Early Jewish efforts to identify the Pentateuch with a historical author such as Moses derived in part from an effort to respond to Greek criticism. The idea of a prophet writing scripture (such as the Book of Genesis) emerged as a late Judean concept, long after the time period of Moses. Similarly, Smith's revelation adds religious depth and authoritative legitimacy to the opening chapters of the Bible.

One of the ancient Jewish texts that parallels the type of structure in the Book of Moses is 1 Enoch. A second-temple Jewish text with literary layers that existed at least as early as the third century BCE, 1 Enoch was originally composed in Aramaic long after the time associated with the biblical Enoch. The book contains five separate segments in a way that reflects the traditional Jewish notion of the Torah consisting of five books.[23] These have been preserved in translation and remain part of the scriptural canon of the Ethiopian Christian church.

1 Enoch features revised segments of the opening chapters of Genesis (including the story of the "Sons of God" in Genesis 6:1–4). These revisions are presented as a vision received by the biblical patriarch Enoch and begin with an editorial superscription or introduction that speaks about Enoch in third person:

> The blessing of Enoch: with which he blessed the elect and the righteous who would be present on the day of tribulation at (the time of) the removal of all the ungodly ones. And Enoch, the blessed and righteous man of the Lord, took up (his parable) while his eyes were open and he saw, and said . . . (1 Enoch 1:1–2a)[24]

The account then transitions to a depiction of Enoch's own words:

> (This is) a holy vision from the heavens which the angels showed me: and I heard from them everything and I understood. I look not for this generation but for the distant one that is coming. (1 Enoch 1:2b)

---

23. For the various elements in 1 Enoch and an analysis of their historical development, see George W. E. Nickelsburg, *1 Enoch: A Commentary of the Book of Enoch Chapters 1–36, 81–108* (Minneapolis: Fortress, 2001), 7–8, 21–26.

24. As translated by E. Isaac in James Charlesworth, ed. *Old Testament Pseudepigrapha*, 2 vols. (Garden City, NY: Doubleday, 1983–87), 1:13.

Following an introduction that runs through 1 Enoch 5, the text transitions to a revised version of the source's story of the Sons of God in Genesis 6:1–4. 1 Enoch, therefore, directly parallels the structure for the Book of Moses. The Book of Moses begins with an editorial introduction that speaks about Moses in third person and then transitions to Moses using direct first person speech followed by a revised version of material found in the Book of Genesis. In so doing, both texts present a revised version of Judean documentary sources as revelations dictated by earlier prophetic figures. Known as pseudepigrapha (meaning "false superscriptions or titles"), this type of literature is a very common feature in ancient Jewish scriptural texts.

Even many of the books in the New Testament are pseudepigraphic works attributed to early Christian leaders. The New Testament, for instance, contains an epistle depicted as a letter written by Paul to his missionary companion Titus. This is one of a series of epistles attributed to Paul that biblical scholars almost universally believe were not written by the apostle, including the epistles to Timothy and the Ephesians. Colossians and 2 Thessalonians are also held by many critical scholars as pseudepigraphic texts. As Bart Ehrman explains,

> Letters allegedly written by Paul continued to be produced in the second and later centuries [i.e. long after his death]; among those that still survive are a third letter to the Corinthians, a letter addressed to the church in the town of Laodicea, and an exchange of correspondence between Paul and the famous Greek philosopher Seneca.[25]

These later texts illustrate how the pseudepigraphical letters of Paul in the New Testament follow a common pattern in early Christian writings. Indeed, the same holds true for other scriptural sources from the New Testament. Most New Testament scholars, for instance, do not believe that Peter was the author of the two epistles ascribed to him in the Bible nor that the Epistle of Jude was written by the brother of Jesus and James.[26]

Other pseudepigraphic texts not included in the traditional New Testament canon include such works as the Gospel of Peter and the Gospel of Judas. In fact, a critical survey of early Christian literature, including

---

25. Bart Ehrman, *New Testament: An Historical Introduction to the Early Christian Writings* (Oxford: Oxford University Press, 2007), 292–93.

26. Historically, Jesus's brother Jude would have been a lower class, Aramaic-speaking Jew. The author of "Jude," however, was highly educated in Jewish apocryphal writings and possessed an ability to write in Greek. The author, for example, cites the book of 1 Enoch as scripture in verse 14.

the books that appear in the New Testament, illustrates that presenting a religious text as the words of a famous Christian leader was not simply a pervasive tradition, it was the norm.

Attributing a literary work to another person who held an important religious role, such as a prophet or apostle, elevated the religious status of the document as sacred literature.[27] In his recent work focusing upon early Christian writings that follow this trend, Ehrman explains:

> The single most important motivation for authors to claim they were someone else in antiquity . . . was to get a hearing for their views. If you were an unknown person, but had something really important to say and wanted people to hear you—not so they could praise you, but so they could learn the truth—one way to make that happen was to pretend you were someone else, a well-known author, a famous figure, an authority.[28]

In other words, claiming that your revelation was actually given to Enoch, Isaiah, Abraham, or Paul gave the work a type of religious credence.

This interpretation of the purpose of pseudepigraphy works well for many of the early Christian examples that Ehrman's study focuses upon. However, imposing the same idea upon the Book of Moses is problematic. Smith did not need to attribute his revelation (Moses 1) to the biblical Moses in order to provide his revelation with greater validity. As prophet of God, in addition to translating the Book of Mormon, Smith was already dictating his own personal revelations as scripture in 1830. There was no need for the Mormon prophet to bolster his religious views by claiming that they were Moses's. Instead, Moses 1 presents the opening chapters of Genesis as a revelation given to Moses on a mountaintop. It therefore elevates the religious authenticity of the Bible, not Smith's revelations. From this angle, the Book of Moses may be defined by believing Latter-

---

27. James C. VanderKam, *From Revelation to Canon: Studies in the Hebrew Bible and Second Temple Literature* (Leiden: Brill, 1999), 23–25; G. W. E. Nickelsburg, "Revealed Wisdom as a Criterion for Inclusion and Exclusion: From Jewish Sectarianism to Early Christianity," in *To See Ourselves as Others See*, ed. J. Neusner and E. S. Frerichs (Atlanta: Scholars Press, 1985), 73–91; G. W. E. Nickelsburg, "The Nature and Function of Revelation in 1 Enoch, Jubilees, and Some Qumranic Documents," in *Pseudepigraphic Perspectives: The Apocrypha and Pseudepigrapha in Light of the Dead Sea Scrolls*, ed. Esther G. Chazon et al. (Leiden: Brill, 1999), 91–120.

28. Bart D. Ehrman, *Forged: Writing in the Name of God—Why the Bible's Authors Are Not Who We Think They Are* (New York: HarperOne: 2012), 31.

day Saints as inspired prophetic midrash. And as illustrated, Smith's work follows an ancient religious literary pattern for scripture.

Yet ancient authors who produced a religious source as the words of an earlier prophet or sage did not always seek to identify the text as a document that ultimately derived from that authoritative figure (though such an attempt was common). Instead, ancient authors occasionally sought to produce a text wherein one who communicated with God could serve as a type of conduit for the disclosure of divine knowledge. This is one of the ways Moses can be understood in Smith's revelation. For those who accept Smith's Book of Moses as inspired scripture, Israel's great lawgiver serves as an instrument or conduit for the disclosure of the divine knowledge that appears in Genesis. The text, therefore, accords with Smith's role as a Restorer, bridging the spiritual and scriptural gaps between the ancient and modern worlds.

Pseudonymous authors legitimize the scriptural authority of the text. In this sense, the pseudonymous writer is "not so much creator or author as he is tradent and guarantor."[29] Hence, the ancient art of pseudepigraphy should not be viewed through modern notions of fraud or forgeries. This point is well-articulated by Annette Yoshiko Reed:

> When grappling with the presence of Pauline pseudepigrapha in the New Testament ... scholars ... have cautioned against assuming that this ancient literary practice was necessarily motivated by any radical intent to replace an earlier text or tradition. Like the prophetic pseudepigraphy that formed second and third Isaiah, for instance, the Pauline pseudepigraphy of the Pastoral Epistles may be better understood in terms of a claim to faithful oral reception and written transmission of Pauline teachings and/or as a claim to the inspired interpretation and faithful continuation of Pauline tradition. Rather than a rebellion against the textual authority of Paul's own writings, this literary choice may reflect a conservativism vis-à-vis received tradition, forged in settings in which its preservation seemed, to some, to be endangered by competing readings of the meanings of Paul's written words.[30]

A Latter-day Saint who accepts the arguments of Higher Criticism could adopt Reed's perspective of pseudepigrapha as a reflection for what the Book of Moses does for Genesis.

---

29. Annette Yoshiko Reed, "Pseudepigraphy, Authorship and the Reception of the 'the Bible' in Late Antiquity," in *The Reception and Interpretation of the Bible in Late Antiquity*, ed. L. DiTommason and L. Turcescu (Leiden: Brill, 2008), 477.

30. Reed, 475–76.

Like Wellhausen and other nineteenth-century critical thinkers, Joseph Smith recognized that the Bible was a product of human hands. Its problems needed to be addressed. Smith identified some of these issues, and he attempted to correct the errors (as he perceived them) via his new translation. However, unlike Wellhausen—whose critical approach to the Bible humanized the work—Smith's critical assessment represents a type of religious conservativism that seeks to elevate the inspired authenticity of the Bible by providing Genesis's prehistory with a new interpretive lens attributed to Israel's great lawgiver.

Adopting this perspective, the Book of Moses can be seen to conceptually parallel Smith's reworking of his United Firm revelations (D&C 78, 82, 92, 96). These revelations show signs of significant revisionary efforts that develop over time. Part of this growth occurred as a result of Smith's desire to keep hidden from outsiders the identities of the men whose names appear in the revelations. The original revelations referred openly to men who were participating in Smith's United Firm, an organization that supervised the management of the Church's financial enterprises and distribution of properties from 1832 to 1834. The changes made to these financial revelations concerning the United Firm included more than simply a substitution of ancient code names. They were intentionally revised in order to sound like ancient texts. Smith changed his own name to Enoch and Gazelam, and he gave "Adamic-like" names to his cohorts: Newel K. Whitney was changed to Ahashdah; Edward Partridge to Alam; John Whitmer to Horah; A. Sidney Gilbert to Mahalaleel; Martin Harris to Mahemson; Oliver Cowdery to Olihah; Sidney Rigdon to Pelagoram; W.W. Phelps to Shalemanasseh; Frederick G. Williams to Shederlaomach; and John Johnson to Zombre.[31] Anachronistic Bible references that originally appeared in the texts were substituted for terms connected with an earlier Adamic setting. The word "Israel" appears changed to a more archaic "Zion." John Johnson's lineage through Joseph of Egypt is changed to that of Seth, and even the name Jesus Christ was switched to describe its Adamic form, "Son of Ahman."[32] These changes allowed the revelations to appear as ancient rather than modern.

---

31. In the words of Christopher Smith, "Significant additions and deletions were made in order to give these revelations an authentically ancient veneer." Christopher C. Smith, "The Inspired Fictionalization of the 1835 United Firm Revelations," *Claremont Journal of Mormon Studies* 1 (2011): 16, 25.

32. Smith, 25.

This objective behind these changes is made clear in the way Joseph revised the revelation that eventually became Doctrine and Covenants 78. In the 1835 version of this revelation, the Prophet added the clause, "the Lord spoke unto Enoch, saying . . ." to the beginning of the revelation. This effectively transformed the *Sitz im Leben* for this nineteenth-century economic text concerning the United Firm to read as if it had been given to the ancient prophet Enoch:

> Hearken unto me saith the Lord your God O ye who are ordained unto the high priests hood of my church, who have assembled [yourselves together]. (Book of Commandments and Revelations)[33]

> The Lord spake unto Enoch, saying, Hearken unto me saith the Lord your God, who are ordained unto the high priesthood of my church, who have assembled yourselves together. (D&C 75:1; 1835 edition)

> The Lord spake unto Joseph Smith, Jun., saying: Hearken unto me, saith the Lord your God, who are ordained unto the high priesthood of my church, who have assembled yourselves together. (D&C 78:1; current edition)

Moreover, the 1835 edition of the revelation Smith published was given the title, "The Order of the Lord to Enoch, for the purpose of establishing the poor." These changes to Joseph's revelations are significant. They illustrate that the Prophet viewed his efforts to express the word of God as a malleable endeavor.

From a historical perspective, an analogy, therefore, can be drawn between Smith's United Firm revelations and the Book of Moses. In both instances, we find Smith reworking previous religious texts into the prophetic vision of biblical figures. In the Book of Moses, Genesis is placed into the context of Moses's revelation; in Smith's United Firm texts, the Mormon prophet's economic revelations were reworked into the vision(s) of Enoch. From a theological perspective, these revised revelations illustrate Smith's understanding of dispensationalism (the idea that history repeats itself in types and shadows from dispensation to dispensation).[34] This unique perspective gave Smith precedence to rewrite scriptural texts (including his own) into the words of ancient prophets.

---

33. Revelation Book 1, p. 196, as published Robin Scott Jensen, Robert J. Woodford, and Steven C. Harper, eds., *Manuscript Revelation Books*, facsimile ed. Vol. 1 of the Revelations and Translations series of *The Joseph Smith Papers*, ed. Dean C. Jessee, Ronald K. Esplin, and Richard Lyman Bushman (Salt Lake City: Church Historian's Press, 2009), 368–69.

34. This thesis is argued in Smith, "Inspired Fictionalization," 30.

A revelation given to Joseph Smith in 1841 depicts God's perspective concerning the prophet: "I give unto you my servant Joseph to be a presiding elder over all my church, to be a translator, a revelator, a seer, and prophet" (D&C 124:125). As a prophet and seer, Smith translated religious texts that Latter-day Saints define as scripture comparable to the Bible. However, that translation process was in most instances non-traditional; most of Smith's translation projects did not involve working with a text in a foreign languages (the Book of Abraham being an obvious exception). In nineteenth-century American English, the verb "translate" carried a variety of nuances (much as it does today). In addition to "the act of turning into another language," it could also mean "interpretation," or a "version." Its primary meaning was "the act of removing or conveying from one place to another."[35] Each of these 1828 definitions works well as a characterization of the Joseph Smith Translation, a revelatory work that created a new interpretation or new version of the Bible.

In his efforts to combine his revelatory work with past dispensations, Smith never produced traditional translations by working with another language.[36] For example, he does not seem to have directly used the plates to produce the Book of Mormon in his act of translation.[37] While Smith made use of the Egyptian papyri to produce the Book of Abraham, the role those papyri directly played in the process in unclear. And we know by both his inspired translation of the Bible and the revealed text "translated from parchment written and hid up by [John the beloved disciple]

---

35. Noah Webster, *American Dictionary of the English Language*; 1828 facsimile ed. (Anaheim: Foundation for American Christian Education, 1967), s. v. "translate."

36. Richard van Wagoner and Steven Walker, "Joseph Smith: 'The Gift of Seeing,'" *Dialogue: A Journal of Mormon Thought* 15, no. 2 (Summer 1982): 48–68.

37. On the translation process, Bushman writes: "By the time Cowdery arrived, translator and scribe were no longer separated. Emma said she sat at the same table with Joseph, writing as he dictated, with nothing between them, and the plates wrapped in a linen cloth on the table. When Cowdery took up the job of scribe, he and Joseph translated in the same room where Emma was working. Joseph looked in the seerstone, and the plates lay covered on the table. Neither Joseph nor Oliver explained how translation worked, but Joseph did not pretend to look at the "reformed Egyptian" words, the language on the plates, according to the book's own description. The plates lay covered on the table, while Joseph's head was in a hat looking at the seerstone, which by this time had replaced the interpreters." Bushman, *Rough Stone Rolling*, 71–72.

himself," found in Doctrine and Covenants 7,[38] that an actual copy of an ancient source was unnecessary for his translations.

Smith's translation work appears to reflect his understanding of divine creation. It is a process whereby structure or order is given to preexistent chaos. In translating, Smith was imitating deity and His creative work. The Mormon Prophet understood "translation" as a process whereby something (or someone) was "carried off" or "moved from one place to another." For example, in his revised version of Genesis, Smith referred to ancient men of faith who entered into the order of the Son of God and were "translated and taken up into heaven" (Gen. 14:32, JST). Thus, in "translating," Smith took something that existed in the physical or temporal world such as the Egyptian papyri he used to create the Book of Abraham (or even the Bible itself) and translated that material into something of increased spiritual importance.

The Book of Moses offers not only correction but additions to the sources from the Bible Latter-day Saints hold as both inspired and imperfect. For example, it provides the opening chapters of Genesis with a new *Sitz im Leben*—a mountain—that repackages the Pentateuch as a temple-based revelation.[39] This new scripture serves an essential role in Smith's effort to not only correct some of the Bible's errors as he saw them, but to spiritually bind previous dispensations with the modern era. As a religious translator, he made known that which was hidden from the world.

As this brief study has shown, the modern advancements in biblical studies carry significant ramifications for a critical assessment of the Book of Moses. While it is true that these insights force us to the conclusion that perhaps some traditional assumptions regarding the nature of Smith's revelatory texts may on some levels be incorrect, the inspired validity of his work is an issue beyond the realm of scientific analysis. In terms of the Book of Moses, Smith sought to raise the Bible's divine authenticity by bringing the book into harmony with his own revelatory experiences. To quote LDS scholar Phillip Barlow, "If certain truths were not originally included in the Bible, they are truths nonetheless and readers will be edified by studying them; it is not the text of the Bible as such, but rather the truths of God that are sacred."[40]

---

38. *Book of Commandments* (Independence, MO: W. W. Phelps 1833) 6:1, http://www.josephsmithpapers.org/paper-summary/book-of-commandments-1833/22.

39. Bokovoy, *Authoring the Old Testament*, 367–69.

40. Barlow, *Mormons and the Bible*, 57.

Ultimately, scripture finds its spiritual worth in the process of actualization, meaning bringing something from the past into the present. It is the power to act rather than theorize. For Joseph Smith, the Bible was a collection of sacred religious texts with imperfections and human error. It needed, therefore, to be "translated correctly." As part of the expanded LDS canon, the Book of Moses helps Latter-day Saint readers actualize the Bible in their own religious quest to "translate."

9

THE ASCENDANCY AND LEGITIMATION OF THE PEARL OF GREAT PRICE

Brian M. Hauglid

In considering the Mormon canon of scripture we find that the Book of Mormon, the Doctrine and Covenants, and the Pearl of Great Price represent a clear expansion beyond the Bible, which itself, for the majority of the Christian world, represents *the* canonical border. But, as David Holland has said, "On one side of that border—the open side—lay both breathtaking liberties and a frightening potential for tyranny; on the other lay remarkable cultural cohesion and the ongoing promise of interpretive conflict."[1]

When applied to the Pearl of Great Price, Holland's observation proves quite perceptive. On the one hand, the Pearl of Great Price leads us to the Bible and well beyond, not just in terms of its textual expansion, but significantly to a mind-stretching contemplation of intellectually charged theological concepts, such as novel creation narratives (cosmogony), astronomical hierarchies (cosmology), eternal intelligence(s) (ontology), salvific covenant making (soteriology), priestly structure and progression (sacerdotalism), and the immanent and transcendent Christ (Christology).

On the other hand, its path towards canonization has, albeit inadvertently, raised observations about the Pearl of Great Price, which may seem to challenge or call into question its legitimacy. This may in large part be due to the fact that what those involved in the canonization process knew and understood about the Pearl of Great Price (especially the Books of Moses and Abraham) in their day (1850–80) pales in comparison to what is known now. For example, we now know much more about what precisely is in the LDS version of the Book of Moses that was imported from the Missouri-based Reorganized Church of Jesus Christ of Latter

---

1. David F. Holland, *Sacred Borders: Continuing Revelation and Canonical Restraint in Early America* (Oxford: Oxford University Press, 2011), 10.

Day Saints (RLDS, now Community of Christ).[2] Further, no one in the nineteenth century could have known that in the twentieth century, Egyptologists would be able to determine that the Book of Abraham may contain translation issues. Issues such as these bring into relief the human aspect of the making of scripture and, at the same time, bring up pertinent questions: What is sacred scripture? How is it made? What role does human filtering play in the reception of revelation?

As fascinating as it would be to explore these theological questions more thoroughly, space will only permit a brief mention of the dynamics that served to propel the Pearl of Great Price into the canon of Mormon scripture, a process that may be viewed as the ascendancy and legitimation of the Pearl of Great Price. But as important as this scripture-making process may have been, it is also worth looking at what happened following the 1880 canonization of the Pearl of Great Price, an era in which challenges to legitimacy gradually emerged, calling into question its authenticity and legitimation, particularly for the Book of Abraham, which gave rise to a robust apologetic that has lasted into the twenty-first century. Interestingly, for some, apologetics has fallen short of its effectiveness, which has led many to consider the ways that sacred scripture may occur at the nexus of both the fallible, imperfect human influence and the divine, revelatory, religious experience.

In terms of its ascendancy towards canonical authority, we find that the Pearl of Great Price has an interesting and unique story. All of its contents were produced during the Joseph Smith period, particularly in the 1830s. However, Smith did not canonize any of it before his death in 1844—unless canonization in his view meant publishing his revelations in Church periodicals, particularly the *Times and Seasons*. It is known that the Doctrine and Covenants was approved as an official church text in General Conference meetings.[3] However, at present, no evidence suggests specific plans of Smith to present any part of what would become the Pearl of Great Price in General Conference for inclusion in the canon of Mormon scripture.

---

2. Scott H. Faulring, Kent P. Jackson, and Robert J. Matthews, *Joseph Smith's New Translation of the Bible: Original Manuscripts* (Provo, UT: Religious Studies Center, 2004). See also, Kent P. Jackson, *The Book of Moses and the Joseph Smith Translation Manuscripts* (Provo, UT: Religious Studies Center, 2005).

3. The modern Mormon notion of canonization did not fully develop until much later, as the Book of Mormon seems to have arisen to canon status *ex post facto* its publication at the official organization of the Church in April 1830.

In 1851, some seven years after the death of Joseph Smith, Franklin D. Richards (a mission president in England at the time) did something that no mission president would be able to do today—he published a miscellaneous collection of Smith's un-canonized revelations for the British Saints without (ostensibly) the explicit, formal approval of Brigham Young and the Twelve. In Richards's defense, a paper shortage in the American Great Basin made it impossible to print materials for the British Mormons, who craved church literature and urged Richards to publish what he had brought with him from America. Apparently, Richards initially desired to provide the English Mormons with the revelations published as a missionary tract and had little or no ambition for seeing it canonized. In a February 1851 letter to his uncle Levi Richards, Franklin D. Richards said, "I thought of issuing a collection of revelations, prophecies &c., in a tract form of a character not designed to pioneer our doctrines to the world, so much as for the use of the Elders and Saints to arm and better qualify them for their service in the great *war*."[4] In this letter Richards lists the contents he had collected from earlier church periodicals, particularly the *Times and Seasons*. These he would include in his 1851 Liverpool collection entitled—for the first time—*The Pearl of Great Price*. Granted, while Joseph Smith had previously designated some of these materials as revelations and prophecies either through direct commentary or through publication, some of Richards's *Pearl* had never been published before, but were printed for the first time in either Richards's 1851 *Millennial Star* or his 1851 *Pearl of Great Price*. (For example, Moses 2:1–4:13a; Moses 4:14–19, 22–25; and D&C 87 were all first published by Richards in England.)[5]

It can be surmised that during the next three decades leading to its formal canonization, the 1851 *Pearl of Great Price* became more and more familiar to the American Mormons through immigration and missionary work.[6] In addition to these influential factors, Apostle Orson Pratt seems

---

4. H. Donl Peterson, *The Pearl of Great Price: A History and Commentary* (Salt Lake City: Deseret Book Company, 1987), 11; emphasis in original.

5. A helpful chart can be found in Peterson, *The Pearl of Great Price: A History and Commentary*, 17–20.

6. Since the 1851 edition was meant to be a missionary tract, it is not unreasonable to assume that it became quite popular in its time and was, perhaps, carried back to America with returning American missionaries. This seems a reasonable assumption for immigrant converts as well. Much work still needs to be done with Mormon nineteenth-century print culture (e.g. journals, diaries) to explore how much Richards's *Pearl of Great Price* was used in both missionary and

to have been a prominent influence in the ascendancy of the *Pearl of Great Price* towards canonization. Over a thirty-year period, he repeatedly quoted, referred to, or commented on its contents in the *Journal of Discourses* and *The Seer*.[7] As early as 1853, we find Pratt, in *The Seer*, quoting extensively from the both the Book of Moses and the Book of Abraham.[8] In doing so he repeatedly described the passages as "inspiration" and "revelation," which no doubt assisted in bolstering its sacred stature.[9]

It is interesting, and perhaps odd, that Orson Pratt's 1878 American edition of the *Pearl of Great Price* appeared only a year after Brigham Young's death and became an official part of the Mormon canon two years later. Young likely approved of the text to a certain degree, since he donated a copy of the 1851 edition to Harvard and placed a copy in the Salt Lake Temple time capsule. But Young's reluctance to canonize the Pearl of Great Price was perhaps due to his suspicions (later confirmed) that the RLDS Church imported material into the Book of Moses not sanctioned by Joseph Smith—a concern he shared with Orson Pratt.[10]

---

immigration scenarios. I have gone through all of the diaries of Richards from the 1840s to 1890s and have, unfortunately, found very little that directly relates to it.

7. Of course, there were others who had some interest in the Pearl of Great Price in Pratt's day, maybe not to the same degree as Pratt, but perhaps enough to add to the growing stature of the text. For examples, see George Q. Cannon, April 21, 1867, and Erastus Snow, April 6, 1879, *Journal of Discourses*, 26 vols. (London and Liverpool: LDS Booksellers Depot, 1854, 86), 12:41 and 20:181.

8. Orson Pratt, "The Pre-existence of Man," *The Seer* 1, no. 4 (April 1853): 51–52; quoting Abraham 3:22–4:2 and Moses 4:1–11. For more references to the Pearl of Great Price in *The Seer*, see Orson Pratt, "The Pre-existence of Man," *The Seer* 1, no. 8 (August 1853): 118–19 and "War," *The Seer* 2, no. 4 (April 1854): 241. Many more references cite Enoch, Moses, and Abraham, which, more than likely, and at least indirectly, derive from the Pearl of Great Price.

9. In addition to the examples in the previous footnote, see the following discourses of Orson Pratt in the *Journal of Discourses*: September 11, 1859 (7:253); November 24, 1872 (15:235, 238); May 18, 1873 (16:50); November 22, 1873 (16:325); December 28, 1873 (16:336); January 27, 1874 (16:362–63); August 25, 1878 (20:64–66, 72); November 12, 1879 (21:201); June 13, 1880 (21:259–60); and July 18, 1880 (21:287). The Pearl of Great Price was canonized in October 1880.

10. James R. Harris, "Changes in the Book of Moses and Their Implications upon a Concept of Revelation," *BYU Studies* 8, no. 4 (1968): 323n23.

The Book of Moses

The Book of Moses seems to divide itself into two broad revelatory categories. The first category could be termed a visionary or auditory revelation such as found in its opening chapter that was first published in the *Times and Seasons* in 1843 with the title "A Revelation to Joseph Smith, jun. given June, 1830." The specific historical provenance for this revelation is now lost to us, but the preamble in the historical record describes Moses 1 as a "precious morsel" received amid many "trials and tribulations."[11] Chapters 2 through 8 appear to be more connected to a second category of revelation, one that was a product of the new translation of the Bible. While Moses 1 is not attested to in the Bible, Moses 2–8 follows the biblical narrative expanding the text and revising or replacing terminology, much as an editorial revision.

All of the Moses material was produced between June 1830 and February 1831 but was published piecemeal between 1832 and 1851. The earliest part of the Moses corpus to be printed appeared in the *Evening and Morning Star* between 1832 and 1833; it encompassed what is now known as Moses 5:1–16a (April 1833); 6:43–68 (March 1833); 7:1–69 (August 1832); 8:13–30 (April 1833). Interestingly, Moses 5:19–23 and 32–40 first appeared in the 1835 Doctrine and Covenants as part of the *Lectures on Faith*. As already noted, Moses 1 appeared in the January 1843 *Times and Seasons*.[12] It is also intriguing that Moses 2:1–4:13a was first published in the March 1851 issue of the *Millennial Star*,[13] while Moses 4:14–19, 22–25 first appeared in the 1851 edition of the Pearl of Great Price.

From the publication record of the Moses material, besides Moses 2–4 the rest of Moses (with the exception of Moses 2–4) was publicly available during the Smith period and likely viewed as imbued with some measure of sacred authoritativeness. A key part of the Moses material that served to elevate it in authority and legitimation, aside from its initial connection to Smith, is the Enoch portion of the text (Moses 6–7), which was also the earliest of the Moses material to be published in the Missouri *Evening*

---

11. "History of Joseph Smith," *Times and Seasons* 4 (January 16, 1843): 71. See also Joseph Smith, et al., *History of the Church of Jesus Christ of Latter day Saints*, ed. B. H. Roberts, 7 vols., 2nd ed. rev. (Salt Lake City: Deseret Book, 1948 printing), 1:98.

12. "History," 71–73.

13. "The First Part of the Book of Genesis," *Millennial Star* 13, no. 6 (March 15, 1851): 90–93.

and Morning Star (1832). The timeliness of this publication should not be underestimated. In July 1831, Joseph Smith received a revelation in which the "land of Missouri" was "appointed and consecrated for the gathering of the saints" and designated "the land of promise, and the place for the city of Zion" (D&C 57:1–2). This gave rise to a fervent socio-economic utopian vision that remained strong up until the late nineteenth and early twentieth centuries.[14]

Significantly, Richard's 1851 *Pearl of Great Price* begins with "extracts from the prophecy of Enoch" (Moses 6:43–7:69). This excerpt focuses on Enoch's Zion, the gathering, and the establishment of Zion in the last days all in anticipation of a thousand-year millennial reign of Jesus Christ, a telling way to begin the Pearl of Great Price that fits quite well within the context of the mid-nineteenth-century Mormon emphasis on the gathering of the saints to Zion.[15] Interestingly, a harbinger to this millenarian emphasis had occurred just two years prior to the publication of the 1851 *Pearl of Great Price* with the creation of the Perpetual Immigration Fund. With the publication of the Enoch material, then, many future British Mormon immigrants could catch the vision of gathering to Zion and access the economic help to realize that vision.

In sum, although the Moses material appears to have been in a fragmented format prior to its inclusion in the 1851 and 1878 editions of the Pearl of Great Price, it seems that Moses 1, 6, and 7 were emphasized during the 1830s and 1840s in such a way as to raise the authority and legitimation of this particular material. For Moses 1 it was its placement within the realm of a formal revelation; for Moses 6 through 7 it was the historical framework of the saints' search for Zion. Significantly, the rest of the Moses material did not attain in authority in the same way as its counterparts. What seems interesting is that Joseph Smith and the early saints focused on select portions of the current Book of Moses, which served to bolster Mormons within specific contexts, such as the gathering to Zion, yet other portions of the Moses material, particularly Moses 2–4, increased in authority and legitimacy in a later doctrinal context, particularly in the early-nineteenth century.

---

14. For an excellent discussion of the early Mormon millenarian vision, see Grant Underwood, *The Millenarian World of Early Mormonism* (Urbana and Chicago: University of Illinois, 1999).

15. James R. Clark, *The Story of the Pearl of Great Price* (Salt Lake City: Bookcraft, 1955), 23, 39–47.

Generally, the Book of Moses has not seen the critical challenges faced by the Book of Abraham and the First Vision. Although one can identify clear historical-critical importations from the biblical text (Moses 1–3) and perceived racist language (Moses 7:8, 22), critics of Smith have generally focused on the Egyptian papyri or multiple accounts of the First Vision when discussing contents of the Pearl of Great Price. Since the publication of the Joseph Smith Translation manuscripts it has become clearer that Orson Pratt compared the RLDS Church's Inspired Version (their title of Joseph Smith's translation of the Bible) with the Book of Moses when creating the 1878 American edition of the Pearl of Great Price. This means that the Book of Moses was compared against Old Testament Revision 2 (OT2), the base text of the Inspired Version, updating the text from Richards's *Pearl of Great Price*, which was based on the earlier Old Testament Revision 1 (OT1). This was certainly a worthy effort. At the same time, Pratt must have trusted the RLDS version of the Book of Moses, because he basically imported the Inspired Version rendition of the Book of Moses wholesale into the 1878 edition, introducing RLDS changes into the Moses text that remain in the LDS version to this day (see, for example, Moses 1:21; Moses 7:29, 41).[16] Most of these changes are rather minor but, again, a critical examination of the Book of Moses could help to assess the breadth and depth of its textual history.

The Book of Abraham

In contrast to the Book of Moses, there is much less historical information describing the origins of the Book of Abraham. It enters Church history sometime in late June or early July 1835 when Joseph Smith purchased four mummies and several rolls of papyri from Michael Chandler, a traveling antiquities dealer. Smith later determined that "one of the rolls contained the writings of Abraham, another the writings of Joseph of Egypt."[17] Since its inception it is by no means an overstatement to say that

---

16. Kent P. Jackson has noted many more RLDS changes Pratt imported into the 1878 Book of Moses in his *The Book of Moses and the Joseph Smith Translation Manuscripts* (Provo, UT: Religious Studies Center, 2005).

17. Dan Vogel, ed., *History of Joseph Smith and The Church of Jesus Christ of Latter-Day Saints: A Source-and Text-Critical Edition* (Salt Lake City: The Smith-Pettit Foundation, 2015), 2:240. Vogel notes that Willard Richards inserted this entry into the *Manuscript History of Joseph Smith* B-1 (596), likely with the help of W. W. Phelps on September 15, 1843.

the Book of Abraham has garnered more questions and criticisms than the Book of Moses.

Even before the Egyptian artifacts arrived in Kirtland, Ohio, during the summer of 1835, Joseph Smith had already developed a fascination with antiquity, which included the study of ancient languages, such as Egyptian.[18] However, it does not appear that material in the Book of Abraham attained the same level of sacred authority and legitimacy in Smith's day as with the Enochian material in the Book of Moses. Although Smith received the papyri in the summer of 1835 he did not publish it until March 1842 in the *Times and Seasons*, and he seems to have never intended it to be a part of the Mormon canon of scripture. In fact, in November 1843 Smith may have been more interested in publishing a "grammar of the Egyptian language"[19] rather than canonizing the Book of Abraham. It seems for the most part that the Book of Abraham increased in its authority and legitimacy subsequent to its inclusion in the 1851 *Pearl of Great Price*, as it became well-known to immigrants and missionaries, especially Orson Pratt.

The Book of Abraham comprises five chapters and, like the book of Moses, includes both biblical and non-biblical materials. Chapters 1 and 3 contain materials not found in the biblical text that function as an expansion of the Abrahamic narrative; chapters 2, 4, and 5, however, appear more like minor revisions and additions similar to those found in Smith's work on the Bible that produced Moses 2 through 8. Unlike the Book of Moses, which was published in various places in a fragmentary manner, the entire Book of Abraham was published serially in the *Times and Seasons* from March to May 1842.

Joseph Smith probably initiated translation work on Abraham in early July 1835 in Kirtland, Ohio, but it is not entirely clear how much of the

---

18. As early as 1831, Smith was interested in obtaining the pure language of Adam. See Robin Scott Jensen, Robert J. Woodford, and Steven C. Harper, eds. *Manuscript Revelation Books*, facsimile ed., vol. 1 of the Revelations and Translations series of *The Joseph Smith Papers*, ed. Dean C. Jessee, Ronald K. Esplin, and Richard Lyman Bushman (Salt Lake City: Church Historian's Press, 2009), 144. It is also likely that Smith viewed the ancient Egyptian language as descending from the pure language of Adam. See Samuel Morris Brown, "Joseph (Smith) in Egypt: Babel, Hieroglyphs, and the Pure Language of Eden," *Church History* 78, no. 1 (March 2009): 36–40.

19. Scott Faulring, ed., *An American Prophet's Record: The Diaries and Journals of Joseph Smith* (Salt Lake City: Signature Books, 1989), 427.

text was produced at that time, nor is it entirely clear how the Book of Abraham was translated from the Egyptian papyri. However, two very different approaches offer their own explanations as to how the translation process occurred. Both take into evidence the surviving Abrahamic and Egyptian manuscripts as well as historical considerations. Also, to one degree or another, both propositions present well-reasoned, logical arguments dealing with important questions: What is the source of the Book of Abraham? How do the Abraham and Egyptian manuscripts relate to each other and the Joseph Smith Papyri? What purpose is behind the production of the Abraham and Egyptian manuscripts? Did Joseph Smith dictate any text contained in the Abraham and Egyptian manuscripts, or do these manuscripts instead represent copied text from earlier exemplars? Was the translation of Abraham chapters 1 through 5 completed in 1835, or were the later chapters (3–5) finished much later in Nauvoo (1842)?[20] It should also be noted that the lines between these positions are rather porous and should not be viewed as an either/or scenario, but only as a useful way to present differing points of view.

One approach (what I call the Imagination Position), fueled by the 1967 rediscovery of eleven of Smith's Egyptian papyri fragments[21] (referred to here as the Joseph Smith Papyri),[22] focuses on the notion that the Book of Abraham is solely a nineteenth-century product of the imagination of Joseph Smith.[23] It underscores that one of the acquired frag-

---

20. Because of the long history of debates concerning questions such as these and the complexities of some the arguments on both sides of the issues, this brief survey of the translation process will only highlight the main points of the approaches with a few sources for further study and not supply numerous sources to debate arguments.

21. These fragments were part of a catalogued collection housed at the Metropolitan Museum of Art in New York City. They are now archived with the Church History Library of the Church of Jesus Christ of Latter-day Saints. For the traditional historical account of events leading up to the 1967 acquisition of the papyri, see Jay M. Todd, *The Saga of the Book of Abraham* (Salt Lake City: Deseret Book Company, 1969), 333–88. See also some important corrections to this account in John Gee, "Some Puzzles from the Joseph Smith Papyri," *FARMS Review* 20, no. 1 (2008): 115–16.

22. Joseph Smith Papyri XI is also known as "The Book of Breathings," the "Breathing Permit," the "Sensen Papyrus," the "Scroll of Horos," the "Scroll of Hor," and the "Document of Fellowship of Isis," depending on author preference.

23. For a general review of the arguments contained in the Imagination Position, see Charles M. Larson, *By His Own Hand Upon Papyrus: A New Look at the Joseph*

ments, which contains a vignette (Joseph Smith Papyri I) that is identical to Facsimile 1 of the Book of Abraham, was once attached to another fragment (Joseph Smith Papyri XI). This latter fragment contains hieratic characters that can be found in the left margin of three 1835 Abraham manuscripts with facing text from the Book of Abraham. This position argues that since Abraham 1:12 says, "I will refer you to the representation [Joseph Smith Papyri I] at the commencement of this record [Joseph Smith papyri XI]," and since the three 1835 manuscripts contain characters from Joseph Smith Papyri XI, they represent the actual translation papers used to produce the Book of Abraham. This position also argues correctly that the hieratic characters do not translate to the facing text from the Book of Abraham.[24] A further elaboration of this approach posits that two of the 1835 Abraham manuscripts contain at least seven nearly identical emendations and therefore represent a simultaneous dictation scenario with Joseph Smith dictating to two scribes at once.[25] Another

---

Smith Papyri (Grand Rapids: Institute for Religious Research, 1992). Complete transcriptions of the Abraham and Egyptian papers can now be accessed on josephsmithpapers.org. The Joseph Smith Papers Project will also be publishing a print edition of these manuscripts tentatively titled *Revelations and Translations, Volume 4: Book of Abraham and Related Manuscripts*, ed. by Robin Scott Jensen and Brian M. Hauglid (Salt Lake City: Church Historian's Press, 2018).

24. In 1912 a number of non-Mormon Egyptologists considered the connection of the Joseph Smith Papyri to the Book of Abraham translation and concluded that the characters do not translate to the Book of Abraham. See F. S. Spaulding, *Joseph Smith, Jr., as a Translator* (Salt Lake City: The Arrow Press, 1912). Later Egyptologist Klaus Baer translated the characters common to Joseph Smith Papyri XI and the 1835 Abraham manuscripts in "The Breathing Permit of Hôr: A Translation of the Apparent Source of the Book of Abraham," *Dialogue: A Journal of Mormon Thought* 3, no. 3 (1968): 130–32. Other non-Mormon Egyptologists have also looked more recently at Joseph Smith Papyri XI from various perspectives. See for example, Robert K. Ritner, "'The Breathing Permit of Hôr' Among the Joseph Smith Papyri," *Journal of Near Eastern Studies* 62, no. 3 (2003): 161–80; and Lanny Bell, "The Ancient Egyptian 'Book of Breathing,' the Mormon 'Book of Abraham,' and the Development of Egyptology in America," in *Egypt and Beyond*, ed. by Stephen E. Thompson and Peter Der Manuelian (Providence: Department of Egyptology and Ancient Western Asian Studies, 2008), 21–39.

25. All references to and designations of the manuscripts hereafter adhere to the schema developed in Brian M. Hauglid, *A Textual History of the Book of Abraham* (Provo, UT: Neal A. Maxwell Institute for Religious Scholarship, 2010). For examples of matching emendations, compare Ab2 folio 1a lines 1, 2, 29 (Hauglid, 67, 69); folio 1b lines 14–15, 29 (Hauglid, 71, 73); folio 2a

more recent argument related to the Imagination Position postulates that Joseph Smith produced Abraham 1:1–3 from an 1835 Egyptian document titled the "Grammar and Aphabet [sic] of the Egyptian Language."[26]

Another approach, referred to here as the Revelation Position, proposes that the Book of Abraham is not a nineteenth-century product of imagination, but the result of God-inspired revelation to Joseph Smith. According to this position, Smith, through revelation, translated the Book of Abraham from a now nonextant long roll of papyri, which was once attached to Joseph Smith Papyri XI.[27] Concerning Abraham 1:12, quoted above, this position argues that this verse was a later redaction by Joseph Smith, who included it to point out Facsimile 1 at the beginning of the Book of Abraham (not Joseph Smith Papyri XI).[28] Also, both the Abraham and Egyptian manuscripts appear to exhibit enough paragraphing, punctuation, and visual copying errors to suggest that they

---

lines 16–17 (Hauglid, 75) with Ab3 folio 1a lines 1, 2 (Hauglid, 87); folio 1b line 17 (Hauglid, 91); folio 2a line 27 (Hauglid, 97); folio 3a line 5 (Hauglid, 103). The scribes for these two manuscripts are Frederick G. Williams (Ab2) and Warren Parrish (Ab3). It should be noted that proponents of the simultaneous dictation theory refer to Ab2 and Ab3 as mss 1a and 1b respectively to underscore their simultaneity. Edward H. Ashment first introduced this theory in "Reducing Dissonance: The Book of Abraham as a Case Study," in *The Word of God: Essays on Mormon Scripture*, ed. Dan Vogel (Salt Lake City: Signature Books, 1990), 221–35. Christopher C. Smith posits that the three Egyptian Alphabet documents are also a product of simultaneous dictation. See his "The Dependence of Abraham 1:1–3 on the Egyptian Alphabet and Grammar," *John Whitmer Historical Association Journal* 29 (2009): 40.

26. Smith, "Dependence of Abraham 1:1–3," 47–52.

27. Mormon Egyptologist John Gee previously proposed that the "long roll" was not related to Joseph Smith Papyri XI; see "A Tragedy of Errors," *FARMS Review* 4, no. 1 (1992): 107–8. More recently Gee has argued that the "long roll" may have been attached to Joseph Smith Papyri XI, citing nineteenth-century eyewitness descriptions of the "long roll," employing a mathematical formula to ascertain the length of the scroll of Horos, and noting ancient Egyptian scroll practices. See Gee, "Some Puzzles from the Joseph Smith Papyri," 119–23. For a much more conservative estimate of the length of the scroll of Horos, see Andrew W. Cook and Christopher C. Smith, "The Original Length of the Scroll of Hôr," *Dialogue: A Journal of Mormon Thought* 43, no. 4 (Winter 2010), 1–4; and Andrew W. Cook, "Formulas and Facts: A Response to John Gee," *Dialogue: A Journal of Mormon Thought* 45, no. 3 (Fall 2012): 1–10.

28. See the sublinear insertion in Ab2 folio 1a, line 37 in Hauglid, *A Textual History*, 69.

were not dictated, but were copied from earlier exemplars. This would mean that the originally dictated Abraham manuscripts did not survive into the twentieth century. Regarding the hieratic characters from Joseph Smith Papyri XI found in the left margin of the three 1835 Abraham manuscripts, the Revelation Position has offered several explanations. One argument proposes that the characters function as a mnemonic device,[29] while another postulates that the characters represent an effort on the part of Joseph Smith's scribes to learn the Egyptian language through reverse engineering.[30] Still another unpublished and untested intertextual study argues that the Book of Abraham was fully extant before the creation of the 1835 Abraham/Egyptian papers.[31]

A key question in both of these approaches concerns how much of the Book of Abraham was translated and when this translation occurred. As noted above, the Revelation Position generally accepts that the entire Book of Abraham (and beyond!) was translated in 1835, perhaps as early as July.[32] However, Joseph Smith's journal records two translation sessions on March 8 and 9, 1842 that employ the term "translation."[33] These entries specify

---

29. See John A. Tvedtnes, "The Use of Mnemonic Devices in Oral Traditions, as Exemplified by the Book of Abraham and the Sensen Papyrus," *Newsletter & Proceedings of the SEHA* 120 (April 1970).

30. This theory argues that the scribes (not Joseph Smith) tried to compare characters from Joseph Smith Papyri XI to the already extant text of the Book of Abraham in an effort to decode the Egyptian. For a more thorough explanation of the characters in the Abraham manuscripts from this point of view, see Hugh W. Nibley, "The Meaning of the Kirtland Egyptian Papers," in *An Approach to the Book of Abraham* (Salt Lake City: Deseret Book and FARMS, 2009), 502–68.

31. William Schryver, "The Meaning and Purpose of the Kirtland Egyptian Papers," a paper delivered at the Twelfth Annual Conference for the Foundation for Apologetic Information and Research (FAIR) in Salt Lake City, Utah, August 6, 2010. Schryver is not trained in intertextual studies, which makes it all the more necessary that his work be carefully peer-reviewed by intertextual specialists if it is to gain any further traction in Book of Abraham studies.

32. John Gee, *A Guide to the Joseph Smith Papyri* (Provo, UT: Foundation for Ancient Research and Mormon Studies, Brigham Young University, 2000), 4–5.

33. Andrew H. Hedges, Alex D. Smith, and Richard Lloyd Anderson, eds., *Journals, Volume 2: December 1841–April 1843*, vol. 2 of the Journals series of *The Joseph Smith Papers*, ed. Dean C. Jessee, Ronald K. Esplin, and Richard Lyman Bushman (Salt Lake City: Church Historian's Press, 2011), 42. See also Brian M Hauglid, "The Book of Abraham and Translating the Sacred," *BYU Religious Education Review* 10, no. 1 (Winter 2017): 13. Even though the term

that this translated material would appear in the tenth number of the *Times and Seasons* (Abraham 2:19—5:21).[34] To have all of the Book of Abraham translated in 1835 (especially in July), one could then assume that the 1835 Abraham/Egyptian Papers has little to do with translating the Book of Abraham. This is what gave rise to Nibley's reverse-engineering theory.

However, if it can be accepted that Abraham 2:18—5:21 was translated in early 1842, then other possible scenarios can be investigated, such as a possible translational relationship between the Egyptian papers and the Book of Abraham,[35] as well as the role the Book of Abraham may have played in the 1842 development of Smith's views on freemasonry and temple theology.

What seems clear at this point is the Book of Abraham has received more questions concerning its authority and legitimation than any of the other texts in the Pearl of Great Price, which, of course, ultimately reflects on Joseph Smith's legitimation as a prophetic translator as well.

Open Dialogue Needed

From the above-mentioned challenges, particularly those related to the Book of Abraham, I have found that both the Imagination and Revelation positions have good points and that the truth is probably somewhere between the two. Open dialogue between those who are reasonable in either position could, in my view, be more productive than what has generally taken place in the past.

Perhaps there are some inclined toward the Imagination Position who would be open to considering the possibility that Joseph Smith used a method of inspired adaptation in his creation of Mormon scripture.[36]

"translation" is used in these entries, Gee argues that "while Joseph slightly revised the translation preparatory to its publication in 1842, there is no other evidence that he worked on the translation of the existing book after 1835" (*A Guide to the Joseph Smith Papyri*, 4).

34. Abraham 1:1—2:18 was published in the ninth issue of the *Times and Seasons*.

35. Brian M Hauglid, "The Book of Abraham and the Egyptian Project: 'A Knowledge of Hidden Languages,'" in *Approaching Antiquity: Joseph Smith and the Ancient World*, ed. Lincoln H. Blumell, Matthew J. Grey, and Andrew H. Hedges (Provo, UT: Religious Studies Center, Brigham Young University, 2015), 473–511.

36. For an interesting theory of inspired pseudepigraphon, see David Bokovoy, *Authoring the Old Testament: Genesis-Deuteronomy* (Salt Lake City: Greg Kofford Book, 2014), 169–173.

And perhaps there are those inclined toward the Revelation Position who would be open to considering the possibility that Smith was fallible and made mistakes in his assumptions, but was still able to be inspired.

We can use the three Facsimiles as an example. We know that examining the three Facsimiles strictly from the perspective of Egyptology creates serious problems for Joseph Smith. Yet if Smith's inspired purpose in using these illustrations was primarily to adapt them to the life of Abraham, then perhaps he could be forgiven for assuming the vignettes dated to the time of Abraham, or that he incorrectly translated certain characters in Facsimile 3. Granted, this approach will not fully please everyone on either side of the questions, but perhaps it could at least open up some room for dialogue, promote more critical thought, and hopefully lead to a more accurate understanding of the realities involved.

Conclusion

It is hoped that this review of the Pearl of Great Price and especially the examination of its two translation texts have shown how the Pearl of Great Price has gone beyond canonical borders. From this we can see that the Mormon open-canon approach rests on the initial authority and legitimacy of Joseph Smith, and that the desire for an open canon increases as sacred material becomes more available to members of the LDS Church. However, it can also be seen from this brief analysis that going beyond the canonical borders can be both a divine and human endeavor, which can be risky or even dangerous, and it can sometimes lead to challenges that threaten the sacred legitimacy that has been fostered in the past.

This dynamic tension in expanding the canon and going beyond the canonical borders can be quite useful in bringing about a type of Hegelian synthesis that Joseph Smith mentioned in a letter to Daniel Rupp: "By proving contraries, truth is made manifest."[37]

---

37. *History of the Church*, 6:428.

10

PIVOTAL PUBLISHING MOMENTS FOR THE BOOK OF MORMON

Paul C. Gutjahr

Introduction

Like every person, books have their own individual histories. They are born, and then as they age, they evolve. The forms they take, the interpretations they inspire, and the level of fame they achieve are all dependent on a complex matrix of factors including historical contexts, the preferences of editors, and the sophistication and interpretative agendas of various readerships. The Book of Mormon is no different.

This essay provides a brief overview of the nearly two-hundred-year life of the Book of Mormon by concentrating on four pivotal moments in its publishing history. To lend a degree of focus to the study, these moments primarily deal with the factors involved in the book's production rather than its reception. In so doing, it argues against the perception that sacred scriptures in general, and this sacred text in particular, are monolithic, frozen entities—unchanged and unchangeable.

By necessity, divine words are often wrought by human hands, and that human touch—guided by a higher power, or not—reveals much about the evolution of religious publishing in the United States and just how complex the life story of any sacred text is. Such a study provides a vivid testimony that sacred scriptures are by necessity mediated hybrids, meshing purported supernatural interventions with more mundane human efforts. Thus, to understand the changing status, form, and message of various sacred scriptures, one must pay close attention to how otherworldly messages take more worldly forms.

First Moment: The 1820s

The Book of Mormon lays claim to a fascinating origin story. Its self-proclaimed "author and proprietor," a twenty-four-year-old farmer, day laborer, and sometimes treasure hunter by the name of Joseph Smith Jr., claimed that he had spent years translating the book from ancient golden tablets he found buried in a nearby hill in upstate New York. These tablets purported to be the record of ancient civilizations that had once inhabited Central and North America from roughly 2500 BCE to 420 CE, and they told the story of Jesus Christ bringing his message of salvation to the Western Hemisphere.

What is important to note here is that while Smith's claim of ancient Jews traveling to the Americas was bolder than many similar claims then circulating in antebellum America, his new sacred scripture was not born in a vacuum and bears many of the cultural markings of the historical moment in which it appeared. These markings take two basic forms: the explosion of printed material in the United States in the 1820s and the massive importance of the Bible in America's pre-Civil War print culture.

The first edition of the Book of Mormon appeared in book form in late March 1830 from the small print shop of E. B. Grandin in Palmyra, New York. A stout octavo volume of nearly six-hundred pages, it was a massive endeavor for a shop that was still using laborious hand presses to print its wares. Grandin produced 5,000 copies of the book. That a small town publisher such as he was willing and able to accomplish a feat that only a handful of the nation's publishers would have even attempted twenty years earlier offers some idea of just how much had changed in American publishing in the opening decades of the nineteenth century.

Since the first North American book—Stephen Daye's *Whole Book of Psalmes*—came off the presses in 1640, there have been two absolutely critical, watershed moments in American publishing. The first of these moments came in the 1820s, the second in the 1980s. While the latter moment will be discussed later, to appreciate fully the appearance of Smith's Book of Mormon in the Spring of 1830, one must first understand the radical changes that marked American print culture in the 1820s. One chief feature of these changes was an almost immeasurable growth in American publishing that began in the 1820s and continued through the rest of the century. At the turn of the nineteenth century, the standard press run for a book or pamphlet was some two thousand copies. By the 1830s, a typical press run had grown to 10,000, with editions of 75,000 or even 100,000 copies becoming ever more common.[1] Other areas of print aside from books were also experiencing unprecedented growth. Whereas some 200 newspapers existed in 1800 (including some 24

---

1. "Authors Among Fruits," *New York Daily Times* 1258 (September 28, 1855): 1.

daily papers), more than 700 were in circulation by 1830 and some 1,200 daily or weekly newspapers were in existence by 1840.[2]

In the area of printed material, no publishing force proved itself more aggressive and committed to growth than the nation's religious press. As the historian David Nord has convincingly argued, passionate missionary impulses drove the religious press to became the first mass media form in the United States.[3] Religious periodicals that had been "virtually nonexistent in 1800 . . . had by 1830 become the grand engine of burgeoning evangelical culture. The Universalist denomination alone cranked out 138 different periodicals in the three decades after 1820."[4] The American Tract Society was publishing and distributing some seventy-seven million pages of tracts annually by 1830.[5]

The explosive growth in American publishing was the result of no single cause, but the confluence of a number of intertwining factors. Some of these factors were tied to technology. The first two decades of the nineteenth century saw significant changes in papermaking, the use of stereotyping, and the perfection of machine-powered presses. Handmade paper using masses of cloth pulp set in cumbersome wood frame forms gave way to machine-made paper.[6] Stereotyping came to replace the traditional practice of setting individual type molds that needed to be reset for each new page.[7] Steam presses came into wide use by the 1830s, allowing

---

2. Michael Schudson, *Discovering the News: A Social History of American Newspapers* (New York: Basic Books, 1978), 13. See also Bernard Bailyn, *The Ideological Origins of the American Revolution* (Cambridge, MA: Harvard University Press, 1967), 1.

3. David Paul Nord, "The Evangelical Origins of Mass Media in America, 1815–1835," *Journalism Monographs* 88 (May 1984): 1–30.

4. Nathan Hatch, "Elias Smith and the Rise of Religious Journalism in the Early Republic," in *Printing & Society in Early America*, ed. William L. Joyce et al. (Worcester, MA: American Antiquarian Society, 1983), 250.

5. Nord, "The Evangelical Origins," 22.

6. Nord, 11–12. Ronald Zboray, *A Fictive People: Antebellum Economic Development and the American Reading Public* (New York: Oxford University Press, 1993), 11. For an excellent treatment of the changing nature of the papermaking industry in the United States, see Judith A. McGaw, *Most Wonderful Machine: Mechanization and Social Change in Berkshire Paper Making, 1801–1885* (Princeton: Princeton University Press, 1987).

7. A good overview of the emergence of stereotyping can be found in George Adolf Kubler, *A New History of Stereotyping* (New York: J. J. Little & Ives Company, 1941).

printers who had been forced to use one or two helpers to print between 200 and 250 pages an hour to instead have a single operator produce 900 pages an hour.[8] Finally, book binding itself changed during the 1820s. Books began to be bound in large batches soon after they had been printed, moving away from the long-held practice of purchasers binding books individually after they bought works in unbound sheets.[9]

Added to these changes in printing technology were certain key cultural factors. The nation's transportation networks were becoming more refined and sophisticated. Roads were becoming better, and the advent of train travel in the 1840s allowed printed material to be distributed more cheaply and more widely than ever before. Perhaps the most important cultural factor, however, was the growing importance of literacy. Literacy rates for both white men and women were on the rise in the decades before the Civil War, and as industrialization took hold people felt an increased need to be able to read and write to perform the ever-growing number of white collar jobs that industrialization demanded.[10] People did not only read for economic gain, however. They also read to be entertained and enlightened, so the novel and a wide range of religious and educative material blossomed in popularity during these years.

Coupled with the massive growth in publishing was the fact that the single most important book in American culture during the opening years of the nineteenth century was the Bible. If families owned any book, it most often was either a Bible or an almanac. The importance and prevalence of the text can be seen in the emergence of the American Bible Society in 1816. What started as a loose confederation of local Bible societies in the early 1800s had become so powerful a religious publishing force by 1828 that it undertook what it called its first "General Supply," a plan to provide every household in America with a Bible. Within a year, the Society was producing the utterly astounding number of 300,000 Bibles a year.[11] They

---

8. Ralph Green, "Early American Power Printing Presses," *Studies in Bibliography* IV (1951–52): 149.

9. H. Steinberg Sigfrid, *Five Hundred Years of Printing* (London: Faber and Faber, 1959), 201–2.

10. The standard treatment of the growing necessity of reading during the antebellum period is William Gilmore, *Reading Becomes a Necessity of Life: Material and Cultural Life in Rural New England, 1780–1835* (Knoxville: The University of Tennessee Press, 1989).

11. Paul C. Gutjahr, *An American Bible: A History of the Good Book in the United States, 1777–1880* (Stanford: Stanford University Press, 1999), 187.

failed to get a Bible into the hands of every American, but the attempt alone underscored just how vitally important many believed the Bible to be in American society.

Into this expanding and highly religious print mileau came the Book of Mormon, a new sacred text. In both its form and its content, it had close ties to the Bible. When it first appeared, the Book of Mormon bore a striking resemblance to the most common Bible editions then being circulated by the American Bible Society in its first General Supply.[12] More than just its binding, however, invoked the sacred inspiration of the Holy Bible. The book itself was divided into separate Bible-like sections bearing names such as Jacob and Alma, and it told a complex historical narrative filled with miracles, epic struggles between the righteous and the sinful, and extended teachings on the way in which to pursue a sanctified life.

The book also told its story in a biblical style. Its very wording was King Jamesean—the most popular English translation of the Bible before the Civil War. Its language was peppered with "eth" endings, so that "suppose" became "supposeth" and "do" became "doeth." Because American English was moving ever further away from such archaic forms in its everyday speech, this choice of wording forcefully linked the Book of Mormon to the sacred cadences found in the King James Bible.

By using such biblical language to tell quasi-biblical historical epics such as those found in biblical books like Exodus, Judges, and Chronicles, Smith's Book of Mormon came to be one of many texts of the period that one historian has called "pseudobiblical" writing.[13] British and then American writers had a long history of copying the Bible's tone and language in works that sought to invoke a pronounced gravity of subject. For example, in 1793 Richard Snowden wrote an earnest—if tedious—history of the American Revolution in the style of the Bible entitled *The American Revolution; Written in the Style of Ancient History*. That this historical/biblical style persisted for decades is seen in how a similar biblically-styled history of the War of 1812 would follow some thirty years later.[14] Countless other pamphlets, poems, and books also capitalized on biblical linguistic and narrative conventions to add emotional and intellectual weight to

---

12. Paul C. Gutjahr, "The Golden Bible in the Bible's Golden Age: *The Book of Mormon* and Antebellum Print Culture," *American Transcendental Quarterly* 12, no. 4 (December 1998): 278.

13. Eran Shalev, *American Zion: the Old Testament as a Political Text from the Revolution to the Civil War* (New Haven, CT: Yale University Press, 2013), 84.

14. Shalev, 94.

their messages. When the Book of Mormon appeared in 1830, it stood on the shoulders of nearly a century of pseudobiblical texts produced on both sides of the Atlantic.[15]

Considering the immense popularity of the Bible and the tremendous growth of America's religious print culture in the opening decades of the nineteenth century, it is not surprising that the Book of Mormon emerged and then gained both attention and influence in the years leading up to the Civil War. The American reverence for the Bible, a long literary tradition of biblically imitative narratives, and a powerful, ubiquitous religious print culture that had led many to believe that "types of lead and sheets of papers may be the light of the world" paved the way for the appearance and striking appeal of the Book of Mormon.[16]

Second Moment: The 1870s

While the first publishing moment helps to make some sense of the appearance and influence of the Book of Mormon as a part of the larger American print culture of the 1830s, the second pivotal moment in the Book of Mormon's publishing history centers not so much on a national print culture, but on a Mormon one. The Church of Jesus Christ of Latter-day Saints's commitment to the use of printed material took many forms. Aside from producing the Book of Mormon, Mormons quickly followed the trend of countless American Protestant denominations and began producing their own periodic newspapers. By the time of Joseph Smith Jr.'s death in 1844, Mormons had been responsible for starting some twelve papers, including *The Evening and the Morning Star* (Independence, Missouri), *Times and Seasons* (Nauvoo, Illinois), and *The Latter-day Saints Millennial Star* (Manchester, England). Along with these early newspapers, Mormons also had a vibrant pamphlet culture, producing a plethora of pamphlets including such well-known treatises as Parley Pratt's *A Voice of Warning* and Orson Hyde's *Prophetic Warning*.[17]

What is important to notice, however, in this strong, early commitment to the evangelistic medium of print is the fact that the early years of American Mormonism was characterized by a certain chaotic mobility

---

15. Shalev, 105.

16. Joan Brumberg, *Mission for Life: The Judson Family and American Evangelical Culture* (New York: New York University Press, 1984), 67.

17. Peter Crawley, "Parley P. Pratt: Father of Mormon Pamphleteering," *Dialogue: A Journal of Mormon Thought* 15, no. 3 (Autumn 1982): 15.

due to persecution and internal dissension. In the late 1830s, Missouri's governor forced Mormons under threat of violence to leave his state, and then in the mid-1840s, Mormons were pressured yet again from their home in Nauvoo, Illinois. Eventually, the largest branch of Mormonism under the leadership of Brigham Young would find greater peace and stability by settling in the Great Basin of the American West. But for decades after Smith's death the printing enterprises of the Church were spread out and only slightly coordinated their efforts.

The exception to the troubled printing enterprises of the Church was found in England, where a lack of violent persecution allowed its English mission to establish a steady printing base of operations in Liverpool.[18] Here many early editions of major Mormon works such as the Book of Mormon (1837, 1849, 1852 editions) and the Pearl of Great Price (1851) were published. It was only in the early 1870s that the Church called for the printing plates for its namesake text to be transported to Salt Lake City. With this move, Salt Lake established its status as the central, premier printing base for the Church.

With the rise of Church printing in Salt Lake City, leaders in the Church determined that it was time to produce a new edition of the Book of Mormon. The task was given to perhaps the Church's greatest living theologian at the time, Orson Pratt.

Pratt was one of Mormonism's earliest converts, being baptized in September 1830 at the age of nineteen. He became a founding member of the Quorum of Twelve Apostles in 1835 and distinguished himself as one of the Church's great early missionaries. He was also one of the first pioneers to enter the Salt Lake Valley in July 1847 and was the principal surveyor in laying out Salt Lake City's structured, grid-like urban plan.[19] He crossed the Atlantic Ocean sixteen times to preach in Great Britain, and there he headed the Church's British mission and its printing enterprises for a number of years.[20] Alongside his strengths in mission work and city-planning, Pratt was a Greek and Hebrew linguist, a philosopher, an educator, a mathematician, and an astronomer. At his core, he was a

---

18. A good overview of early Mormon printing practices can be found in David J. Whittaker, *Early Mormon Pamphleteering* (Provo, UT: Joseph Fielding Smith Institute for Latter-day Saint History and BYU Studies, 2003), 20–21.

19. Breck England, *The Life and Thought of Orson Pratt* (Salt Lake City: University of Utah Press, 1985), 110–40.

20. England, x.

scientist whose mathematically-bent mind loved to find pattern and order in every field of intellectual and practical endeavor.

By the 1870s, Pratt was in the final decade of his life, and he turned his attention to an editorial project that might leave a lasting legacy for Mormonism: a new edition of the Book of Mormon. His resultant 1879 edition of the text set a standard trajectory for almost all future editions of the book in three areas: (1) a careful practice of collation and proofreading to cull out errors in pursuit of the most accurate text possible; (2) format and apparatus changes that systemized and helped interpret the text; and (3) geographic linkages between the historical record found in the book and ancient North and South American civilizations.

Pratt began his work by carefully comparing the previous editions of the Book of Mormon to remove printing errors and inconsistencies from the book's core text.[21] He then began to work on certain new organizing principles and explanatory apparatus for the text. He created what would become the standard chapter and verse markings to the text, as well as adding an extended table of contents and internal cross-references at the bottom of each page.

One of Pratt's most striking innovations was the roughly seventy-five footnotes he included that directly linked events in the narrative to specific geographic locations. The practice of linking various North and South American sites to events recorded in the Book of Mormon can be traced all the way back to Joseph Smith, Jr., who connected many locations referenced in the Book of Mormon to specific locations in the Americas.[22] Pratt used his footnotes to continue Smith's practice of fusing the text with actual geography. His footnotes revealed that the "promised land" mentioned in 1 Nephi 18:23 was "believed to be on the coast of Chili, S. America," and the Church's new home in the Great Basin was none other than "the elevated regions of the Rocky Mountains" alluded to in 1 Nephi 21:10's phrase "pastures . . . in all high places."[23] For the first time in a Book of Mormon edition, Pratt offered Mormons specific textual linkages to actual geography.

Even though Pratt's geographic references did not survive when the text was once again revised and re-released in 1920, his practice of link-

---

21. England, 255.

22. "Zarahemla," *Times and Seasons* 3, no. 23 (October 1, 1842): 927. See also Terryl L. Givens, *By the Hand of Mormon: The American Scripture that Launched a New World Religion* (New York: Oxford University Press, 2002), 99.

23. Book of Mormon (1879), 47, 53.

ing the text with Central and North American geography has persisted in various forms in most later editions of the Book of Mormon. Perhaps the most important way this emphasis on the geographic integrity of the book's narrative has continued is found in the illustrations the LDS Church has placed in later editions of the Book of Mormon. The 1963 edition boasted the first illustrations to ever accompany the text, and the content of these illustrations directly mirrors Pratt's wish to link actual locations to the Book of Mormon's historical narrative. Five of the eleven illustrations placed before the book's core text unabashedly link the Book of Mormon with the Americas with such images as Peruvian golden plates and "Egyptian-like murals found on temple walls in Mexico."[24] More recent editions of the Book of Mormon have not included all the illustrations found in the 1963 edition, but they do include various pictures depicting Christ and other characters from the narrative in Mesoamerican settings, once again fusing the stories found in the Book of Mormon to various ancient South American civilizations.

The 1870s proved to be a pivotal decade for the Church's publishing enterprises as they were moved from England and centralized in Salt Lake City. To this day, both English and foreign-language editions of the Book of Mormon are printed almost entirely in Salt Lake City. These editions are all clear heirs in terms of their formatting strategies and their subtle links between text and geography to Pratt's vitally important 1879 edition of the book.

Third Moment: The 1980s

The third pivotal moment in Book of Mormon publishing returns us to a broader consideration of American print culture. It concerns the second great watershed moment in American publishing: the 1980s. American publishing at this time underwent a profound change for one simple reason: the widespread adoption of computer technology in printing.[25] For over a century, though printing machines had become faster and larger, they still worked on the same basic mechanical principals. Writing practices, translation work, and editing had also changed little.

---

24. Book of Mormon (1963), prefatory illustrations and their captions.
25. For an overview of the technological changes in printing during the last half of the twentieth century, see Edward Webster, *Print Unchained: Fifty Years of Digital Printing, 1950–2000 and Beyond—a Sage of Invention and Enterprise* (New Castle, DE: Oak Knoll Press, 2000), 129–81.

Beginning in the 1970s and finally taking hold of the publishing industry in the 1980s, computerization changed these traditional publishing practices. Computers facilitated new ways to layout and typeset books. Gone were the days of time-intensive and cumbersome tools such as light tables, photographic copying, large sheets of graph paper, tape, glue, rulers, and scissors. During the 1980s, writers, translators, and editors also began to widely adopt ever more efficient evolutions of computer software to compose and manipulate text and formats.

The LDS Church took full advantage of these changes when it released its 1981 landmark edition of the Book of Mormon. This edition was special for many reasons, but chief among these was the way in which it presented a core text that had taken into account all previous important editions of the Book of Mormon, and how the 1981 edition's apparatus was synced with the other three key scriptural texts of the Mormon tradition: The King James Bible, the Doctrine and Covenants, and the Pearl of Great Price. Emphasizing their unity and equality as scripture, these books are often bound together in a single volume. (When the Book of Mormon is bound with the Doctrine and Covenants and the Pearl of Great Price, the volume is known as the "Triple Combination." If the Church's edition of the King James Bible is bound with these three standard Mormon texts, it has come to be known commonly as the "Quad.")

LDS Church scholars painstakingly compared and collated previous editions of the Book of Mormon as they set out to produce a new, definitive edition of the book in 1981. Up until that date, the Book of Mormon was largely based off the second (1837) edition of the book that the Church's earliest missionaries had taken to England, as it had been favored as the core reference text to create all subsequent editions of the book prior to 1981. As scholars began their work on the text in the 1970s, they considered not only the editions so influenced by the 1837 edition of the text, but Joseph Smith's final 1840 edition as well. (British missionaries had left for England before Smith had produced his final version of the text, and thus many of Smith's final changes to the text had been overlooked in later editions.) The 1981 edition rectified this neglect.

The LDS Church also wished to produce not only the most accurate possible English translation of the Book of Mormon in its 1981 edition, but it wanted to give its members the most complete and helpful system of cross-referencing between the tradition's sacred texts that had ever been presented. Thus, with the release of the 1981 edition, members could quickly see connections between passages in the Book of Mormon and related passages located in the Pearl of Great Price, the Doctrine and Covenants, and the Bible.

Computerization and newer printing technologies also offered the LDS Church the opportunity to more aggressively pursue their missionary translation agenda. By the end of the 1970s, the Church had translated the Book of Mormon into thirty-nine languages in its 140-year history. Decisions by the Church's leadership in the 1980s to place an ever-greater emphasis on the Book of Mormon coupled with the radical changes in publishing practices brought on by computerization led to the appearance of an astounding forty-nine new language editions during the 1980s.[26] In a single decade, the Church more than doubled the translation work it had done in the previous century and a half. Thus, the 1980s marked a pivotal turning point for the Book of Mormon both in terms of the sophistication of its English translation and the breadth of its presence in foreign languages.

Fourth Moment: The 2010s

The last pivotal publishing moment to consider functions on a slightly different register. It moves from an emphasis resting mainly on printing technologies to an examination of delivery systems of written discourse. Put more simply, it focuses on the advent of electronic books and various other electronic text formats, which are in one sense but an extension of the computerization of print media that took control of the publishing industry in the 1980s. In 1997, the LDS Church began to disseminate its scriptures through its official website. Website versions of the English text were then upgraded in 2006 and 2010, but the most important electronic textual moment for the Book of Mormon (following its initial 1997 online offering) came in 2013 when the Church released a newly edited version of the Book of Mormon in a variety of electronic media formats. Although the Church published an electronic version of the text fairly early on, it is of particular interest to note the slow and measured way the Church adopted other electronic platforms to make the Book of Mormon available. While the technology was in place as early as the mid-1990s to publish texts in various electronic book formats and then a decade later in a variety of smart phone platforms, it was only in the 2010s that the

---

26. Paul C. Gutjahr, *The Book of Mormon: A Biography* (Princeton: Princeton University Press, 2012), 205–7.

Church fully embraced these electronic print technologies to deliver its sacred text to the masses.

Taken in the broader view of how religious traditions often view their sacred practices and scriptures, such a relatively slow adoption is perfectly understandable. Scholars such as James Deetz have demonstrated that such traditions have a high regard for ritual and stability, thus making them less likely to change the items and practices they consider most sacred.[27] The Book of Mormon certainly falls into this category. Since 1830, members of the Mormon Church had their signature text almost entirely in printed form. Much like the Bible, this printed book had taken on a totemic quality for Mormons. In their eyes, it is not just another book, and it should not be treated like one. Thus, there was considerable unease among older Church members when the idea of reading their scriptures—particularly in official meetings such as Church services—from non-print platforms such as electronic tablets and smart phones was first introduced. The book was a book, not some electronic device, and the fact that the Church's highest levels of leadership were older and less familiar with the daily uses of electronic textual devices also slowed the adoption of disseminating the Book of Mormon in newer electronic formats.

In this way, the LDS Church in certain areas of electronic print put itself roughly ten to twenty years behind other institutions, some of these religious, in adopting new electronic media to get their message out. For example, in 2005, the New Electronic Translation (NET) of the Holy Bible was released as the first World Wide Web-only English Bible translation project. Released with the intention of being constantly updated by an editorial team of some twenty scholars sponsored by the Biblical Studies Foundation, the NET was innovative both as a Bible translation and distribution project. The goal was quite simple: to provide a new, accurate Bible translation that was free of any copyright and printing costs made available to users for free on the Web. Because the translation was released without any paper-bound production costs, the edition became famous not only for its interdenominational flavor, but also for its over sixty thousand footnotes, many of which are quite lengthy.

The LDS Church's leadership has always treated the Church's namesake text with the utmost care. Any changes to the text, whether those changes be in the book's content or format, are only made after extensive

---

27. James Deetz, *In Small Things Forgotten: The Archaeology of Everyday Life* (New York: Doubleday, 1977), 50–51, 88. See also Binford, "Archaeology as Anthropology," *American Antiquity* 28, no. 2 (Oct. 1962), 217–25.

and careful deliberation at the highest levels of Church leadership. This markedly conservative approach makes the new 2013 text of the Book of Mormon a momentous event. On March 1, 2013, the highest ruling body of the Church, its First Presidency, announced that the 1981 landmark edition of the text had been updated after a decade of careful editorial work. The 2013 edition included new maps, new illustrations, new footnotes incorporating scholarship on the most recent historical scholarship, and adjusted chapter and sections headings. It also included changes in the text itself, including updated spellings to replace certain archaic renderings of words, as well as corrections to previous typesetting and punctuation errors. Even with all these changes, the LDS Church acknowledged its deliberate and measured relationship to the text by making sure that the pagination of the 2013 edition exactly matched that of the 1981 edition. Thus, both editions could continue to be referenced in a seamless manner among the Church's membership.

What is particularly noteworthy when it comes to the 2013 edition of the Book of Mormon was the Church's decision to bring forth this new standard edition first in different electronic formats and only then in traditional printed formats several months later. In so doing, the Church credentialed the electronic form of the text as every bit as worthy and acceptable for use as the printed form. In this way, the Church fully endorsed and entered the electronic media age of scripture distribution.

Conclusion

Since E. B. Grandin published the first edition of the Book of Mormon in 1830, some twenty English editions and well over one hundred foreign language translations have appeared. Nestled within these myriad editions is the fact that four key moments have proven absolutely pivotal in defining the constantly evolving editorial and publishing practices that have marked its production and distribution. It is impossible to fully appreciate either the Book of Mormon as a divinely inspired text or a sacred material artifact without considering the book in the context of these four historical moments. The pivotal moments discussed in this essay stand as a vibrant testimony that divine messages are always bound by the motivations, technologies, and inclinations of their human messengers. In this way, the divine tongue is forever bound by human hands.

11

RELISHING THE REVISIONS: THE DOCTRINE & COVENANTS AND THE REVELATORY PROCESS[1]

Grant Underwood

The purpose of this chapter is to explore how the textual revisions preserved in the manuscript revelation book titled "A Book of Commandments and Revelations" (BCR) shed light on the process by which Joseph Smith received, recorded, and published his revelations.[2] I will use the phrase *revelation texts*, rather than just *revelations*, to preserve a distinction between the Prophet's inner experience of divine revelation and the words he used to express that revelation. Sometime in 1830 or early 1831, Joseph Smith decided to have his revelation texts copied or "transcribed," as was commonly said at the time, into a single manuscript record book we are now calling the BCR. John Whitmer was the volume's principal scribe and caretaker until its "completion" in 1835. Not long after Whitmer and Oliver Cowdery carried the BCR to Missouri in late 1831 to serve as the basis for publishing the Book of Commandments, another record book was acquired for additional revelation texts, which Frederick G. Williams began transcribing. This volume, simply titled "Book of Revelations" and sometimes known as the "Kirtland Revelation Book," was maintained from 1832 to 1834. Revelations first transcribed there would subsequently

---

1. This chapter combines material that appeared previously in my "The Dictation, Compilation, and Canonization of Joseph Smith's Revelations," in *Foundational Texts of Mormonism*, ed. Mark Ashurst-McGee, Robin Scott Jensen, and Sharalyn D. Howcroft (New York: Oxford University Press, 2018), 101–23; and "Revelation, Text, and Revision: Insights from the Book of Commandments and Revelations," *BYU Studies* 48, no. 3 (2009): 67–84.

2. The BCR is available in a facsimile edition in Robin Scott Jensen, Robert J. Woodford, and Steven C. Harper, eds., *The Joseph Smith Papers, Revelations and Translations Series: Manuscript Revelation Books* (Salt Lake City: The Church Historian's Press, 2009) (hereafter cited as *Manuscript Revelation Books*).

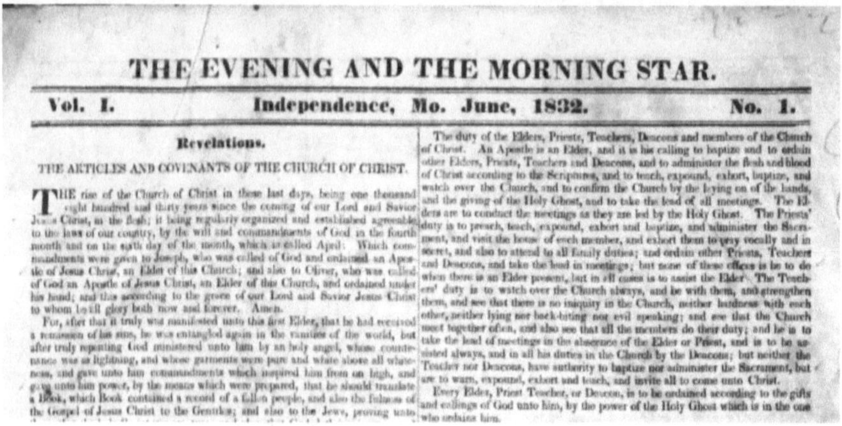

THE EVENING AND THE MORNING STAR.

Vol. I. Independence, Mo. June, 1832. No. 1.

Revelations.

THE ARTICLES AND COVENANTS OF THE CHURCH OF CHRIST.

THE rise of the Church of Christ in these last days, being one thousand eight hundred and thirty years since the coming of our Lord and Savior Jesus Christ, in the flesh; it being regularly organized and established agreeable to the laws of our country, by the will and commandments of God in the fourth month and on the sixth day of the month, which is called April: Which commandments were given to Joseph, who was called of God and ordained an Apostle of Jesus Christ, an Elder of this Church; and also to Oliver, who was called of God an Apostle of Jesus Christ, an Elder of this Church, and ordained under his hand; and this according to the grace of our Lord and Savior Jesus Christ to whom be all glory both now and forever. Amen.

For, after that it truly was manifested unto this first Elder, that he had received a remission of his sins, he was entangled again in the vanities of the world, but after truly repenting God ministered unto him by an holy angel, whose countenance was as lightning, and whose garments were pure and white above all whiteness, and gave unto him commandments which inspired him from on high, and gave unto him power, by the means which were prepared, that he should translate a Book, which Book contained a record of a fallen people, and also the fulness of the Gospel of Jesus Christ to the Gentiles; and also to the Jews, proving unto

The duty of the Elders, Priests, Teachers, Deacons and members of the Church of Christ. An Apostle is an Elder, and it is his calling to baptize and to ordain other Elders, Priests, Teachers and Deacons, and to administer the flesh and blood of Christ according to the Scriptures, and to teach, expound, exhort, baptize, and watch over the Church, and to confirm the Church by the laying on of the hands, and the giving of the Holy Ghost, and to take the lead of all meetings. The Elders are to conduct the meetings as they are led by the Holy Ghost. The Priests' duty is to preach, teach, expound, exhort and baptize, and administer the Sacrament, and visit the house of each member, and exhort them to pray vocally and in secret, and also to attend to all family duties; and ordain other Priests, Teachers and Deacons, and take the lead in meetings; but none of these offices is he to do when there is an Elder present, but in all cases is to assist the Elder. The Teachers' duty is to watch over the Church always, and be with them, and strengthen them, and see that there is no iniquity in the Church, neither hardness with each other, neither lying nor back-biting nor evil speaking; and see that the Church meet together often, and also see that all the members do their duty; and he is to take the lead of meetings in the absence of the Elder or Priest, and is to be assisted always, and in all his duties in the Church by the Deacons; but neither the Teacher nor Deacons, have authority to baptize nor administer the Sacrament, but are to warn, expound, exhort and teach, and invite all to come unto Christ.

Every Elder, Priest Teacher, or Deacon, is to be ordained according to the gifts and callings of God unto him, by the power of the Holy Ghost which is in the one who ordains him.

Figure 1. First issue of *The Evening and the Morning Star.*

be recopied and taken to Missouri, where Whitmer recorded them in the BCR. A rare notation in the BCR preserves the transmission story for what is now Doctrine and Covenants 86: "Kirtland December 6, 1832 given by Joseph the Seer & written by Sidney the Scribe & councellor & transcribed by Frederick assistant Scribe & councellor. & copied by Orson Hyde the clerk of the presidency And Recorded by John Whitmer the Lords Clerk."[3]

By November 1831, over seventy revelation texts had been copied into the BCR, and the decision was made to publish them as a printed volume. A half-dozen men, including Rigdon, Whitmer, and Cowdery, were designated by revelation as a "Literary Firm" to oversee all church publications, including the projected Book of Commandments. By early 1832, a press had been purchased and transported to Independence, Missouri, and in June the inaugural issue of the Church's first periodical, *The Evening and the Morning Star*, came off the press. The *Star*, as it was known among the Saints, regularly published revelation texts in its columns over the next year. Indeed, as seen in Figure 1, the first page of the first issue was entirely devoted to the Church's foundational "Articles and Covenants," known today as Doctrine and Covenants 20. Meanwhile, work was moving forward on producing the Book of Commandments. However, in July 1833, before the printed volume could be completed, a group of antagonistic neighbors broke into the Missouri print shop and vandalized it. Undaunted, Joseph Smith and his associates regrouped and within two years published a new compilation under the title *Doctrine and Covenants of the Church of the Latter Day Saints.*

3. *Manuscript Revelation Books*, 331.

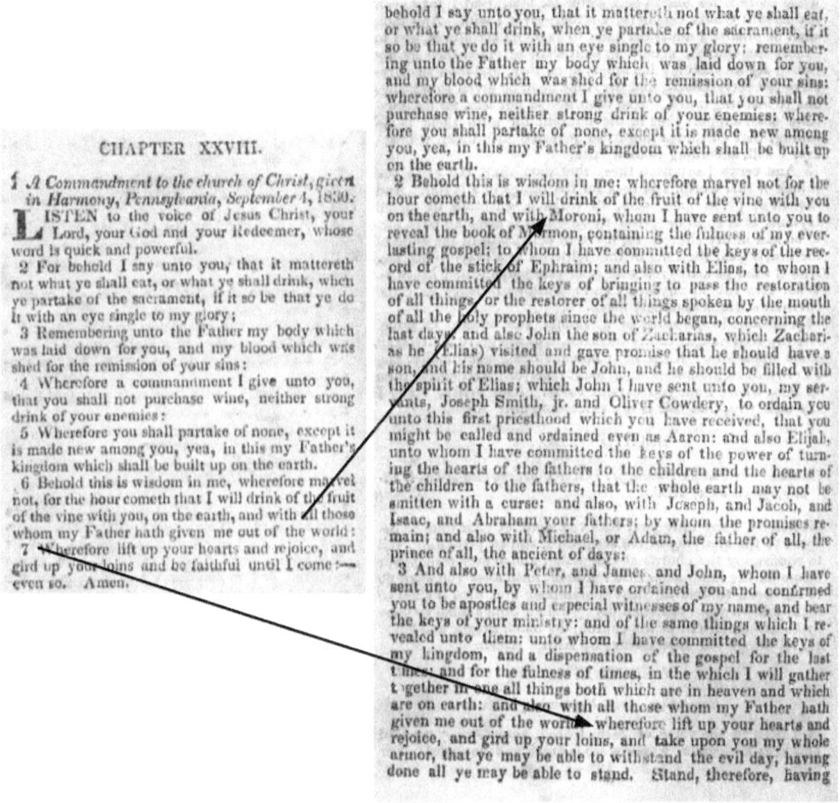

CHAPTER XXVIII.

1 *A Commandment to the church of Christ, given in Harmony, Pennsylvania, September 4, 1830.*

LISTEN to the voice of Jesus Christ, your Lord, your God and your Redeemer, whose word is quick and powerful.

2 For behold I say unto you, that it mattereth not what ye shall eat, or what ye shall drink, when ye partake of the sacrament, if it so be that ye do it with an eye single to my glory;

3 Remembering unto the Father my body which was laid down for you, and my blood which was shed for the remission of your sins:

4 Wherefore a commandment I give unto you, that you shall not purchase wine, neither strong drink of your enemies:

5 Wherefore you shall partake of none, except it is made new among you, yea, in this my Father's kingdom which shall be built up on the earth.

6 Behold this is wisdom in me, wherefore marvel not, for the hour cometh that I will drink of the fruit of the vine with you, on the earth, and with all those whom my Father hath given me out of the world:

7 Wherefore lift up your hearts and rejoice, and gird up your loins and be faithful until I come:—even so. Amen.

behold I say unto you, that it mattereth not what ye shall eat, or what ye shall drink, when ye partake of the sacrament, if it so be that ye do it with an eye single to my glory: remembering unto the Father my body which was laid down for you, and my blood which was shed for the remission of your sins: wherefore a commandment I give unto you, that you shall not purchase wine, neither strong drink of your enemies: wherefore you shall partake of none, except it is made new among you, yea, in this my Father's kingdom which shall be built up on the earth.

2 Behold this is wisdom in me: wherefore marvel not for the hour cometh that I will drink of the fruit of the vine with you on the earth, and with Moroni, whom I have sent unto you to reveal the book of Mormon, containing the fulness of my everlasting gospel; to whom I have committed the keys of the record of the stick of Ephraim; and also with Elias, to whom I have committed the keys of bringing to pass the restoration of all things, or the restorer of all things spoken by the mouth of all the holy prophets since the world began, concerning the last days: and also John the son of Zacharias, which Zacharias he (Elias) visited and gave promise that he should have a son, and his name should be John, and he should be filled with the spirit of Elias; which John I have sent unto you, my servants, Joseph Smith, jr. and Oliver Cowdery, to ordain you unto this first priesthood which you have received, that you might be called and ordained even as Aaron: and also Elijah, unto whom I have committed the keys of the power of turning the hearts of the fathers to the children and the hearts of the children to the fathers, that the whole earth may not be smitten with a curse: and also, with Joseph, and Jacob, and Isaac, and Abraham your fathers; by whom the promises remain; and also with Michael, or Adam, the father of all, the prince of all, the ancient of days:

3 And also with Peter, and James and John, whom I have sent unto you, by whom I have ordained you and confirmed you to be apostles and especial witnesses of my name, and bear the keys of your ministry: and of the same things which I revealed unto them: unto whom I have committed the keys of my kingdom, and a dispensation of the gospel for the last times: and for the fulness of times, in the which I will gather together in one all things both which are in heaven and which are on earth: and also with all those whom my Father hath given me out of the world: wherefore lift up your hearts and rejoice, and gird up your loins, and take upon you my whole armor, that ye may be able to withstand the evil day, having done all ye may be able to stand. Stand, therefore, having

Figure 2. 1833 Book of Commandments 28 (left) and 1835 Doctrine and Covenants 50 (right).

It has long been recognized that between the earliest printing of the revelation texts in the *Star* or Book of Commandments and the Doctrine and Covenants a number of revisions were made to the wording of the texts. For instance, Figure 2 reveals a significant textual amplification of what is now Doctrine and Covenants 27. Less well-known is that the revelation texts were also edited *prior* to initial publication in the *Star* or Book of Commandments, and what was entirely unknown until the BCR was published in 2009 is the *extent* of those earliest revisions. Literally hundreds of redactions, as they are also called, usually involving only a word or two but sometimes comprising an entire phrase or more, were inscribed in the BCR between 1831 and 1833. These early redactions were primarily grammatical or stylistic in nature, or they sought to clarify meaning. Later revisions—those made while preparing the texts for publication in the Doctrine and Covenants—often had as their objective to

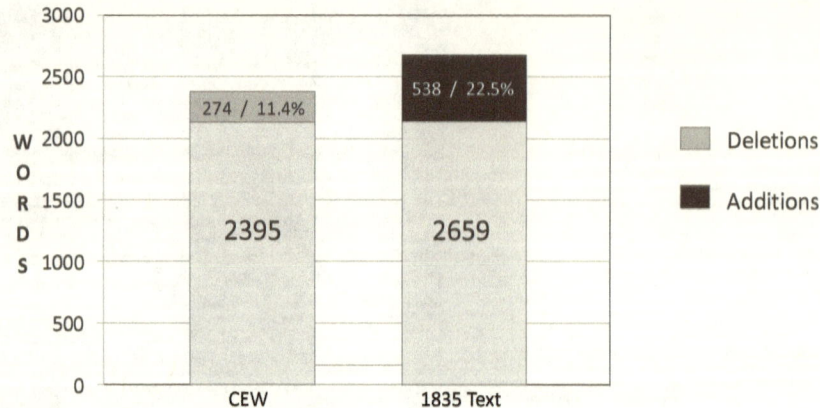

Figure 3. Total word count of Doctrine and Covenants 42 in both the Consensus Earliest Wording (CEW) and 1835 Doctrine and Covenants 13.

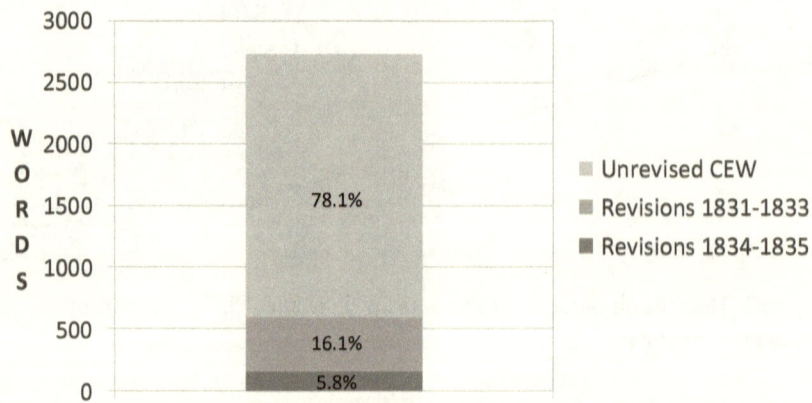

Figure 4. Proportion and dating of unrevised to revised text of Doctrine and Covenants 42 (1835 Doctrine and Covenants 13).

update and amplify the revelation texts to reflect emerging church polity, practice, or doctrine.

From one perspective, the presence of textual revisions in the BCR is valuable because it allows us to look behind those revisions to an earlier wording not previously known. For individuals interested in getting as close as possible to the original dictation texts of the revelations, virtually none of which have survived, the BCR is crucial, providing, as it does, the earliest known version of dozens of revelation texts. But my objective here is not to promote the original. Rather, it is to relish the revisions!

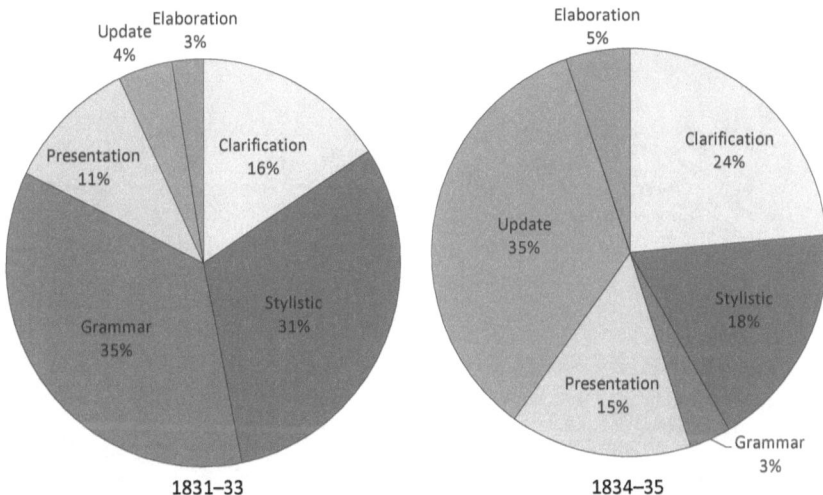

Figure 5. Types of revisions made to Doctrine and Covenants 42 between 1831 and 1835.

To gain some sense of the scope and nature of the revisions, let us first consider the results of a detailed analysis of textual revisions made to one of the longest and most important early revelation texts, really two texts that became one—the "Laws of the Church of Christ," now Doctrine and Covenants 42. Figure 3 compares the overall size difference in terms of word count between the Consensus Earliest Wording (CEW)—a designation I chose because we only have early manuscript copies to work with rather than the actual dictation text—and the final 1835 text. It also shows the breakdown of word-count differences between textual deletions and additions: 274 CEW words were deleted and 538 new words were added to the Doctrine and Covenants text. Figure 4 shows *when* the wording changes were made, indicating that the bulk of the revisions occurred in the later period. This difference in the quantity of redactions made between the two periods is consistent with most other revelation texts. Although not the focus of our discussion here, it also illustrates that most of the wording in the revelation texts was unchanged from initial dictation to publication in the Doctrine and Covenants. Figure 5 is a rough attempt at classifying the *kinds* of revisions made to the Law in both periods. Preliminary review suggests that it, too, is representative of the general pattern for other revelation-text revisions, that is, the earliest redactions tended to be grammatical and stylistic, while the later revisions

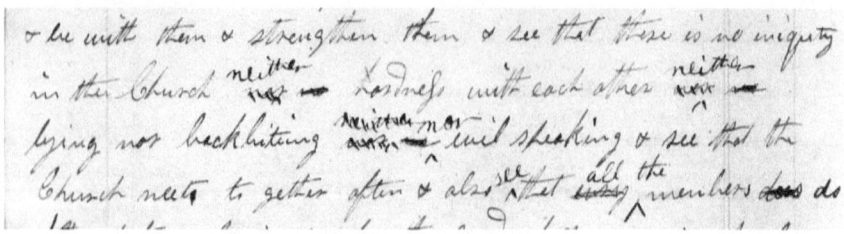

Figure 6.

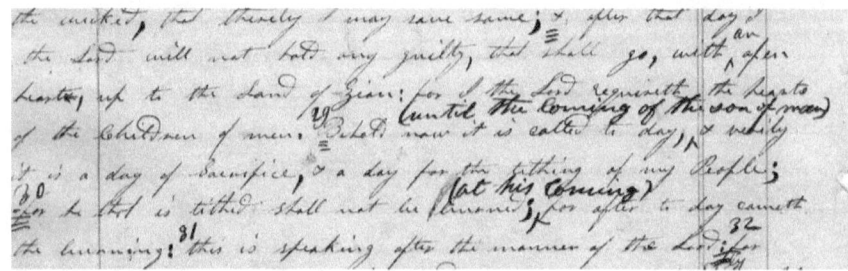

Figure 7.

contemporized and amplified the revelation texts. In both periods, a concern to clarify wording or make it more publicly presentable is manifest.

Space will permit only a brief look at the various types of revisions. The "Articles and Covenants" provides an example of *grammatical* revision. When discussing the duties of ordained teachers the CEW reads, "see that there is no iniquty in the Church nor no hardness with each other nor no lying nor backbiting nor no evil speaking." Figure 6 shows redactions in Oliver Cowdery's handwriting where he changes "nor no" to "neither," as well as additional refinements by John Whitmer.[4]

Figure 7 shows an example of *clarification* in what is now Doctrine and Covenants 64. The CEW reads, "Behold now it is called to day & verily it is a day of sacrifice & a day for the tithing of my People; for he that is tithed shall not be burned." Notice that the later insertion "until the coming of the son of man" clarifies what is meant by "to day." And "at his coming" clarifies "shall not be burned." Handwriting experts tell us these particular revisions are among relatively few that are in the hand of Joseph Smith.[5]

---

4. *Manuscript Revelation Books*, 83.
5. *Manuscript Revelation Books*, 193.

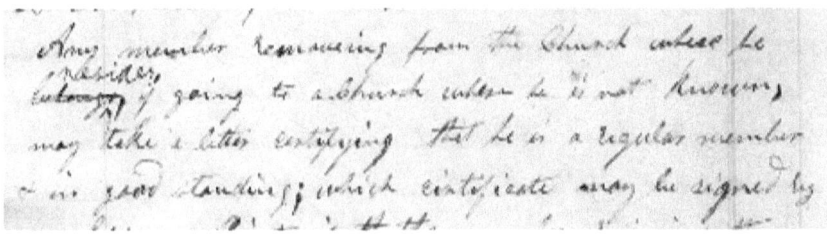

Figure 8.

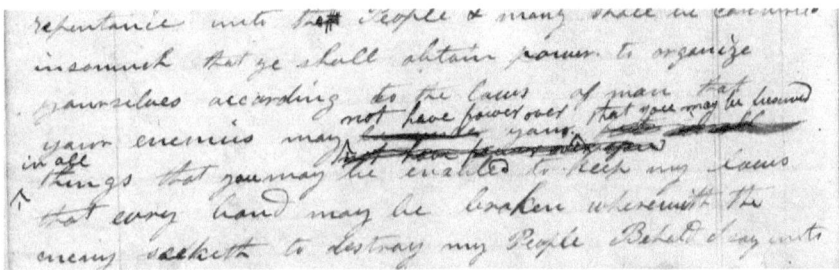

Figure 9.

Stylistic changes are redactions that neither correct demonstrably poor grammar nor actually clarify meaning; they merely smooth out the style. Figure 8 shows a simple word change from the final paragraph in the "Articles and Covenants" talking about church member relocation. The phrase "where he belongs" is changed to "where he resides."[6]

Ten to fifteen percent of the revisions fit in a category designated *presentation*. These changes seem to simply restate the same basic idea in more refined language. Figure 9 is an example from what is now Doctrine and Covenants 44. The text promises the Saints power to organize themselves according to the laws of man "that your enemies may be under your feet in all things." At some point the potentially inflammatory nature of this language was recognized, and in the handwriting of Sidney Rigdon the passage was revised to read "that your enemies *may not have power over you that you may be preserved* in all things."[7]

Some revisions, classified as *elaborations*, seem to have no other purpose than merely to enrich and extend the text. In Doctrine and Covenants 41:6, the CEW says that "it is not meet that the things which belong to

---

6. *Manuscript Revelation Books*, 87.
7. *Manuscript Revelation Books*, 113; emphasis added.

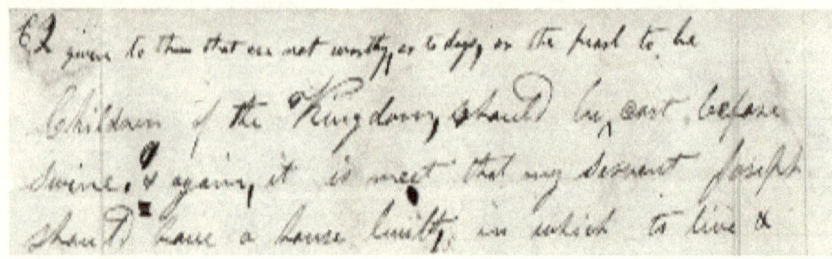

62 given to them that are not worthy, or to dogs, or the pearl to be
children of the kingdom should be cast before
swine. & again, it is meet that my servant Joseph
should have a house built, in which to live &

Figure 10.

to minister even according to the first wherefore it shall be an
high priest who is worthy & he shall be appointed by the presidency of
high priests & again, no Bishop, or high priest who shall be set apart
for this ministry shall be tried or condemned for any crime save
it be before the first presidency of the church & inasmuch as he is found guilty
before this presidency by testimony that cannot be impeached
he shall be condemned or forgiven according to the covenants of the church

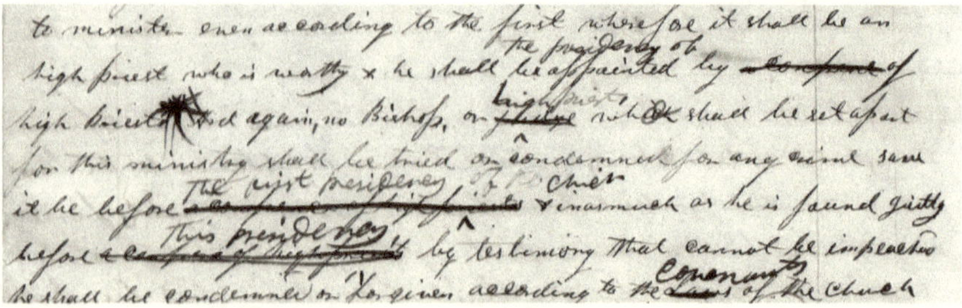

Figure 11.

the children of the kingdom should be cast before swine." (See Figure 10.) As is, the sentence is intelligible, grammatically correct, even literary, but between "shall be" and "cast before swine," John Whitmer inserted an additional line of text: "given to them that are not worthy, or to dogs, or the pearl to be."[8] Presumably, it was felt that the text should more fully echo the Sermon on the Mount, where Christ says "Give not that which is holy unto the dogs, neither cast ye your pearls before swine" (Matt. 7:6).

Although there were some redactions in the early period that can be classified as "updating" the text, a much larger percent of the revisions in the 1834-35 period fall into this category. Joseph and his associates seemed anxious to ensure that the revelation texts published in the Doctrine and Covenants were current both in terms of doctrine and ecclesiastical procedure, rather than serving as outdated museum pieces of past Church polity. In Figure 11, for instance, "the first presidency of the Church" and "this presidency" replace the earlier "conference of high priests."[9] A conference of high priests was the church's highest governing body in 1831 when

8. *Manuscript Revelation Books*, 94–95.
9. *Manuscript Revelation Books*, 201.

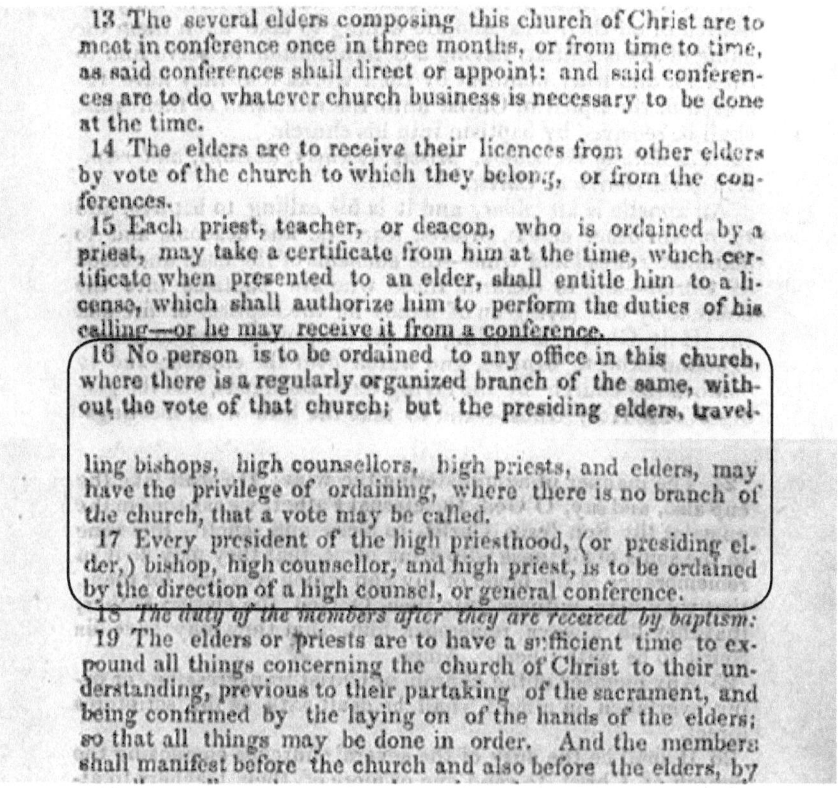

> 13 The several elders composing this church of Christ are to meet in conference once in three months, or from time to time, as said conferences shall direct or appoint: and said conferences are to do whatever church business is necessary to be done at the time.
> 14 The elders are to receive their licences from other elders by vote of the church to which they belong, or from the conferences.
> 15 Each priest, teacher, or deacon, who is ordained by a priest, may take a certificate from him at the time, which certificate when presented to an elder, shall entitle him to a license, which shall authorize him to perform the duties of his calling—or he may receive it from a conference.
> 16 No person is to be ordained to any office in this church, where there is a regularly organized branch of the same, without the vote of that church; but the presiding elders, travelling bishops, high counsellors, high priests, and elders, may have the privilege of ordaining, where there is no branch of the church, that a vote may be called.
> 17 Every president of the high priesthood, (or presiding elder,) bishop, high counsellor, and high priest, is to be ordained by the direction of a high counsel, or general conference.
> 18 The duty of the members after they are received by baptism:
> 19 The elders or priests are to have a sufficient time to expound all things concerning the church of Christ to their understanding, previous to their partaking of the sacrament, and being confirmed by the laying on of the hands of the elders; so that all things may be done in order. And the members shall manifest before the church and also before the elders, by

Figure 12.

this revelation was dictated, but by 1835 the First Presidency had been formed and was handling the matters discussed in this revelation text.

In a few cases, lengthy passages were added to bring procedures up to date. In Figure 12, the boxed text (now Doctrine and Covenants 20:65–67) is new to the 1835 printing of the "Articles and Covenants." The offices of bishops, high councilors, high priests, and presidents of the high priesthood simply did not exist when the "Articles and Covenants" was first issued in 1830. Yet, they had become crucial to the Church's governance by 1835.

Some revisions can be classified as doctrinal updates. For instance, Joseph Smith dictated a revelation text bearing the date of March 1, 1832, that includes the perfectly acceptable phrase "saith your Redeemer even Jesus Christ." Sometime later that month an unusual document was created titled "A Sample of Pure Language." This brief item revealed that in the "pure language," the name of God was Ahman and the name of Jesus

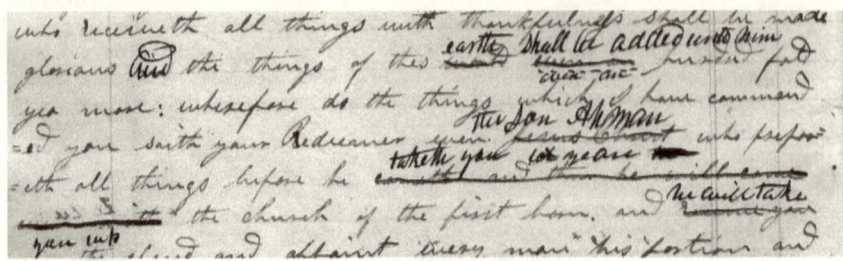

Figure 13.

Christ was "Son Ahman."[10] Several weeks later a copy of the text, along with others Joseph had dictated since Whitmer and Cowdery departed the previous November, was taken to Missouri. At some point thereafter, W. W. Phelps changed "your Redeemer even Jesus Christ" to "your Redeemer even the Son Ahman."[11] (See Figure 13.)

Later, when the revelation text was being revised for the 1835 Doctrine and Covenants, yet more newly revealed doctrine was included. This time to "Lord God, the Holy One of Israel" was added: ". . . who hath established the foundations of Adam-ondi-Ahman; who hath appointed Michael, your prince, and established his feet, and set him upon high; and given him the keys of salvation under the counsel and direction of the Holy One and so forth." The earthly identity of Michael was first revealed at the end of 1833 and the first documented use of Adam-ondi-Ahman occurred in spring 1835. Thus, the textual amplification shown here was likely inscribed sometime in 1835.

By now, the reader will have noticed that often the textual revisions are in the handwriting of individuals other than Joseph Smith. Indeed nearly all the redactions in the BCR are in the handwriting of his scribal associates John Whitmer, Oliver Cowdery, Sidney Rigdon, and W. W. Phelps, each of whom was a member of the Church's Literary Firm. The widespread involvement of these men sheds important light on Joseph Smith's role in revising the revelation texts. Just as we have reason to believe he dictated, rather than wrote, most of the original revelation texts, it is possible that he dictated many of the revisions, particularly those made in November 1831 after being specifically charged in a council meeting to "correct those errors or mistakes which he may discover by the holy spirit

---

10. *Manuscript Revelation Books*, 265.
11. *Manuscript Revelation Books*, 269.

while reviewing the revelations and commandments."[12] There is also evidence that he later occasionally edited the revelation texts as well. A brief journal entry for December 1, 1832, reads simply: "wrote and corrected revelations &c."[13]

Still, *most* of the 1832–33 redactions found in the BCR were made by Whitmer, Cowdery, or Phelps, apparently without Joseph's direct involvement. Significantly, he rarely revised or removed their revisions later on. To this day, their revisions stand as part of the official Doctrine and Covenants. This reality invites us to adjust our assumptions about Joseph's role in revising the revelation texts and, therefore, about how he viewed the revelatory process itself. The data suggest that in getting the revelation texts into print, Joseph focused on the message, the ideas, or what he called "the sense" of the revelation he received, and he welcomed assistance from members of the Literary Firm in refining the language or enriching the texts to include all that God had revealed to him.

To be sure, Joseph recognized that he had the ultimate responsibility. He was, after all, the "revelator." That reality had been formally recognized in the November 1831 decision to have him lead out in revising the revelation texts where prompted. Five months later, however, Joseph presided at a council meeting in Missouri at which "brs. William [Phelps], Oliver [Cowdery] & John [Whitmer] [were] appointed to review the Book of Commandments [BCR] & select for printing such as shall be deemed by them proper, as dictated by the spirit & make all necessary verbal corrections."[14] Based on the evidence now available in the BCR, "verbal corrections" primarily, though not exclusively, meant grammatical and stylistic revisions. Although the word "correction" often implies changing the wording to match a "correct" original, the Missouri editor-printers construed their commission from the Prophet more broadly to include a variety of textual improvements or revisions. Because such redactions had the potential to spill over into substantive changes in meaning, several months later Joseph warned Phelps regarding the revelation texts to "be careful not to *alter the sense* of any of them."[15] Significantly "altering the

---

12. "The Conference Minutes and Record Book of Christ Church of Latter Day Saints," [commonly known as the "Far West Record" and hereafter FWR], 16.

13. Dean C. Jessee, et al., *The Joseph Smith Papers, Journals, Volume 1: 1832–1839* (Salt Lake City: The Church Historian's Press, 2008), 10.

14. FWR, 16 (April 30, 1832).

15. "Letter to William W. Phelps, 31 July 1832," in Matthew C. Godfrey, Mark Ashurst-McGee, Grant Underwood, Robert J. Woodford, William G.

sense" of the revelations was the boundary line, and analysis of the BCR revisions made by members of the Literary Firm in 1832 and 1833 shows that most redactions respected that boundary.

That Joseph gave the Literary Firm some linguistic leeway in preparing the revelation texts for publication is implicit in another statement made in his July 1832 letter to Phelps: "You mention concerning the translation [of the Bible.] I would inform you that they will not go from under my hand during my natural life for correction, revisel or printing and the will of [the] Lord be done therefore you need not expect them this fall."[16] What is noteworthy here is Joseph's expectation that once the Bible translation texts went out "from under [his] hand," they would experience "correction, *revisel* [and] printing." The BCR data cause us to take notice of this statement in a way that we may not have before. "Revisel," as well as "correction," seems to be precisely what Literary Firm editor-printers Phelps, Cowdery, and Whitmer were doing with the revelation texts. As long as the fundamental "sense" of the revelations was not altered, Joseph apparently allowed these trusted associates to make whatever textual "revisels" they felt impressed by the Spirit to make. Joseph seems to have had a healthy awareness of the inadequacy of finite, human language, including his own, to perfectly communicate an infinite, divine revelation. As he pled on one occasion: "Oh Lord God deliver us in thy due time from the little narrow prison [of] . . . a crooked broken scattered and imperfect language."[17]

What does all this suggest about the revelatory process that eventually produced the final edited version of the revelation texts? Examination of the BCR and the history of the Doctrine and Covenants revelation texts from dictation to final form lead us to a richer, more nuanced view—one that sees Joseph as more than a mere human fax machine through whom God communicated finished revelation texts composed in heaven. Joseph had a role to play in the revelatory process. His contemporary Orson Pratt believed that Joseph received messages from God and then had to "clothe those ideas with such words as came to his mind."[18] Elder John A. Widtsoe

---

Hartley, eds., *The Joseph Smith Papers, Documents, Volume 2: July 1831–January 1833* (Salt Lake City: The Church Historian's Press, 2013), 266; emphasis added. Hereafter *JSP Documents*.

16. *JSP Documents*, 2:267.

17. "Letter to William W. Phelps, 27 November 1832," in *JSP Documents*, 2:320.

18. Orson Pratt, "Minutes of the School of the Prophets," Salt Lake Stake, December 9, 1872, Church History Library, The Church of Jesus Christ of Latter-day Saints, Salt Lake City.

of the Quorum of the Twelve Apostles explained: "Seldom are divine revelations dictated to man. . . . Instead, ideas are impressed upon the mind of the recipient, who then delivers the ideas *in his own language.*"[19] If, therefore, Joseph's diction, vocabulary, and grammar, and even that of some of his associates, are discernible in the revelation texts, believers may consider that impressive testimony to the fact that even in communicating his word and will to his prophets, God does not override their humanity. The Church of Jesus Christ of Latter-day Saints has no official statement on the nature of the interaction between Divine Revealer and human revelator in the genesis of scripture, but, as we have seen, a number of its leaders have offered explanations of the revelatory process that allow for Spirit-aided, yet still mortal, articulation and refinement of the divine message.

Many Christian scholars who accept the Bible as the Word of God have come to the same conclusion about the Holy Scriptures. They borrow from an ancient Christological axiom to affirm that Scripture can be viewed as both fully divine *and* fully human. In the words of one book title, the Bible is the "word of God in words of men."[20] Renowned Catholic scholar Raymond E. Brown has observed regarding the scriptural word of God: "The fact that the 'word' of the Bible is human and time-conditioned makes it no less 'of God'."[21] Otherwise, notes New Testament scholar Donald Hagner, "the genuinely human factor of the biblical documents is in effect denied in favor of a Bible that floated down from heaven by parachute, untouched by human hands or the historical process."[22] Clearly, that is *not* what happened with the revelation texts of the Doctrine and Covenants. Seeing scriptural texts as both fully divine *and* fully human allows ample room for regarding as inspired both their earliest wording and their subsequent revisions. In the end, as F. Henry Edwards reminds believers, the revelation texts should be seen as a "gateway" to God rather than an idol that replaces Him.[23]

---

19. John A. Widtsoe, "The Articles of Faith: X. Eternal Increase," *Improvement Era* 40 (October 1937): 600–601; emphasis added.

20. Jean Levie, S. J., *The Bible, Word of God in Words of Men* (New York: P. J. Kenedy & Sons, 1966).

21. Raymond E. Brown, "'And the Lord Said'? Biblical Reflections on Scripture as the Word of God," *Theological Studies* 42 (March 1981): 18.

22. Donald Hagner, "The Battle for Inerrancy," *The Reformed Journal* 34 (April 1984): 21.

23. F. Henry Edwards, *The Edwards Commentary on the Doctrine and Covenants* (Independence, MO.: Herald Publishing House, 1986), 17–18.

12

SPIRITUALIZING ELECTRONIC SCRIPTURE IN MORMONISM

Blair G. Van Dyke

For millennia many holy sayings ascribed to Deity and chronicles of God's dealings with humanity have been engraved on stone and metal, written on wood, papyrus, vellum, cloth, and, eventually, printed on paper. Generally known as scripture, billions of religious adherents spiritualize these writings and situate their content in authoritative, other-worldly, and godly domains.[1] Simply, the inscribed, written, or printed text itself is holy, distinct, and set apart from the mundane.

Determining what, if anything, an adherent esteems to be holy is critical to grasping the world-view of those that profess to follow God. As Philip Barlow has noted, "notwithstanding the difficulty of the task, understanding a people's conception and employment of scripture can contribute much toward comprehending their religious essence."[2] One need look no further than an earnest Muslim washing his hands before touching the Qur'an, the reverential placement of the Torah in the Ark of a Jewish synagogue (signifying the light and presence of Jehovah that emanates from his word), or a Protestant drawing priesthood authority from the Bible, to see the spiritualization of printed scriptural texts.

However, the bend of the arc of technological advancement has, in recent years, intersected with the arc of holy writ, thus compelling religious institutions and individuals to consider whether an iPad, iPod, tablet, or smart phone may be spiritualized to the extent that its electronic

---

1. Robert E. Van Voorst, *Anthology of World Scriptures* (Belmont, CA: Thomson Wadsworth, 2006), 4–9. See also Terryl L. Givens, *People of Paradox: A History of Mormon Culture* (Oxford: Oxford University Press, 2007), 37–51.

2. Philip L. Barlow, *Mormons and the Bible: The Place of the Latter-day Saints in American Religion* (Oxford: Oxford University Press, 2013), xii. See also, Terryl L. Givens, *By the Hand of Mormon: The American Scripture that Launched a New World Religion* (Oxford: Oxford University Press, 2002), 218.

display of scriptural text can still be viewed in the same other-worldly and divinely inspired way as are the scriptural texts in tangible print. For our purposes, spiritualization is a process wherein authoritative and divine favor is dispensed through declaration, ritual, or practice that is binding at individual and, where applicable, institutional levels insomuch that it transforms the status of a concept, ritual, or object from ordinary to holy. Can electronic scripture go through this process and be endowed with the sacral credibility that printed texts have enjoyed for centuries?

Leaders and adherents of the world's religions continue to ask and answer this question. For example, is it appropriate for a Jew to read an electronic display of Torah from an iPad or some other device on Shabbat? For many Jews, the answer is no. Daniel Nevins, a rabbi in Conservative Judaism, explained that employing electronic devices to access the Torah "violated the spirit of the Sabbath and the holidays, traditionally viewed as a sanctuary from the workday world." However, for another Conservative rabbi the answer is yes. Rabbi Elie Spitz explained that use of electronic versions of Torah and other holy writings of Judaism is "inevitable." He continued: "The codes of Jewish law take up an entire wall of bookshelves, but I can have the entire thing in the palm of my hand on my phone. This is a real revolution of access."[3]

Similar dialogue is occurring in Islam. For instance, a mufti (juris consult—expert in the Qur'an that provides interpretations and directives relative to religious applications in contemporary society) in the United Arab Emirate issued a fatwa (Islamic legal opinion) that authorized Muslims to read the Qur'an in electronic formats. The fatwa expressed the need to read the Qur'an by whatever means possible and that reading electronic versions of the Qur'an is better than not reading at all. However, the ruling did place printed text above electronic formats because ultimately, reading from the actual holy book in printed form is the most favored approach. Furthermore, due to the noise or vibration they may produce, electronic devices have the potential to disrupt or even negate some ritual acts of worship like prayer (salat) or ritual circumambulating of the Ka'ba at Mecca (Tawaf). Hence, while electronic versions of the Qur'an are acceptable in many parts of the Islamic world, they still maintain a lesser status than a printed copy of the holy book.[4]

---

3. Rabbi Daniel Nevins and Rabbi Elie Spitz, as reported by Jennifer Medinar, "A Question For Seder: What Role For Screens?" *The New York Times*, April 14, 2014.

4. Rym Ghazal, "Fatwa allows Quran Reading on Smartphones," *The National UAE,* March 29, 2012, http://www.thenational.ae/news/uae-news/fatwa-allows-quran-reading-on-smartphones.

Mormonism, unlike Judaism and Islam, is governed by a central hierarchy of leaders. They place high value on global unity and church correlation. The Church's First Presidency and the Quorum of the Twelve Apostles determine not only how scriptures will be employed throughout the world but, in the face of technological developments such as electronic literature, the acceptable mediums of scripture for use in Church worship services and formal Church instruction.

With this in mind, technology within Mormonism shares a complex and often conflicted interplay that ranges from strains of technophilia to bursts of technophobia. Technophilia is manifest in a long tradition of declarations by high-ranking Mormon leaders that expound the virtues of technological advances from the steam engine to the microchip, claiming that such marvels of modernism are inspired by God to further the advancement of Joseph Smith's restoration. Elder David A. Bednar of Mormonism's Quorum of the Twelve Apostles explained:

> We are blessed to live, learn, and serve in this most remarkable dispensation. An important aspect of the fullness that is available to us in this special season is a miraculous progression of innovations that have enabled and accelerated the work of salvation: from trains to telegraphs to radios to automobiles to airplanes to telephones to transistors to televisions to computers to satellite transmissions to the internet—and to an almost endless list of technologies and tools that bless our lives. All of these advancements are part of the Lord hastening His work in the latter days.[5]

Mormons generally possess a strong belief that they are stewards of technological discoveries and advancements. Indeed, they commonly believe that a fullness of truth belongs to Mormonism.[6] Thus, the principal utility of modern discoveries is to push forward the work of God throughout the world: if those discoveries and modern inventions can be used for other purposes, they are ancillary and secondary to the work of God. This perspective also extends to scientific, social, historical, educa-

---

5. David A. Bednar, "To Sweep the Earth as with a Flood," address delivered at Brigham Young University's Education Week, August 19, 2014, available at http://www.lds.org/prophets-and-apostles/unto-all-the-world/to-sweep-the-earth-as-with-a-flood. See also Joseph Fielding Smith, *Doctrines of Salvation* (Salt Lake City: Bookcraft, 1976), 1:180–81.

6. Dean C. Jessee, ed., *Personal Writings of Joseph Smith* (Salt Lake City: Deseret Book, 2002), 438. See also Brigham Young, April 24, 1870, *Journal of Discourses*, 26 vols. (London and Liverpool: LDS Booksellers Depot, 1854–86), 13:335; John Taylor, *Gospel Kingdom* (Salt Lake City: Bookcraft, 1964), 93.

tional, philosophical, and other realms of discovery. In this light, Socrates, Plato, Aristotle, Columbus, Hobbes, Locke, Luther, Calvin, Madison, Jefferson, the Wright brothers, Ford, and many others are acknowledged by Mormon prophets to have been inspired by God to play a role in preparing the world for global exposure to Joseph Smith's restoration of the Gospel.[7] The development of computer technologies that made electronic scripture possible may be seen through this same lens.

Mormon technophobia, on the other hand, may be illustrated in an anecdotal account of instruction by a local LDS leader to a large congregation of Mormon men and boys: "Brethren," the leader warned, holding an iPod above his head, "I.P.O.D. is an acronym for *Instant Pornography On Demand,* and such a device in your possession places your soul in grave danger!"[8] This leader's admonition echoes scores of warnings from high-ranking leaders of the Church about the pernicious dangers of pornography.[9] It highlights a very real dimension of the Mormon experience vis-a-vis technological advancements. Mormons believe that mortality is a testing ground wherein their ultimate opponent, Satan, works to deter them from the sacred and divine. In Mormon belief, Satan can and does use technological advancements to oppose goodness. He hopes to generate vice and chaos where God intends virtue and order. Mankind possesses free will to choose between the two.

From this vantage, certain aspects of scientific advancements, technological inventions, and social evolutions may be viewed as the opening of Pandora's Box—unleashing great uncertainty and spiritual peril. Mormons generally believe that safety may be found in established religious, spiritual, and cultural moorings that are carefully correlated by

---

7. See "Statement of The First Presidency Regarding God's Love for All Mankind," February 15, 1978, photocopy available at http://www.dovesandserpents.org/wp/wp-content/uploads/2011/10/First_Presidency_Gods_Love_1978.pdf.

8. The author was present when this warning was given at a general stake meeting in Utah County in 2012.

9. Warnings about pornography have been a common occurrence in General Conference sermons since the 1970s. The first decade of the twenty-first century has seen the greatest number of warnings from the pulpit thus far. The word "pornography" was used in General Conferences of the Church over four hundred times since its first usage in 1959, including four times by Ezra Taft Benson. During the 1960s it was used four times; 1970s, 74 times; 1980s, 43 times; 1990s, 62 times; 2000s, 165 times; and from 2010 to 2017, 61 times. See LDS General Conference Corpus, s.v. "pornography," at https://www.lds-general-conference.org/x.asp?c=gc&q=65694291.

central Church authorities. Advancements in technology present a means for Satan to introduce instability into an otherwise stable spiritual community, and nowhere is this threat felt more acutely in contemporary Mormonism than in the realm of internet technologies—the application of which is commonly individualistic, correlation-defying, and globally pervasive. Thus, the advancements that made electronic scripture possible must also be seen through this lens.

These examples illustrate the paradoxical relationship between Mormonism and the digital age. On one hand, the Church accepts technological advances as a manifestation of God's miraculous power to move Mormonism effectively into the future. On the other hand, the Church sternly ascribes certain uses of the cyber-world to Satan—most commonly pornography and anti-Mormon writings.[10] Several institutional and personal religious considerations are embedded in this dualism. Perhaps the most significant consideration is the honorific position printed scriptural texts have enjoyed in Mormonism. For example, the 1981 edition of the LDS scriptures was heralded as a fulfillment of Ezekiel's prophesy that the stick of Judah and the stick of Joseph would be united in a future day (Ezek. 37:15–19).[11] That esteem persisted even as access to electronic texts came to saturate what was once a print-only culture. However, I am persuaded that the spring 2013 release of a new edition of LDS scriptures in an electronic format without a hard-copy companion marked a deliberate tipping point in Mormonism from which there is likely no return: the use of electronic scriptures will continue to wax while the use of hard-copy scripture will continue to wane. The purpose of this essay is to explore how the spiritualization of electronic scriptures occurred in Mormonism. The technological gadgets referred to in this essay are of little significance. Indeed, at the rate technologies advance, specific devices mentioned herein

---

10. Internet pornography and anti-Mormon writings are two prominent concerns within Mormonism. However, they are not the only concerns. On May 3, 2009, Elder David A. Bednar of the Quorum of the Twelve Apostles warned college-age Mormons about the dangers of excessive online gaming. He also warned about the expanding digital fantasyland known as Second Life, where participants assume a new identity, create an avatar for themselves, purchase virtual property, own a virtual pet, explore virtual religiosity, engage in virtual relationships, and enter into virtual marriages with other participants through their avatars and pseudonyms. See David A. Bednar, "Things As They Really Are," *Liahona*, June 2010, 22–31.

11. Boyd K. Packer, "Scriptures," *Ensign*, November 1982, 53.

will likely be out-of-date sooner rather than later. However, this transitory time period in Mormonism provides a singular opportunity to observe how the hierarchy of the Church bestows institutional and sacral favor.

Confronting Digital Frontiers, 1997–2010

Electronic versions of the scriptures have been available to Mormons for decades. The Church released its first version of LDS scriptures online in 1997. Individual private use for study and research has always been acceptable. For approximately twenty years, electronic scriptures predated high speed internet and hand-held portable devices that could store and access large data files. Hence, their initial use was primarily limited to desktop computers. Scholars used them advantageously, but they were not widely used by rank and file Mormons.[12] Desktop computers began to appear in Mormon meetinghouses in North America in the early 1990s but were only used in administrative offices to facilitate financial purposes (to account for weekly tithes and offerings) and for pastoral functions (to maintain records of leadership structures and membership data). Family History Centers soon followed, wherein genealogical research was carried out on computers via the internet, vicarious work for the dead in Mormon temples being the intended outcome. Amidst these and other advances, the use of electronic scriptures in formal worship and instruction was a practical impossibility because the afore-mentioned arc of technological advancement had not yet intersected with the arc of holy writ in ways that would make electronic versions of the scriptures practical in day-to-day use.

The year 2000 serves as a general marker for the point in time that portability (of laptops, tablets, smart phones, and so forth), user-friendly applications, and scriptural texts came together for the first time, making it possible and appealing for many Mormons to consider leaving printed scriptures at home and instead bring electronic copies of the scriptures to worship services. However, leaders and teachers did not rush to use

---

12. Possibly the most influential and widely known example of research that utilized electronic scriptures in the early years was Susan Ward Easton's (later Susan Easton Black) analysis of the frequency of the names of Christ in the Book of Mormon compared to the biblical text. In a summary of her research that appeared in the *Ensign* magazine, she wrote: "In a word-by-word study, I have found some form of the Lord's name mentioned an average of every 1.7 verses in the Book of Mormon." See Susan Ward Easton, "Names of Christ in the Book of Mormon," *Ensign*, July 1978, 60–61.

electronic scriptures in formal church settings. Even after the ubiquitous spread of portable technology, printed texts carried spiritual cache in Mormonism that the same text on an electronic screen did not. As will be illustrated, they lacked sacral character in large measure because electronic devices that supported e-scriptures and accessed the internet were viewed with suspicion by high ranking leaders of the Church due to certain sinister uses—especially pornography.

The President of the Church from 1995 to 2008 was Gordon B. Hinckley. As a Church employee working with media from 1935 until he was called as a General Authority in 1958, Hinckley pioneered many of the Church's earliest enterprises with emerging technologies of the twentieth century, including radio, television, and film.[13] Among other things, his presidency was characterized by progressive institutional use of computer technologies, accompanied by grave warnings—especially to men and boys—about private use of the internet. Hinckley was simultaneously the architect of a new brand of Mormon inclusiveness of an ever-expanding pluralism in the world and a staunch defender of traditional moral values espoused by his pioneer forebears.[14] Concerning the latter, he preached stinging sermons against what he determined were the mounting evils of pornography. A representative example is his 2004 LDS General Conference declaration that pornographic ills were "compounded by the internet." He continued:

The National Coalition of the Protection of Children and Family states that

> "approximately 40 million people in the United States are sexually involved with the internet. . . . Three million of the visitors to adult websites in September 2000 were age 17 or younger. . . . [And] sex is the number 1 topic searched on the internet." . . . Suffice it to say that all who are involved [with internet pornography] become victims. Children are exploited, and their lives are severely damaged. The minds of youth become warped with false concepts. Continued exposure leads to addiction that is almost impossible to break. Men, so very many, find they cannot leave it alone. Their energies and their interests are consumed in their dead-end pursuit of this raw and sleazy fare. . . . I know that I am speaking directly and plainly. I do so because

---

13. J. B. Haws, *The Mormon Image in the American Mind: Fifty Years of Public Perception* (Oxford: Oxford University Press, 2013), 159. See also, "In Memoriam: President Gordon B. Hinckley 1910–2008," *Ensign*, March 2008, 6.

14. Matthew Bowman, *The Mormon People: The Making of an American Faith* (New York City: Random House, 2012), 245–46.

the Internet has made pornography more widely accessible, adding to what is available on DVDs and videos, on television and magazine stands. It leads to fantasies that are destructive of self-respect. It leads to illicit relationships, often to disease, and to abusive criminal activity.[15]

Again, this is representative of many sermons preached during these years to stem the tide of growing use of internet pornography in Mormonism. In their efforts to reclaim those experimenting with or addicted to online pornography and to persuade all others to turn away from "this raw and sleazy fare," reformation rhetoric was employed by Mormonism's hierarchy that painted personal internet use in private space in a very foreboding light. One outgrowth of this rhetoric was that private use of the internet came to be almost synonymous with risky or ominous moral behavior. Therefore, the comparatively few Mormons that did use e-scriptures at church and in Mormon educational settings did so for personal use only and, at times, were the recipients of minor criticism by leaders, teachers, and congregants that questioned their appropriateness. As will be seen, leanings against the use of the internet and associated electronic devices in formal church settings persisted until 2011 or later.

About midway through the first decade of the new millennium, electronic scriptures at church were not forbidden by the Mormon leadership, but because of the unacceptable uses of portable digital devices, electronic scriptures were not encouraged. Notwithstanding, the popularity, accessibility, affordability, convenience, and continually expanding utility of electronic portable devices created greater use in larger demographics than ever anticipated. Soon it was more common than not for Mormons in economically developed areas of the world to own and use these devices extensively—including electronic scriptures. And yet, their use remained limited in formal worship services relative to speaking and teaching. The tensions revolved around the above-mentioned hierarchy that governs Mormonism. Since Mormon leaders, specifically the First Presidency and the Quorum of the Twelve Apostles, had not implicitly or explicitly endorsed the use of electronic scriptures (and their attendant portable devices) in formal church settings, ecclesiastical expectations eclipsed individual preferences. Simply, wholesale spiritualization of electronic scriptures was essential to creating wide-spread acceptance within Mormon worship communities, and that could only be granted by the First Presidency and

---

15. Gordon B. Hinckley, *Discourses of President Gordon B. Hinckley Volume 2: 2000–2004* (Salt Lake City: Deseret, 2005), 252–53.

the Quorum of the Twelve Apostles. But this wholesale endorsement was slow to come, leaving questions of acceptability in limbo.

Local Leaders

Since high-ranking leaders of the Church did not definitively weigh in on the institutional acceptability of this new format of the canon, local leaders were left to wrestle with the question. For many, perhaps most, the dualism of the cyber world exceeded tolerable limits. How could a device that possibly accessed internet pornography, sexting, anti-Mormon literature, or online gambling on Saturday night be allowed into Mormonism's sacred Sabbath rituals and meetings less than twenty-four hours later? Among other reasons, the fact that portable devices like iPads, iPods, tablets, and any variety of smart phones can morph from mundane to sacred to sinful in a matter of seconds was disconcerting to many leaders. Furthermore, texting, telephoning, and imaging capabilities of these devices could detract from individual and communal worship and learning, and this served as one more justification for some leaders to formally ban electronic scriptures in local congregations.

Conversely, other local leaders embraced portable electronic scriptures in their congregations with varying degrees of enthusiasm. These leaders carved out space for electronic scripture, independent of other e-publications. This position recommended that just as printed pornography does not taint printed scripture, electronic pornography does not taint electronic scripture. Also, some felt that distractions associated with electronic devices were likely no more aggravating than those found in the non-virtual world. However, even leaders sympathetic to the use of electronic scriptures did not feel at liberty to allow their use by speakers and leaders at the pulpit or by teachers in the classroom. That would not occur without clear endorsement from Mormonism's highest tier of leadership.

The Members

The discussion among members themselves about electronic scriptures was a reflection of the disparate views held by local leaders. A quick perusal of any number of internet "chat rooms" at the time where Mormons discussed this topic is revealing. Many Mormons maintain that the study of electronic scripture does not yield the same spiritual benefits as the study of physically printed scripture. Also, some Mormons bestow a recreational status upon electronic scripture. That is to say, one may read e-scripture at the beach, park, or while taking a break in the office lounge. However, *serious* study of scripture should be accomplished with printed scripture. It is not a recreational pursuit but demands disciplined demeanor and protocol suitable to the undertaking. Electronic scriptures are associated by some to be closer to video gaming than godly communion and therefore lack the discipline and spirit to attain desired spiritual fulfillment. On the other hand, the virtues of portability are trumpeted by many members who find that they can study scripture at almost any time or place because the Mormon canon now fits in their pocket.[16]

Church Hierarchy

On December 15, 2007, Elder M. Russell Ballard of the Quorum of the Twelve Apostles delivered a commencement address at Brigham Young University—Hawaii. Within seven months an adaptation of the address was published in the *Ensign*, the Church's flagship publication to its members. In this speech Ballard explained:

> There are perhaps few inventions that have had a greater impact on the world than the printing press, invented by the inspired Johannes Gutenberg around 1436. The printing press enabled knowledge, including that contained in the Holy Bible, to be shared more widely than ever before. Today we have a modern equivalent of the printing press in the Internet. The Internet allows everyone to be a publisher, to have his or her voice heard, and it is revolutionizing society. . . . The emergence of new media is facilitating a worldwide conversation on almost every subject, including religion, and nearly everyone can participate. This modern equivalent of the printing press is not reserved only for the elite.[17]

As part of his comments, Ballard provided warnings about the dangers of electronic technologies and how quickly and easily they can be used to purvey "the filth and sleaze of pornography."[18] But his concerned expressions were so brief when compared to his extensive and effusive praise of the internet and mediums of new media that his words stood as a significant ecclesiastical endorsement. According to his instruction, the benefits of electronic media far outweighed the potential risks associated with their use. He encouraged members of the Church to embrace technological advances and employ them to "join the conversation" on the internet. In

---

16. See Trent Toone, "Digital vs. Print: Which Scriptures Do You Use?" *Deseret News*, April 18, 2013, http://www.deseretnews.com/article/865578467/The-standard-works-digital-vs-print-What-works-for-you.html.

17. M. Russell Ballard, "Sharing the Gospel Using the Internet," *Ensign*, July 2008, 60.

18. Ballard, 60.

fact, he stated that Mormons cannot "stand on the sidelines while others, including our critics, attempt to define what the Church teaches."[19]

This landmark address and subsequent publication on the virtues of internet communication created new levels of acceptability and enthusiasm among Mormons. At the time the speech was given, Mitt Romney, a prominent Mormon, was engaged in his first campaign for President of the United States. The Church hosted its first online press conference to request that the nation's news reporters provide clarity for misunderstandings about the Church that had arisen from heightened exposure due to a Mormon running for the highest political office in America.[20] Within two years, the Church's Public Affairs department entered the blogosphere through its website (MormonNewsroom.org/blog). Lyman Kirkland, then Senior Manager Newsroom/New Media for the Church, explained that one purpose of this blog is "to supplement the Newsroom Web site with additional stories from the Church that may not lend themselves to a news release, and to provide additional context and background on stories that appear in the news media."[21] Another purpose is to "provide journalists, bloggers and the public with additional context and information regarding public issues and news stories involving the Church."[22]

Finally, the Church moved quickly to pilot programs with missionaries to experiment with proselytizing through social media platforms such as Facebook. This necessitated distributing iPads to thousands of young missionaries.[23] With this general context in mind, it is apparent that Ballard's BYU-Hawaii speech was not given in a vacuum, for many technological developments were transpiring behind the scenes. Even so, at the time the BYU-Hawaii speech was delivered, neither Ballard nor any of his peers in Quorum of the Twelve or First Presidency provided a specific sanction for

---

19. Ballard, 61.

20. Peggy Fletcher Stack, "In the Romney Spotlight, LDS Church goes Online to Brief Religion Press," *Salt Lake Tribune*, October 2, 2007, http://archive.sltrib.com/article.php?id=7062785&itype=NGPSID.

21. Lyman Kirkland, "Welcome to the Newsroom Blog," *Mormon Newsroom* (blog), August 18, 2009, http://www.mormonnewsroom.org/blog/welcome-to-the-newsroom-blog.

22. Kirkland.

23. Peggy Fletcher Stack, "LDS Church Sees Potential in Proselytizing Online," *Salt Lake Tribune*, July 16, 2010, http://archive.sltrib.com/article.php?id=10212967&itype=storyID.

the use of electronic scriptures in formal church settings. That discussion continued to percolate.

In October 2009, just over one year after Ballard's BYU-Hawaii commencement address was published in the *Ensign*, Elder Richard G. Scott of the Quorum of the Twelve Apostles granted an interview to Sheri Dew, president and chief executive officer of Church-owned Deseret Book Company. At the time of the interview, Scott served as the Chair of the Church Audio-visual Committee and, according to Dew, is "always up on the latest [technological advancements] and very open to embracing various kinds of technology to help spread the gospel and teach the gospel and so forth."[24] Dew invited Scott to speak about the pros and cons of technology. He launched immediately into a discussion about electronic scriptures, saying:

> Well, let's take a negative thing about technology. It's very easy with a computer if you're going to give a talk to word search the scriptures and pick out scriptures and find and organize it. It might help in writing a talk but it is a very poor way of learning the gospel. *There is nothing like hefting the book in your hand*, reading and marking your own volume of scriptures, and if that isn't happening, and people are using only *the scriptures that are in a computer*, they are missing the richness of the feelings that come and the ability to write it in the margins, impressions that surely come as we read passages of scripture. So there is the difficulty. There are great blessings that can come from proper use of technology. That's the reason that I've been interested in it. There isn't any subject that you can imagine that we can't find information with the tools that are available through technology in today's world. We have the ability to learn and to find out exciting and interesting things that would not have been within our reach except for technology. So

---

24. "Elder Richard G. Scott and daughter Linda Mickle - Episode 6," *Mormon Channel*, October 5, 2009, http://www.mormonchannel.org/conversation/6. It may appear from Scott's comments that electronic formats of the scriptures in 2009 did not allow a user to mark and annotate their scriptures in a way commensurate to traditional printed texts. However, there were several apps and programs available prior to this time. Rob Jex, Director of Scriptures Coordination for the Church, explained that the first LDS scripture app that allowed users to mark and annotate was introduced in 2008. Prior to that official release there were several private entities that developed apps and programs with these capabilities for use with Mormon scriptures. Rob Jex, personal communication with the author, August 27, 2014. See also, Aaron Shift, "Digital Scriptures are Popular," *Deseret News*, August 13, 2009, http://www.deseretnews.com/article/705378520/Digital-scriptures-are-popular.html.

the proper use of it is a very powerful tool for someone who wants to learn in today's world.²⁵

Like Ballard, Scott's endorsement of the proper use of technology is unmistakable. However, it is equally clear that, at the time, he drew a line to separate printed scripture from electronic scripture. Scripture that is "in the computer" lacks richness and feeling for certain sacral purposes—this "is the difficulty." Printed scripture, on the other hand, may be hefted, marked, and written upon in a way that facilitates greater spiritual enlightenment.

As the first decade of the new millennium came to a close, computer technology and social networking were being endorsed like never before by the hierarchy of the Church. However, electronic scriptures still lacked sacral status and were not being used broadly at an institutional level. "Hefting" the printed word remained preferable to "clicking" on an icon.

Spiritualizing Electronic Scripture in Mormonism

Explicit spiritualization of electronic scriptures came without formal announcement or fanfare. It was gradual and transpired in a way that accentuated unity within the highest ranks of Church leadership. This was essential because significant shifts and changes in practice and policy in Mormonism are made by the First Presidency and the Quorum of the Twelve Apostles, who are sustained by Church members as prophets, seers, and revelators. At the core, what this means is that Mormons generally view their highest leaders through an Old Testament lens. They believe that as Moses spoke for the Lord anciently, modern prophets and apostles speak for the Lord today and are authorized to pronounce a principle, practice, or doctrine of the Church to be beneficial, benign, or malignant. Therefore, no matter how saturated society were to become with other electronic texts, electronic scripture could not be used widely in Mormon worship until they were spiritualized by the First Presidency and the Quorum of the Twelve Apostles, and this would need to be clearly communicated to the Church.²⁶

---

25. "Elder Richard G. Scott"; emphasis added.

26. In Mormonism, spiritualization at the institutional level is a process that requires receipt of revelation by high-ranking members of Church hierarchy. See Givens, *People of Paradox*, 37–51. See also Grant Hardy, "Introduction," in *The Book of Mormon: The Earliest Text*, ed. Royal Skousen (New Haven: Yale University Press, 2009), vii-xxviii; and Armand L. Mauss, *The Angel and the Beehive* (Urbana: University of Chicago Press, 1994), 106–8. Mauss describes

In hindsight, it is apparent that a significant step toward spiritualizing electronic scripture occurred late in 2010. In November, the First Presidency and the Quorum of the Twelve Apostles announced that the second volume of the *Church Handbook of Instructions* would be immediately available online and could be freely accessed by anyone world-wide, member or non-member. Prior to this time, this handbook could only be viewed by members of the Church that held particular leadership positions within Melchizedek Priesthood quorums and auxiliary organizations. The first volume could also be accessed online but only by high-ranking priesthood leaders (including bishops, stake presidents, mission presidents, and general authorities). Assessing the significance of the decision to release the second volume to the public involves a series of developments within the Church ecclesiastically, theologically, sociologically, and so forth. For example, sociologist Armand Mauss observed that granting full access to this handbook "removes the veil of secrecy from a lot of [Church] operation. That's healthy."[27] Julie Smith, a biblical scholar, added that free access is particularly important so that everyone—not just those in leadership callings—may come to know the specific policies employed to govern the Church.[28] A full exploration of the importance of this administrative decision exceeds the scope of this essay.

For our purposes, the fact that the handbook was made available to the general public in an electronic format and not in print is an indicator of developments within the Church relative to using technology, and it serves as an important precursor to the eventual release of the new electronic edition of the scriptures. Indeed, few documents rise to the level of import in Mormonism to rival the *Church Handbook of Instructions*. Elder Dallin H. Oaks of the Quorum of the Twelve Apostles explained: "While handbooks do not have the same standing as the scriptures, they do represent the most current interpretations and procedural directions of

---

the Mormonization of the King James Version of the Bible culminating in the 1981 LDS edition of the scriptures. This edition also necessitated written and spoken statements from members of the First Presidency and the Quorum of the Twelve Apostles that created cultural and spiritual legitimacy for the new scriptures. Spiritualization and Mormonization (as used here by Mauss) are essentially synonymous. I employ the former term herein.

27. As quoted in Peggy Fletcher Stack, "LDS Church Handbook On Social Issues Available Online," *Salt Lake Tribune*, November 26, 2010, http://archive.sltrib.com/article.php?id=12085646&itype=storyID.

28. Stack.

the Church's highest authorities."²⁹ Church President Thomas S. Monson has explained that "there is safety in the handbooks."³⁰ Furthermore, the introduction of volume two states: "These instructions can facilitate revelation if they are used to provide an understanding of principles, policies, and procedures to apply while seeking the guidance of the Spirit."³¹ From these statements it is evident that this volume is of utmost import to Church governance and serves as an impetus to understanding, to spiritual safety, and to revelation for adherent Mormons. Publishing volume two of the handbook online communicated to the Church and others that the Mormon hierarchy was comfortable utilizing electronic formats for their most sacred and important publications—save scripture. However, scripture was next. But more needed to be done to accomplish this purpose.³²

Beginning in 2011, Elder L. Tom Perry, a senior apostle, began conducting training meetings with no printed scriptures in hand. He worked entirely from his iPad for notes, and when he desired to read passages of scripture he clicked on his scripture icon and read the text from his electronic device. News that an apostle was using electronic scriptures in formal church meetings spread quickly among Mormons and was seen by many as an apostolic endorsement.³³

---

29. Dallin H. Oaks, "'Overview of the Handbooks,' *2010 Worldwide Leadership Training Meeting*," Church of Jesus Christ of Latter-day Saints (website), http://www.lds.org/broadcasts/article/worldwide-leadership-training/2010/11/overview-of-the-new-handbooks.

30. Thomas S. Monson, "'Opening Remarks,' *2010 Worldwide Leadership Training Meeting*," Church of Jesus Christ of Latter-day Saints (website), http://www.lds.org/broadcasts/article/worldwide-leadership-training/2010/11/opening-remarks.

31. "Introduction," *Handbook 2: Administering the Church*, 2010, http://www.lds.org/handbook/handbook-2-administering-the-church/introduction.

32. It is important to note that in December 2010 the First Presidency authorized changes to chapter headings in the online version of the Book of Mormon. These changes pertained to racial references in chapter headings that had been altered for the 2004 Doubleday publication of the Book of Mormon. The changes to the online version were in line with the Doubleday printed publication and did not constitute a new edition of scripture. Since online scriptures were not used by the vast majority of the general membership of the Church at this time, the changes went largely unnoticed.

33. Documenting apostolic endorsement at this early stage of spiritualizing electronic scriptures and associated portable devices is challenging because the response was organic and emerged from Mormons in the blogosphere without capturing a great deal of attention by writers or reporters that covered Mormonism.

In concert with Perry's efforts, Elder David A. Bednar, then a junior member of the Quorum of the Twelve Apostles, conducted several training meetings with live audiences that were broadcast by satellite. Like Perry, Bednar used his iPad in these meetings as if it were a printed copy of scriptures. He also received and answered questions texted to him in real time by members of the viewing audience that were not in the room where the satellite transmission originated. At this time, being trained by Bednar was not just a religious or spiritual undertaking—for many it represented a clear embrace of a new and enthusiastic marriage between religiosity and technology in Mormonism that unquestionably included the entire canon of scripture in digital formats.

Furthermore, in spring 2012, Oaks spoke at a devotional in Asia. At one point in his comments, he searched for a scripture on his iPad. During the search, he rehearsed that Elder Boyd K. Packer, then President of the Quorum of the Twelve Apostles, had directed the entire quorum to get iPads. Oaks noted that he found electronic scriptures "a much more convenient and light way to carry his scriptures." He also added that the scriptures were the only app he had on his iPad at the time.[34] It appears from Oaks's comments that apostolic use of electronic scriptures was at least encouraged and almost certainly coordinated by quorum leadership. Given the weight Mormons give to the teachings and directions of these high-ranking leaders, the significance of Oaks's report of complete unity within the Quorum of the Twelve Apostles with respect to using electronic scriptures in formal church meetings cannot be overstated.

The result of multiple apostles using electronic scriptures in formal church meetings, along with the reported approval of the President of the Quorum of the Twelve, was the rapid disappearance of postures that opposed electronic scripture in church and the portable devices that support them. Generally speaking, Mormons had been fastidiously clinging to Gutenberg-style hard copy print as orthodox until apostolic authorities spiritualized electronic scripture through use in their own ministries. Once their endorsement was openly observed, hesitations associated with electronic scriptures dissipated at virtually every level of the Church. However, one development remained in order to securely fix the process

---

34. Reported in "Reactions to an Apostle's Words," *Wheat & Tares*, May 29, 2012, http://www.wheatandtares.org/8220/reactions-to-an-apostles-words/. See also, Peggy Fletcher Stack, "Call them iApostles—LDS Leaders Pack High-tech Scriptures," *Salt Lake Tribune*, May 29, 2012, http://archive.sltrib.com/article.php?id=21338285&itype=storyID.

of spiritualization of electronic scripture in Mormonism: privileging the digital release of the updated Standard Works.

The 2013 Edition of the LDS Scriptures

On March 1, 2013, the Church released a new edition of the LDS scriptures—the first since 1981. After nearly eight years of preparation, it is significant that this new edition was only available in electronic format (a printed version followed approximately five months later). The 2013 edition updates archaic spellings and corrects many minor typographical errors in spelling and punctuation. It is noteworthy that 99 percent of the changes are in the study materials such as the Bible Dictionary, footnotes, Topical Guide, maps, and so forth.[35] Some adjustments were made to headings and historical overviews of sections of the Doctrine and Covenants. The intent of these changes was

> to provide a clearer context for the scriptures. For example, in the Doctrine and Covenants some of the section headings have been revised and introductory headings have been added to both official declarations to provide the reader with a better understanding of the purposes of those revelations and the Church's doctrine related to them.[36]

The question has been posed: Did the 2013 LDS edition of the scriptures expand the Mormon canon? The answer is both yes and no. Responding negatively to the question is accurate because no new revelations were added to the canon itself. However, responding in the affirmative is reasonable because introductory statements, chapter headings, historical overviews, and depictions of geography on maps including physical and political borders all communicate important information that is officially endorsed by the Church at the canonical, or highest, levels of scrutiny and care for Mormon thought, doctrine, and orthodoxy.

This is particularly evident in the changes made to the introduction to Official Declaration 2, which announced the revelation ending the priesthood and temple restriction of black Latter-day Saints. The 1981 edition introduces the declaration as follows: "June 8, 1978. To all general and local priesthood officers of The Church of Jesus Christ of Latter-day Saints throughout the world" (OD 2 [1981]). For decades before and after June 1978, justifications for the priesthood ban were circulated formally

---

35. "Church Announces 2013 Edition of English Scriptures," *Mormon Newsroom*, March 1, 2013, http://www.mormonnewsroom.org/article/scriptures-digital-2013.

36. "Church Announces."

through correlated instructional materials used in the Church and informally through unofficial writings of some members of the First Presidency and the Quorum of the Twelve Apostles. Explanations ranged from blacks lacking valiancy in the pre-existence (Mormon conception of life prior to mortal birth) to the biblical curse of Cain to Joseph Smith's receipt of a revelation that he privately passed on to Brigham Young.[37] Was the ban Church doctrine, policy, or merely an outgrowth of the racially charged nineteenth-century American society from which Mormonism sprang? Even after the ban was lifted in 1978, justifications for the ban remained opaque. No formal explanations were provided by the Church historically, socially, or theologically. Largely, the Church attempted to establish benign racial postures amidst increasing pluralism while simultaneously reserving accolades for prophetic personalities that instituted, upheld, and in some cases, vigorously defended the ban.

With this in mind, consider the following synopsis of the much lengthier and ground-breaking introduction found in the 2013 edition of Official Declaration 2 that captures nine religious ideas, historical considerations, and doctrinal positions concerning race and Mormon priesthood: first, "all are alike unto God" (2 Ne. 26:33); second, people of every race and ethnicity have been baptized throughout the world and lived faithfully in the Church; third, Joseph Smith presided over the ordination of blacks to the priesthood when he was alive; fourth, following the death of Joseph Smith, early Church leaders stopped ordaining blacks to the priesthood; fifth, no clear origin of the ban is evident; sixth, Church leaders believed that a revelation was needed to alter the ban; seventh, President Spencer W. Kimball received a revelation to lift the ban in the Salt Lake Temple on June 1, 1978; eighth, other leaders of the Church were also present during this revelatory experience; and ninth, the revelation removed all restrictions with regard to race that had applied to the priesthood (OD 2 [2013]).[38]

---

37. Paul W. Reeve, *Religion of a Different Color Race and the Mormon Struggle for Whiteness* (Oxford: Oxford University Press, 2015), 188–214. See also Armand L. Mauss, *All Abraham's Children Changing Mormon Conceptions of Race and Lineage* (Urbana: University of Illinois Press, 2003), 212–30.

38. It is noteworthy that the introduction of Official Declaration 2 closely follows language employed by an official statement released by the Church almost one year prior to the announcement of the 2013 edition of scriptures. That statement, entitled "Race and the Church: All Are Alike Unto God," was apparently a response to a Washington Post interview with a Brigham Young University professor of religion. The professor responded to questions about the Church's justifications

The singularity of expressions in the revised introduction of Official Declaration 2 is expansive, and the strength of the language is bold in light of LDS Church history relating to race relations and priesthood. This is particularly the case with the first, third, fourth, and fifth points of the introduction. Formal admission that the founder of the Church ordained blacks but that Mormons today lack clarity regarding the origins and justifications surrounding the ban—in a scriptural introduction—is both instructive and more transparent. Indeed, these were the first formal declarations of their kind to be attached to scriptural text. To be clear, this introduction is not considered scripture by Mormons. However, it is immensely influential and is an excellent example of Barlow's observation that interpretive apparatus such as introductions, chapter headings, footnotes, topical guides, and cross referencing "conditions how the Saints understand the text."[39] In this way, some answers to questions regarding the priesthood ban were simultaneously provided and spiritualized by their placement in the new edition of the scriptures.[40] A similar introduction was added to Official Declaration 1, which ended the practice of plural marriage. These introductions are one way that the 2013 edition expanded the canon in quasi-scriptural ways.

It seems apparent that the release of the electronic edition of the scriptures several months prior to the print edition was intentional. It certainly would not have been difficult to wait a few months to release them simultaneously. Releasing the digital version first clearly moved e-scripture out of the shadow of questionable realms of the electronic cyber-world. It would be difficult for the First Presidency and the Quorum of the Twelve

---

for banning blacks from holding the priesthood from the 1850s to June 1, 1978. The professor's explanations were so far eschew from the contemporary perspectives of Mormonism's hierarchy that an official statement was released to correct misinformation and clarify the Church's current position. See "Race and the Church: All Are Alike Unto God," *Mormon Newsroom*, February 29, 2012, http://www.mormonnewsroom.org/article/race-church.

39. Barlow, *Mormons and the Bible*, xliv.

40. In December 2013 the Church released the Gospel Topics essay "Race and the Priesthood" on its website. This document places the priesthood ban in historical and religious context and is part of a series of essays published by the Church intended to answer challenging questions related to the rise of Mormonism. "Race and the Priesthood," *Church of Jesus Christ of Latter-day Saints* (website), December 2013, https://www.lds.org/topics/race-and-the-priesthood. It is significant that before this landmark document was released, findings similar to those expressed in the essay had been published earlier that year in the 2013 introduction to Official Declaration 2.

Apostles to more convincingly communicate the acceptability of electronic scripture than by releasing the first new edition of the scriptures in over three decades in an electronic format. As such, the 2013 electronic edition of the scriptures stands fully clothed in authority and Mormon orthodoxy. Electronic scripture has been thoroughly spiritualized by the First Presidency and the Quorum of the Twelve Apostles.[41] This was a watershed moment in the history of Mormonism that largely ended years of doubt and discussion over the acceptability of using electronic scriptures in formal worship services.[42] Remarkably, the men and teenage boys that the Mormon leader so gravely warned about "*Instant Pornography on Demand*" may now freely stand at the pulpit in a Mormon worship service and use their iPod, tablet, smart phone, or other device as if it were a printed and bound book of scripture. However, since all of the negative aspects of using electronic devices persist, the wholesale spiritualization of electronic scripture was a step squarely onto turf that is both promising and pernicious.[43] As Terryl Givens explained, the challenge—when

---

41. Just over one month after the release of the 2013 edition of the LDS scriptures, Richard G. Scott spoke in the General Conference of the Church and, in a show of apostolic unity, addressed how electronic scriptures and attending portable devices could enhance communication through the Holy Ghost. To Scott, "clicking" a scripture icon was now as acceptable as "hefting" the scriptures. After warning about the deterrents of the digital age, Scott explained: "Be wise how you embrace technology. Mark important scriptures on your device and refer back to them frequently. If you young people would review a verse of scripture as often as some of you send text messages, you could soon have hundreds of passages of scripture memorized. Those passages would prove to be a powerful source of inspiration and guidance by the Holy Ghost in times of need." Richard G. Scott, "For Peace at Home," *Ensign*, May 2013, https://www.lds.org/ensign/2013/05/for-peace-at-home.

42. The willingness of Mormon authorities to formally spiritualize electronic scripture and encourage the use of associated electronic devices that support the 2013 edition of the scriptures goes hand in hand with the Church's missionary department's utilization of these tools and technologies. According to Elder David F. Evans, the First Presidency and the Quorum of the Twelve Apostles are expanding the use of mobile devices among full-time missionaries. By early 2015, the Church planned to have approximately forty thousand missionaries equipped with iPad minis or similar mobile devices. See "Church Expands Use of Digital Devices for Missionary Work," *Mormon Newsroom*, July 2, 2014, http://www.mormonnewsroom.org/article/church-expands-use-of-digital-devices-for-missionary-work.

43. David F. Holland, *Sacred Borders Continuing Revelation and Canonical Restraint in Early America* (Oxford: Oxford University Press, 2011), 1–15. One

simultaneously faced with temptation and promise—is to "exploit the accoutrements of that host culture without suffering contamination or loss of mission and identity in the process. The difficulty in 'spoiling the Egyptians' has ever been the same: to turn the plundered riches into temple adornments rather than golden calves."[44] Redefining the digital arc in order to productively harness the digital age is unquestionably one of the great opportunities and challenges of Mormonism as a church and people.

Conclusion

Mormons experience a paradoxical relationship between their faith and the digital age. Historically, a love for, and a tension with, digital technologies has abounded in Mormonism. However, the First Presidency and the Quorum of the Twelve Apostles of the Church have made culture-wrenching efforts to spiritualize electronic scriptures and validate technological devices necessary to employ them. I have proposed that the culmination of this process was the release of the 2013 edition of the LDS scriptures in an electronic format that precluded its printed version. For Mormons, this was the intersection wherein the arc of scriptural text and the arc of technological advancement met. Did Monson, Packer, Perry, Oaks, Bednar, and other members of the First Presidency and the Quorum of the Twelve Apostles expand the canon of sacred texts in Mormonism? No, not in the sense that new revelations were added to the 2013 edition of the LDS scriptures, but they played an indispensable role in expanding interpretive tools such as the introduction to Official Declarations 2 and the acceptable mediums through which sacral texts could be freely employed in sacred Mormon space. This is a clear example of one way Mormon hierarchy functions—especially in how it bestows sacral value within the Church. In sum, Mormons have entered a new era wherein electronic scripture enjoys complete legitimacy in private and public venues. The spiritualization of electronic scriptures is a seminal event in the history of sacred texts in Mormonism.

---

of Holland's principal points in these pages is that the openness necessary to make adjustments of any kind to the canon of scripture may "corrode any meaningful sense of canonicity" (p. 3). That risk is generally noted with varying degrees of sobriety by religionists—this is certainly the case with leaders of Mormonism.

44. Givens, *People of Paradox*, 62.

13

THE ART OF SCRIPTURE AND SCRIPTURE AS ART: THE PROCLAMATION ON THE FAMILY AND THE EXPANDING CANON

Boyd J. Petersen and *David W. Scott*

In his 1967 essay "What the Church Means to People Like Me," Richard Poll classified Latter-day Saints into two groups, comparing them to two objects described in the Book of Mormon: obedience-driven saints he compared to the Iron Rod, an extended handrail that provided stability and safety to those who grasped it, as described in 1 Nephi 8; and independent-minded saints he compared to Liahonas, referring to the ancient brass ball described in 1 Nephi 16 that provided GPS-like directions upon prayerful request. While both Iron Rod and Liahona saints participate fully in the Church, Poll believed they often have trouble understanding each other. Iron-Rod saints are confident about their access to inspiration through scripture, prophets, and the Holy Spirit. They do not question, and they regard those who do question as having an imperfect faith. Liahonas, on the other hand, are preoccupied with questions and skeptical of answers. They often regard Iron Rod saints as closed-minded, blindly obedient followers.[1] We might characterize Liahona Mormons as those who focus more on a personal religiosity, emphasizing private spiritual practices and promptings with less concern for dogma; while Iron Rod Mormons might be characterized as emphasizing institutional religious practice, which focuses on denominational worship and loyalty to the church as an institution. More recently, Terryl Givens has shifted the locus of the Iron Rod/Liahona tension from the external community to the internal individual Latter-day Saint: "the divide Poll describes is

---

1. Richard Poll, "What the Church Means to People Like Me," *Dialogue: A Journal of Mormon Thought* 2, no. 4 (Winter 1967): 107–17.

one that, at some level, operates *within* thoughtful Mormons as much as *among* them."[2]

Perhaps this tension is exacerbated by the fact that Mormons have three sources of authority—scripture, prophetic utterance, and individual revelation—with no specific distinction in weight between them and with the distinct possibility that they may conflict with one another. This tension between Iron Rodders and Liahonas is certainly apparent in the way Church members think about the 1995 statement by LDS leaders, "The Family: A Proclamation to the World." Many see it as divinely inspired, but not everyone gives it the same weight. Some see it as equal to scripture, while others see it as counsel. Some see it as binding on their personal beliefs and behavior, while others regard it as open to individual interpretation and inspiration. At the same time, an inner Liahona/Iron Rod tension is apparent in the ways individual members struggle to make sense of the Proclamation's application to the gay marriage debate.

In the first half of this chapter, we address three questions: What is a proclamation in the context of LDS Church history? What are the origins of the Proclamation on the Family? And, finally, how has the Proclamation become so authoritative in Mormon thought and devotion? In the second half, we examine Church members' complex views on the Proclamation in more detail and how it influences their attitudes toward gay marriage.

What is a Proclamation?

In English usage, the word "proclamation" has roots in the British legal system; a proclamation was originally a "formal order issued by a monarch or other legal authority" to the public.[3] However, it has come to mean any authoritative statement made by anyone, but especially government leaders. Presidents, governors, and mayors all issue proclamations. In Mormon usage, the term carries no specific definition. In the *Encyclopedia of Mormonism*, Robert Matthews defines a proclamation as a "solemn," "sacred," "formal written" document designed to "bring forth, build up, and regulate the affairs of the Church as the kingdom of God on the earth." Whether addressed to the members of the Church or to the entire world, they provide "instruction on doctrine, faith, and history; warnings of judgments to come; invitations to assist in the work; and statements of

---

2. Terryl Givens, *People of Paradox: A History of Mormon Culture* (New York: Oxford University Press, 2007), 17.

3. *Oxford English Dictionary*, 2nd ed. (1989), s.v. "proclamation."

Church growth and progress." Written prior to the 1995 proclamation, Matthews's article identifies only four proclamations, but it is careful to emphasize that this is not a complete list.[4] Over the course of its history, the LDS Church has issued a number of documents that might be considered proclamations, and it has never articulated any distinction between them and documents with titles like "Official Declaration," "Doctrinal Exposition," and "Epistle." One former employee of the Church History Library said that, when the Proclamation on the Family was issued, "[w]e were receiving calls from all over the place from people wanting to know how many proclamations existed. That was difficult to determine because we could find no clear definition of what a proclamation was exactly and how it differed from 'official declarations' or letters from the First Presidency and the Twelve. . . . [Ultimately], we were told not to try to compile a list of official proclamations to send out."[5] Evidently Church leaders felt more comfortable with ambiguity than they did about making any official distinctions. The four documents included in Matthews's list are the following:

- A Proclamation of First Presidency to Saints Scattered Abroad, signed by Joseph Smith, Sidney Rigdon, and Hyrum Smith on January 15, 1841. This document summarizes the Church's early history and describes the gathering to Nauvoo, Illinois.
- A Proclamation of the Twelve Apostles, published on April 6, 1845 in New York City, and on October 22, 1845 in Liverpool, England. This sixteen-page pamphlet was addressed to the rulers and people of all nations, apparently in response to Doctrine and Covenants 124, which commands Joseph Smith proclaim the gospel "to all the kings of the world, to the four corners thereof, to the honorable president-elect, and the high-minded governors of the nation in which you live, and to all the nations of the earth scattered abroad" (D&C 124:3).
- A Proclamation of the First Presidency and the Twelve Apostles, dated October 21, 1865, and printed in both the *Deseret News* and *Millennial Star*. This document repudiated Orson Pratt's views

---

4. Robert J. Matthews, "Proclamations of the First Presidency and the Quorum of the Twelve Apostles," in *Encyclopedia of Mormonism*, ed. Daniel H. Ludlow (New York: Macmillan, 1992), http://eom.byu.edu/index.php/Proclamations_of_the_First_Presidency_and_the_Quorum_of_the_Twelve_Apostles.

5. Mike Hunter, email message to author, April 26, 2011.

of God and established official channels for conveying Mormon doctrine.

- A Proclamation of the First Presidency and Quorum of the Twelve, issued on April 6, 1980 in commemoration of the 150th anniversary of the Church.

History of the Proclamation on the Family

"The Family: A Proclamation to the World" was introduced to the Church by then-President Gordon B. Hinckley at the General Relief Society Meeting on September 23, 1995. While few Church members at the time were aware of the Church's involvement in the emerging same-sex marriage debate, the timing and use of the document suggest the Proclamation had a deliberate political function. Nevertheless, the document's content did not significantly deviate from twentieth-century Church leaders' discourses and writings. President Hinckley introduced the Proclamation by stressing that it was "a declaration and reaffirmation of standards, doctrines, and practices relative to the family which the prophets, seers, and revelators of this church have repeatedly stated throughout its history."[6] The Proclamation not only states "that marriage between a man and a woman is ordained of God," but it goes on to define gender roles. It stresses that father and mother are "equal partners" in marriage, but it also specifies specific duties for fathers and mothers. According to the Proclamation, the father's duty is to preside, provide, and protect his family, while the mother's duty is to nurture her children. Such a bifurcation of gender roles is not new in Church teachings. They were second-nature to the stereotypical Mormon family of the 1950s and 1960s. But second-wave feminism and the fight over the Equal Rights Amendment (ERA) drove Mormon Church leaders to reaffirm "traditional" values. Few Church leaders were as vocal as Apostle Ezra Taft Benson. Representative of Benson's views is a talk he gave at the October 1981 General Conference:

> Contrary to conventional wisdom, a mother's place is in the home! I recognize there are voices in our midst which would attempt to convince you that these truths are not applicable to our present-day conditions. If you listen and heed, you will be lured away from your principal obligations.

---

6. Gordon B. Hinckley, "Stand Strong against the Wiles of the World," *Ensign*, November 1995, 100, https://www.lds.org/ensign/1995/11/stand-strong-against-the-wiles-of-the-world?.

Beguiling voices in the world cry out for "alternative life-styles" for women. They maintain that some women are better suited for careers than for marriage and motherhood. These individuals spread their discontent by the propaganda that there are more exciting and self-fulfilling roles for women than homemaking. Some even have been bold to suggest that the Church move away from the "Mormon woman stereotype" of homemaking and rearing children. They also say it is wise to limit your family so you can have more time for personal goals and self-fulfillment.[7]

After becoming Church president in 1987, Benson repeated almost verbatim much of this talk in a special fireside for parents. "In the beginning, Adam—not Eve—was instructed to earn the bread by the sweat of his brow," stated Benson. "Contrary to conventional wisdom, a mother's calling is in the home, not in the market place."[8] A *Parents Guide* that was published in 1985 confirmed these gender roles and gave specific instruction that "[g]irls ought to be taught the arts and sciences of housekeeping, domestic finances, sewing, and cooking. Boys need to learn home repair, career preparation, and the protection of women."[9] The Proclamation on the Family thus reaffirms teachings of Church leaders during the second half of the twentieth century, but at the close of that century, with gains in women's rights and changing cultural mores, many of those teachings seemed more antiquated.

By the 1990s, the perceived threat to "traditional" gender values was not coming from the ERA but from the prospect of gay marriage. The Church's concerns about the legalization of same-sex marriage originated a full decade prior to the Proclamation. In August 1984, newly-called apostle Dallin H. Oaks submitted a memorandum to Church leaders that outlined "Principles to Govern Possible Public Statement on Legislation Affecting Rights of Homosexuals." In that document, Oaks stressed his opinion that "the interests at stake in the proposed legalization of so-called

---

7. Ezra Taft Benson, "The Honored Place of Woman," *Ensign*, October 1981, https://www.lds.org/ensign/1981/11/the-honored-place-of-woman.

8. Ezra Taft Benson, "To the Mothers of Zion," address delivered at the Fireside for Parents, February 22, 1987, Salt Lake City. See also Lavina Fielding Anderson, "A Voice from the Past: The Benson Instructions for Parents," *Dialogue: A Journal of Mormon Thought* 21, no. 4 (Winter 1988): 103–13.

9. *A Parent's Guide* (Salt Lake City: LDS Church, 1985), https://www.lds.org/manual/a-parents-guide/chapter-4-teaching-children-from-four-to-eleven-years.

homosexual marriages are sufficient to justify a formal Church position and significant efforts in opposition."[10]

When the Proclamation was issued in 1995, the LDS Church had been actively involved in a campaign against same-sex marriage in Hawaii. In 1990 three same-sex couples sued the state of Hawaii for refusing them marriage licenses. After the circuit court dismissed the case, the couples appealed to the Supreme Court of Hawaii, which ruled that, while the Hawaiian constitution did not guarantee a right to same-sex marriage, denying marriage to a couple based on sexual orientation amounted to discrimination in violation of the constitution's guarantee of equal protection. The judges further required that the government must show a "compelling public interest" in denying marriage to same-sex couples and sent the case back to the lower court for further review.[11] On February 14, 1994, the First Presidency of the LDS Church issued a statement declaring "marriage between a man and a woman is ordained of God," signaling its opposition to "any efforts to give legal authorization to marriages between persons of the same gender," and urging members of the church to "appeal to legislatures, judges and other government officials to preserve the purposes and sanctity of marriage between a man and a woman."[12] A week later, the LDS Church's Hawaii Public Affairs Council announced its intention to petition the court to become a co-defendant

---

10. Dallin H. Oaks, "Principles to Govern Possible Public Statement on Legislation Affecting Rights of Homosexuals," August 7, 1984, https://goo.gl/HZZRsN. Oaks was called as an apostle on April 7, 1984 and the memorandum is dated August 7, 1984. In that memorandum, Oaks speculates that the Equal Rights Amendment may have been used to usher in gay marriage and he also notes the potential "irony" inherent in the Church issuing a statement against same-sex marriage: the Supreme Court case that established that marriage is between one man and one woman is the 1878 Reynolds anti-polygamy decision that ruled against the LDS Church's practice of plural marriages.

11. Richley Crapo, "Chronology of Mormon/ LDS Involvement in Same-Sex Marriage Politics, *Mormon Social Science Association*, January 4, 2008, https://www.mormonsocialscience.org/2008/01/04/richley-crapo-chronology-of-mormon-lds-involvement-in-same-sex-marriage-politics/; Baehr v. Lewin, 74 Haw. 530, 852 P.2d 44 (1993), reconsideration and clarification granted in part, 74 Haw. 645, 852 P.2d 74 (1993).

12. "First Presidency Statement Opposing Same Gender Marriages," Church of Jesus Christ of Latter-day Saints (website), February 1, 1994, https://www.lds.org/ensign/1994/04/news-of-the-church/first-presidency-statement-opposing-same-gender-marriages. It was reiterated in "Church Supports Call for Constitutional

in the Hawaii lawsuit. In that petition, the Church expressed fears that if same-sex marriages became legal the Church might lose its right to issue marriage licenses and that it might be subject to discriminatory lawsuits. However, the court rejected the Church's argument, stating that since state laws force no minister to marry anyone, any lawsuit filed against the Church would be considered frivolous.[13] Around this same time, the LDS Church joined the Roman Catholic Church to form a lobbying group called Hawaii's Future Today.

The Proclamation on the Family was created within this conflict. No author is credited on the document, but it was likely a committee project just as many recent statements issued by the Church have been. It does, however, show strong parallels with Elder Boyd K. Packer's October 1993 General Conference talk, "For Time and All Eternity." In that discourse, Packer states that God's plan requires "the righteous union of male and female," and he described "gender" as existing prior to mortality in the preexistence. While he emphasized that men and women are equal in God's sight, he also stressed that "[b]oth the scriptures and the patterns of nature place man as the protector, the provider," while woman is "the primary nurturer of the children." The Proclamation on the Family not only makes similar points, it uses similar rhetoric.

The Church has consistently employed the Proclamation as a political tool. Soon after the Proclamation was issued in September 1995, it was attached as an appendix to an amicus brief the Church filed with the Hawaii Supreme Court.[14] In November 1995 President Hinckley and Elder Neal A. Maxwell of the Quorum of the Twelve Apostles presented President Bill Clinton and Vice President Al Gore with a copy of the Proclamation on the Family as they met in the White House to discuss ways to strengthen

---

Amendment," *Ensign*, July 2006, http://www.lds.org/ensign/2006/07/news-of-the-church/church-supports-call-for-constitutional-amendment.

13. Kaimipono David Wenger, "'The Divine Institution of Marriage': An Overview of LDS Involvement in the Proposition 8 Campaign," *Journal of Civil Rights and Economic Development* 26, no. 3 (2012), http://ssrn.com/abstract=2254634. The Church appealed the court's decision, and in January 1996 the Hawaii Supreme Court rejected the Church's appeal for standing.

14. Amicus Curiae Brief of The Church of Jesus Christ of Latter-day Saints, Baehr v. Lewin, Hawaii Supreme Court, 91-1394-05, April 14, 1997. It can be found at the The Queer Resources Directory at http://www.qrd.org/qrd/usa/legal/hawaii/baehr/1997/brief.mormons-04.14.97; see also Laura Compton, "From Amici to 'Ohana: The Hawaiian Roots of the Family Proclamation," Rational Faiths, May 15, 2015, https://rationalfaiths.com/from-amici-to-ohana/

families.¹⁵ In March 1997, copies of the Proclamation (in Czech, English, French, Spanish, German, and Russian) were distributed in Prague at the UN World Congress of Families.¹⁶ Framed copies of the Proclamation have been presented to heads of state, foreign dignitaries, and high-ranking U.S. officials, including General Colin Powell, then-Texas governor George W. Bush, then-Idaho governor Dirk Kempthorne; presidents of Mexico, Italy, and French Polynesia; the prime minister of South Korea; the King of Tonga; and political leaders in Brazil and Australia.¹⁷

Likewise, the Church often cites the Proclamation in official public statements about same-sex marriage. When the U.S. Senate considered an

---

15. See "News of the Church," *Ensign*, February 1996, https://www.lds.org/ensign/1996/02/news-of-the-church.

16. "LDS to be at World Congress of Families," *Church News*, February 15, 1997, http://www.ldschurchnewsarchive.com/articles/29738/LDS-to-be-at-World-Congress-of-Families.html; "Church Delegates Attend World Congress of Families," *Ensign*, June 1997, http://www.lds.org/ensign/1997/06/news-of-the-church/church-delegates-attend-world-congress-of-families.

17. "Mission President Visits with Italian Leader," *Church News*, December 7, 1996, http://www.ldschurchnewsarchive.com/articles/27667/Mission-president-visits-with-Italian-leader.html; Michael Leonard, "Apostles Meet with Prominent Media Leaders and Executives," *Church News*, February 8, 1997, http://www.ldschurchnewsarchive.com/articles/29556/Apostles-meet-with-prominent-media-leaders-and-executives.html; "From around the World," *Church News*, December 20, 1997, http://www.ldschurchnewsarchive.com/articles/29539/From-around-the-World.html; "News of the Church," *Ensign*, February 1998, http://www.lds.org/ensign/1998/02/news-of-the-church; Christopher K. Bigelow, "Australia: Coming Out of Obscurity Down Under," *Ensign*, December 1998, http://www.lds.org/ensign/1998/12/australia-coming-out-of-obscurity-down-under; "News of the Church," *Ensign*, June 2000, http://www.lds.org/ensign/1998/02/news-of-the-church; "Solomon Islands Prime Minister Presented with Family Proclamation," *Church News*, February 11, 2011, http://www.lds.org/church/news/solomon-islands-prime-minister; "South Korea," *Ensign*, August 2011, http://www.lds.org/ensign/2011/08/small-and-simple-things/south-korea; "Tonga's LDS Note King's Birthday," *Church News*, July 11, 1998, http://www.ldschurchnewsarchive.com/articles/30890/Tongas-LDS-note-kings-birthday.html; "President Monson Dedicates Temple, Meets with Vice President in Brazil," *Liahona*, October 2008, http://www.lds.org/liahona/2008/10/news-of-the-church/president-monson-dedicates-temple-meets-with-vice-president-in-brazil; Walter Cooley, "Hosts Give Warm Welcome to Visiting Dignitaries," *Ensign*, March 2006, http://www.lds.org/ensign/2006/03/news-of-the-church/hosts-give-warm-welcome-to-visiting-dignitaries.

amendment to the Constitution to protect marriage in 2006, the Church issued a statement. Citing the Proclamation, the Church reaffirmed its opposition to gay marriage and urged members to "express themselves . . . to their elected leaders."[18] Elder Russell M. Nelson referenced it in a speech at a press conference for the Alliance for Marriage at the U.S. Capitol building.[19] It was also featured prominently in the 2008 debate over California's Proposition 8, including in a commentary by the Church's Newsroom.[20]

The Proclamation on the Family certainly motivated members of the Church to participate in the Prop. 8 campaign. Protect Marriage, a political action group opposed to same-sex marriage, estimated that Mormons contributed over half of the $40 million raised to support the amendment and represented between 80 to 90 percent of the early canvassing volunteers.[21]

The Proclamation's Authority

The LDS Church recognizes three authoritative sources of inspiration: the scriptures, the words of modern prophets, and personal revelation. With an open (but relatively set) canon of scripture, the Church anticipates the possibility that its leaders may introduce revelations for the membership to vote to accept as scripture "by common consent" (D&C 26:2; 28:13). Though common in early Mormonism, this practice has become relatively uncommon in the twentieth and twenty-first centuries.[22] Seen as modern prophets, Church leaders can speak for God; however, just what is consid-

---

18. "Religious Marriage Coalition," Mormon Newsroom, April 24, 2006, http://www.mormonnewsroom.org/article/religious-marriage-coalition.

19. "Church Leader Speaks at the U.S. Capitol to Protect Marriage," Mormon Newsroom, June 5, 2006, http://www.mormonnewsroom.org/article/church-leader-speaks-at-the-u.s.-capitol-to-protect-marriage.

20. "The Divine Institution of Marriage," Mormon Newsroom, August 13, 2008, http://www.mormonnewsroom.org/article/the-divine-institution-of-marriage.

21. Jesse McKinley and Kirk Johnson, "Mormons Tipped Scale in Ban on Gay Marriage," *New York Times*, November 15, 2008, http://www.nytimes.com/2008/11/15/us/politics/15marriage.

22. Only two sections of the Doctrine and Covenants have been added in the twentieth century, and one of those was a previously uncanonized revelation of Joseph Smith from 1836. The other was a 1918 revelation by Smith's nephew, Joseph F. Smith, who was president of the Church during the first two decades of the twentieth century. Additionally, Official Declaration 2, which extended the priesthood to all men regardless of race, was added in 1978. None have been added so far in the twenty-first century.

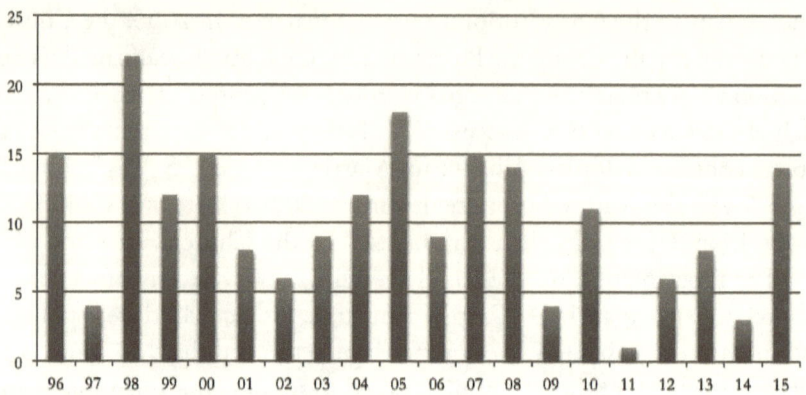

Figure 1. The Proclamation on the Family in LDS Conference Addresses

ered inspired is left to individual members to decide. In 1954, J. Reuben Clark cited a canonized revelation that "whatsoever [Church leaders] shall speak when moved upon by the Holy Ghost shall be scripture, shall be the will of the Lord, shall be the mind of the Lord, shall be the word of the Lord, shall be the voice of the Lord, and the power of God unto salvation" (D&C 68:2–4). Then Clark went on to note that "the very words of the revelation recognize that the Brethren may speak when they are not 'moved upon by the Holy Ghost'; yet only when they do speak as 'moved upon' is what they say considered scripture." In short, Clark argued, "[w]e can tell when the speakers are 'moved upon by the Holy Ghost' only when we, ourselves, are 'moved upon by the Holy Ghost.'"[23]

While it has never been accepted as scripture, the Proclamation on the Family is regarded more authoritatively among Latter-day Saints than any of the other proclamations listed in Robert Matthews's *Encyclopedia of Mormonism* article. Three factors have contributed to its status: references to the Proclamation by leading Church leaders in General Conference addresses, its inclusion in Church curricula and manuals, and its design as an object of religious material culture.

General Conference References to the Proclamation

Since its announcement in 1995 through 2015, the Proclamation on the Family has been mentioned over 160 times in LDS General Conference

---

23. J. Reuben Clark, "When Are the Writings and Sermons of Church Leaders Entitled to the Claim of Scripture?" (address to Seminary and Institute Personnel, Brigham Young University, Provo, UT, July 7, 1954.

Scripture Study		
Marriage		
D&C 42:22	D&C 132:7	"The Family: A Proclamation
D&C 49:15	Genesis 2:24	to the World"
D&C 131:1–4	Ephesians 5:25	
Family		
Mosiah 4:14–15	D&C 130:2	"The Family: A Proclamation
3 Nephi 18:21	1 Timothy 5:8	to the World"
Teach Children		
Alma 56:47	D&C 68:25–30	Ephesians 6:4
Alma 57:21	Moses 6:55–62	Proverbs 22:6

Figure 2. *Preach My Gospel* (2004)

addresses (see figure 1). To put that into context, a similarly designed document that carries the signature of the First Presidency and Quorum of the Twelve, "The Living Christ: The Testimony of the Apostles," has only been mentioned nineteen times within that period since its release at the beginning of the new millennium on January 1, 2000. It is also significant that the frequency of references to the Proclamation on the Family peaked during 2008's debate surrounding California's Proposition 8.

The Proclamation in Church Curricula

The Proclamation is also featured prominently in Church curricula and is found in the following manuals: *Family Home Evening Resource Guidebook*, *Family Guidebook*, *Duty to God* (for young men), *Daughters of My Kingdom* (for young women), *Duties and Blessings of Priesthood* (Melchizedek Priesthood), *The LDS Woman* (Relief Society), *Marriage and Family Relations*, *Eternal Marriage Student Manual* (Church Education Service), and *Preach My Gospel* (the missionary lessons). Significantly, in the *Preach My Gospel* manual the Proclamation is listed in boxes labeled "Scripture Study" (see figure 2), thus equating the Proclamation with scripture in the minds of Church members. And in an October 2010 General Conference talk entitled "Cleansing the Inner Vessel," Packer (then acting as president of the Quorum of the Twelve) stated, "Fifteen years ago, with the world in turmoil, the First Presidency and the Quorum of the Twelve Apostles issued 'The Family: A Proclamation to the World,' the fifth proclamation in the history of the Church. It qualifies according to definition as revelation, and it would do well to members of the Church

> # THE FAMILY
> ## A PROCLAMATION TO THE WORLD
>
> THE FIRST PRESIDENCY AND COUNCIL OF THE TWELVE APOSTLES
> OF THE CHURCH OF JESUS CHRIST OF LATTER-DAY SAINTS
>
> WE, THE FIRST PRESIDENCY and the Council of the Twelve Apostles of The Church of Jesus Christ of Latter-day Saints, solemnly proclaim that marriage between a man and a woman is ordained of God and that the family is central to the Creator's plan for the eternal destiny of His children.
>
> ALL HUMAN BEINGS—male and female—are created in the image of God. Each is a beloved spirit son or daughter of heavenly parents, and, as such, each has a divine nature and destiny. Gender is an essential characteristic of individual premortal, mortal, and eternal identity and purpose.
>
> IN THE PREMORTAL REALM, spirit sons and daughters knew and worshipped God as their Eternal Father and accepted His plan by which His children could obtain a physical body and gain earthly experience to progress toward perfection and ultimately realize their divine destiny as heirs of eternal life. The divine plan of happiness enables family relationships to be perpetuated beyond the grave. Sacred ordinances and covenants available in holy temples make it possible for individuals to return to the presence of God and for families to be united eternally.
>
> THE FIRST COMMANDMENT that God gave to Adam and Eve pertained to their potential for parenthood as husband and wife. We declare that God's commandment for His children to multiply and replenish the earth remains in force. We further declare that God has commanded that the sacred powers of procreation are to be employed only between man and woman, lawfully wedded as husband and wife.
>
> WE DECLARE the means by which mortal life is created to be divinely appointed. We affirm the sanctity of life and of its importance in God's eternal plan.
>
> HUSBAND AND WIFE have a solemn responsibility to love and care for each other and for their children. "Children are an heritage of the Lord" (Psalm 127:3). Parents have a sacred duty to rear their children in love and righteousness,
> to provide for their physical and spiritual needs, and to teach them to love and serve one another, observe the commandments of God, and be law-abiding citizens wherever they live. Husbands and wives—mothers and fathers—will be held accountable before God for the discharge of these obligations.
>
> THE FAMILY is ordained of God. Marriage between man and woman is essential to His eternal plan. Children are entitled to birth within the bonds of matrimony, and to be reared by a father and a mother who honor marital vows with complete fidelity. Happiness in family life is most likely to be achieved when founded upon the teachings of the Lord Jesus Christ. Successful marriages and families are established and maintained on principles of faith, prayer, repentance, forgiveness, respect, love, compassion, work, and wholesome recreational activities. By divine design, fathers are to preside over their families in love and righteousness and are responsible to provide the necessities of life and protection for their families. Mothers are primarily responsible for the nurture of their children. In these sacred responsibilities, fathers and mothers are obligated to help one another as equal partners. Disability, death, or other circumstances may necessitate individual adaptation. Extended families should lend support when needed.
>
> WE WARN that individuals who violate covenants of chastity, who abuse spouse or offspring, or who fail to fulfill family responsibilities will one day stand accountable before God. Further, we warn that the disintegration of the family will bring upon individuals, communities, and nations the calamities foretold by ancient and modern prophets.
>
> WE CALL UPON responsible citizens and officers of government everywhere to promote those measures designed to maintain and strengthen the family as the fundamental unit of society.
>
> *This proclamation was read by President Gordon B. Hinckley as part of his message at the General Relief Society Meeting held September 23, 1995, in Salt Lake City, Utah.*

Figure 3. The Family: A Proclamation to the World (1995)

to read and follow." However, when the talk was published online and in the *Ensign*, Packer's words were revised, stating that the Proclamation "is a guide that members of the Church would do well to read and to follow."[24] Responding to media reports about the revised talk, Church spokesman

---

24. Boyd K. Packer, "Cleansing the Inner Vessel," *Ensign*, November 2010, https://www.lds.org/ensign/2010/11/cleansing-the-inner-vessel.

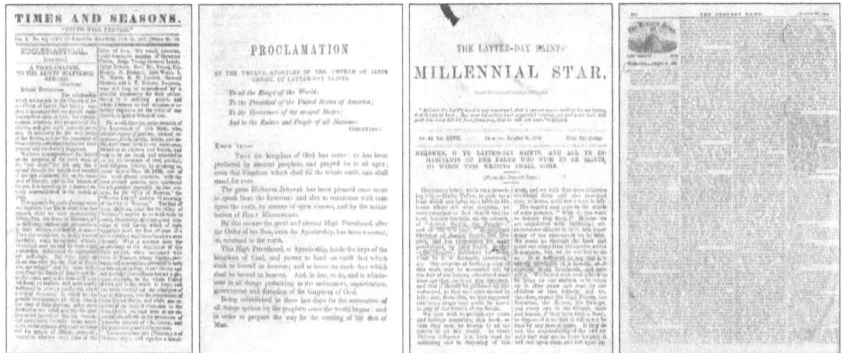

Figures 4–7. Proclamation to Saints Scattered Abroad (*Times and Seasons* 1841); Proclamation of the Twelve to Rulers and People of World (1845); Proclamation of First Presidency and Twelve Apostles on Doctrine (*Millennial Star* 1865); Proclamation of First Presidency and Twelve Apostles on Doctrine (*Deseret News* 1865)

Scott Trotter stated that "the Monday following every general conference, each speaker has the opportunity to make any edits necessary to clarify differences between what was written and what was delivered or to clarify the speaker's intent. . . . President Packer has simply clarified his intent."[25]

Material Presentation of the Proclamation

The authority of the Proclamation is further reinforced by its official-looking design, which has rendered it a "material" manifestation of belief. The document was formatted to look like an official-looking one-page broadsheet in the style of the Declaration of Independence or some other government-issued document (see figure 3). Prior to the 1995 proclamation, the Church had printed no other document quite like it. The proclamation of 1841 was published in the LDS periodical *Times and Seasons* (see figure 4). The proclamation of 1845 was published as a sixteen-page pamphlet both in Liverpool, England, and in New York City (see figure 5). The proclamation of 1865 was published in the Church's Salt Lake City newspaper *The Deseret News* and in its Liverpool-based periodical *Millennial Star* (see figures 6 and 7). And the 1980 proclamation was published in the Church's *Ensign* magazine. While we did find a copy of the 1980 proclamation printed as a one-page broadside (see figure 8), we have not discovered its origins nor any other copies of it. It certainly was not

---

25. "Mormon Church Clarifies Intent of President Boyd K. Packer's Talk," *Deseret News*, October 8 2010, http://www.deseretnews.com/article/700072230/Mormon-church-clarifies-intent-of-President-Boyd-K-Packers-talk.html.

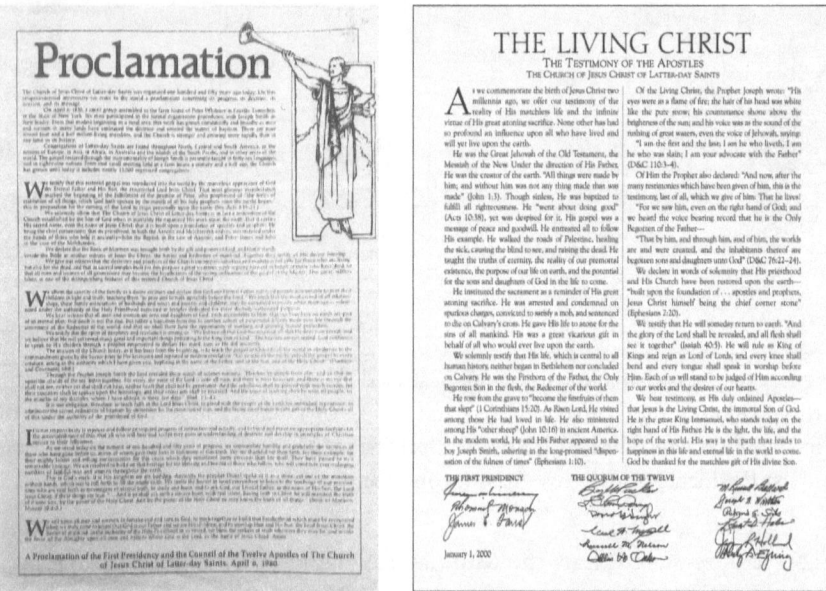

Figures 8–9. Proclamation to the World on 150th Anniversary of Church (1980; BYU Harold B. Lee Library); The Living Christ (2000)

widely disseminated. On the other hand, "about one month" after President Hinckley announced the Proclamation on the Family, the Church Public Affairs department requested that it be available in both 11" x 17" and 8" x 12" printed formats. Approximately three years later, at Packer's request, the Proclamation was also made available as a brochure and sent to priesthood leaders. The Church Education System made the first request to have it framed.[26] By 1998, missionaries in Argentina were inviting members to frame copies of the Proclamation and hang it on their walls.[27] A 2009 "Random Sampler" article from the *Ensign* discusses a display at Salt Lake's Temple Square featuring the Proclamation that was illustrated with pictures of families. Inspired by the exhibit, one Church member reported on how she created a 12-by-12-inch Proclamation scrapbook with family photos. Today, framed copies of the Proclamation, often personalized with or surrounded by family photographs, hang in LDS homes throughout the world.

Interestingly, the Church's statement on "The Living Christ" was formatted in a very similar style to that of the Proclamation on the Family (see figure 9); however, it has received significantly less attention from

---

26. Val Edwards, email message to author, April 29, 2011.

27. Judy C. Olsen, "Argentina's Bright and Joyous Day," *Ensign*, February 1998, http://www.lds.org/ensign/1998/02/argentinas-bright-and-joyous-day.

both Church leaders and members. It is clear that the design elements of the document are not the most significant factor in it becoming such a strong force in LDS culture, but the design does reinforce Church leaders' statements about the Proclamation and its frequent use in curricula.

The status of the proclamation, as we shall see, remains somewhat ambiguous in the minds of Latter-day Saints. Some see it as scripture, some as divine counsel, and others as an expression of institutional position on political matters.

Religion and Cultural Practice

Certainly, Latter-day Saints have internalized the principles enumerated in the proclamation by displaying it in their homes. A class project at Utah Valley University illustrates the relationship many Latter-day Saints have with the proclamation and how we can understand religion as a cultural practice. The class on Mormon Culture centered on Peter Berger's idea of religion as a social construct. In *The Sacred Canopy*, Berger argued that because "the world is built up in the consciousness of the individual by conversation with significant others," our realities are premised on precariously thin threads of conversation.[28] Berger further contends that when these relationships with significant others are interrupted (such as when spouse dies or when we go off to college), those plausibility structures begin to falter. This constructivist idea is particularly relevant in our understanding of the role of the Proclamation because this document has not been canonized—its status is a function of the discursive practices of numerous Latter-day Saints. Furthermore, it arises within a broader spectrum of religious, psychological, cultural, and political discourses regarding gender roles in particular.

Another cultural practice from which to examine the Proclamation is its role as a material artifact. Many Mormons hang the Proclamation on the walls of their homes as a work of art. Such practices affirm David Morgan's claim that material artifacts are important in creating religious identity. Morgan writes: "Language and vision, word and image, text and picture are in fact deeply enmeshed and collaborate powerfully in our sense of the real."[29] The religious community reinforces this material di-

---

28. Peter L. Berger, *The Sacred Canopy: Elements of the Sociological Theory of Religion* (New York: Doubleday, 1967), 17.

29. David Morgan, *Visual Piety: A History and Theory of Popular Religious Images* (Berkeley: University of California Press, 1998), xv.

mension of religious practice. In fact, as noted by Colleen McDannell, much of the discourse and habits engendered in a religious community is attached to the material dimension of religion—access to physical artifacts in turn strengthens one's commitment to religious values and attachment to normative rules.[30] Of course, the Proclamation, as a written (and often framed) document, represents a physical dimension of LDS practice that might reflect such norms, beliefs, and attitudes.

Another dimension of religious practice examined in the Mormon Culture class centers on the distinction (and occasional tension) between institutional (or denominational) religious practice and personal (or spiritual) religiosity. While not mutually exclusive, these elements of religious practices are becoming more and more distinguishable in practice. Institutional religious practice centers on adherence to denominational worship and adherence and loyalty to a church as an institution or body. Personal religiosity emphasizes religion practiced in private or without adherence to dogma or churches per se. Robert Wuthnow's study of religious practice in the United States shows that Americans have been moving away from denominational religion while maintaining deeply held personal religious beliefs since the close of the Second World War.[31] This potential tension between the two approaches is especially relevant among Latter-day Saints because the church functions as a top-down institution with authority-centered discourses from Salt Lake City while at the same time it encourages the populist view of a lay ministry of local congregants.

How do we compare institutional and private religious practice among Mormons? In the Mormon practice, institutional worship might be indicated by references to the prophet and apostles, priesthood authority, priesthood keys, church attendance, paying tithing, obedience (conformity), having a temple recommend, "the Church" or "doctrine," or belief in the historicity and validity of scripture. Personal religiosity, on the other hand, centers on relationship building between the worshiper and deity. In the LDS perspective, signs of private worship might emphasize personal revelation, personal prayer, and belief in God, angels, miracles, charity, or faith.

This distinction between institutional and personal religious practices brings us full circle to our discussion of Liahona Mormons and Iron Rod

---

30. Colleen McDannell, *Material Christianity: Religion and Popular Culture in America* (New Haven: Yale University Press, 1995).

31. Robert Wuthnow, *The Restructuring of American Religion* (Princeton: Princeton University Press, 1988).

Mormons. The Proclamation is a document that can be viewed either through cultural practices that emphasize institutional worship (e.g., Iron Rod Mormons) or personal religious practices (e.g., Liahona Mormons). On the one hand, the institutional foundation of the document is particularly strong. It was presented at a General Relief Society meeting by Church president Gordon B. Hinckley and was signed by the fifteen highest leaders in the Church. It is continually referenced in official publications of the Church, in lesson manuals, and by LDS leaders in General Conference talks. It contains a "prophetic warning" and is often presented to newlyweds after they are sealed in LDS temples. On the other hand, the Proclamation might be read as something that promotes personal religiosity. It isn't canonized, and it doesn't seem to be presented as revelation. Also, it adds a material dimension to religious practices because it is sometimes used as decoration for people's homes (kitsch?). Additionally, much of its content emphasizes personal relationships. The document itself and its history gives rise to potential tension arising between these two religious practices as Latter-day Saints participate in defining their own subjectivity in the context of its message and functioning role as a material object in their homes.

Mormon Culture Class Project

Initially, the Mormon culture class assignment required students to interview couples to learn about the role of material artifacts in their homes. This assignment gave the students an opportunity to observe evidence of the religious subjectivities (personal or institutional) of the Latter-day Saints they interviewed. This wasn't an academic study in the context of having a set of standardized questions and procedural practices typical of academic research. However, as the students filed in with their papers and discussed what they learned, it became apparent that within the LDS culture there was evidence of tension arising between Liahona and Iron-Rod Mormon constructs of the Proclamation.

The class parsed out three major themes that arose in the context of examining the interview transcripts. First, we found that the Proclamation functions both as art and as material proof of religious commitment for some. Second, we learned that in this case, the document was read primarily from an institutional perspective (i.e., most members emphasized the authority of the church and the document itself). One motif was that of fear ("us versus the world") and the other centered on obedience and church authority. Finally, we saw evidence that some Latter-day Saints felt that the Proclamation validated their faith (in terms of spiritual and institutional practices).

Given that the students were interested in how practicing Mormons use art in their homes, it comes as no surprise to learn that the Proclamation functions as a work of art for many of the people interviewed. We discovered a number of dominant themes regarding the Proclamation as a work of art that might be framed and hung in LDS homes. For some who displayed the Proclamation, it served as a personal "reminder" of their beliefs and also as a means of instruction for family members. Furthermore, for some, a physical copy of the Proclamation was displayed to demonstrate their "values" and beliefs to any visitors who might enter their homes. The Proclamation functioned not only to identify one's piety but also as a "missionary tool" that could be used to encourage conversations with visiting non-Mormons. In fact, a few people expressed guilty feelings because they had not hung or displayed the Proclamation in their homes.

One institutional interpretation of the document centered on *fear*— the idea that the Proclamation functions like armor to protect church members from the wicked world outside their homes. This motif gave rise to an "us versus them" rationale with particular emphasis on the politics of same-sex marriage. Here are a few examples:

> "[I]n the world, the wicked world in which we live, a lot of groups are trying to get us to see that there is nothing wrong with being with a homosexual . . . or living that kind of life."

> "The gay business and lesbian set up is so much more pronounced now, even more than it was back then [when the Proclamation was given. . . . And so [the Proclamation] was just given for a little more reinforcement and backbone to that principle. That the church doesn't tolerate that baloney."

Other comments are indicative of the function of the Proclamation as a divine mandate from church leaders. Some saw it as scripture or as revelation. In these examples, members placed emphasis on obedience to leaders and to the authority of the Church itself. These Iron-Rod Mormons where quick to defer to authority figures:

> "[W]e believe that the prophet has given us guidance in strengthening the family, because if the family falls the structure of society is at risk."

> "When my kids say to me, Why are we putting these things up? Because the prophets have asked us to do that."

Others felt that the content of the Proclamations wasn't unique (that it already aligned with what they already had grown up believing as Latter-day Saints), but that it further validates the authority of LDS leaders and the church itself:

> "This was a pretty neat thing for the prophet to come out and say 'All right, world, *this* is what we're saying is a family.' Y'know, so that was kind of a cool thing—at first, I thought 'Well, gee, that's kind of a no-brainer. Why do you have to have a proclamation?' Well, that made it official."

> "You know, we always said that we want to teach our family to be like this, but now it's like we *have* to explicitly teach [our daughter] these things."

For these members, the "common-sense" appeal of the Proclamation was reinforced by appeals to the authority of church leadership.

The third theme centered on members' feeling that the Proclamation itself validated their religious conviction. In other words, it enhanced their faith (at both the institutional and personal levels). For these people, the Proclamation was divinely commissioned and served as evidence of both God's love for them and the prophetic role of the church president. Here are some examples:

> "And I just think that Heavenly Father wanted us to have this Proclamation."

> "Right after it came out, you know, they tried to legalize gay marriage in Hawaii. The Lord knew what was coming."

> "I remember when this came out . . . and this was before so much had come out about same-sex marriage and all that, and I thought, you know the prophet could see what was coming. . . . I mean I know there's been gays and lesbians and stuff for years, but it had not been public and so prominent as it has been since the Proclamation came out."

These interviews conducted by the Mormon Culture class offer insight into the tension arising between denominational (Iron Rod) and private (Liahona) religious practices among the Latter-day Saints they interviewed. These conversations further indicate that many church members are unaware of how the Proclamation came to be. This demonstrates that the document has become canonized in the minds of some Latter-day Saints, not officially, but through repeated references and the discursive practices of church leaders and laity frequently referring to it. Finally, we see indicators that the document appears, at least in these instances, to validate institutional practices more than personal nodes of religiosity, and that for many, this document is seen as a call to arms to fight against gay marriage.

14

PATRIARCHAL BLESSINGS IN THE PROPHETIC DEVELOPMENT OF EARLY MORMONISM

Gordon Shepherd and Gary Shepherd

Bestowing and receiving patriarchal blessings is a religious practice well-known to Latter-day Saints. Outside of LDS circles, however, this practice is not well-known and even less appreciated for its historical connections with the development of early Mormonism. In this chapter, we summarize our argument that patriarchal blessings emerged as a distinctive Mormon ritual for propagating restorationist doctrines and reinforcing the religious commitment of Mormon converts in the face of growing antagonism from religious competitors and secular opponents.[1] The larger conceptual framework of our study concerns the survival problems facing new religions that encounter strong opposition to religious heresy—especially prophetic religions that proclaim new revelation as the basis for their guidance and authority.

The Problem of Commitment in Heretical New Religions

In the face of fierce opposition by established religious traditions and secular authorities—opposition that often includes extra-legal violence as well as relentless legal prosecutions—we may ask: How do heretical new religions sustain their resilience; how do they sustain the resolute commitment of their members? By heretical, of course, we don't mean intrinsically wrong or wicked. We simply mean doctrines and corresponding practices

---

1. These topics are addressed at book-length depth in Gordon Shepherd and Gary Shepherd, *Binding Earth and Heaven: Patriarchal Blessings in the Prophetic Development of Early Mormonism* (University Park: The Pennsylvania State University Press, 2012).

that are at variance with the authority of established orthodoxies.[2] It will not do to simply say that such groups consist of deluded fanatics in the thrall of ego-maniacal leaders. This explains very little.[3] Embattled new religions that endure, and even flourish over time, must effectively appeal to the religious aspirations of some segment of what Rodney Stark and William Bainbridge call a "religious economy."[4] An active religious economy can exist when religious freedom, and therefore religious choice, is countenanced by the political institutions of the state. For a new religion to attract and then retain converts in a religious economy, it must, in the first instance, have market appeal—it must appeal to religious con-

---

2. More specifically, we are employing the term "heretical" from a detached perspective that simply describes (without making a value judgment or implying a technical theological distinction) the way particular religious groups are, in fact, judged by majoritarian or establishment religious denominations. In sociology generally, this would be analogous to the way the concept of social "deviance" is used. Sociologists are not condemning or morally evaluating behavior that is categorized as "deviant." They are simply distinguishing behavior that is socially defined as violating the established norms of a given group from behavior that conforms with the norms of that group. Another closely parallel example would be the way that sociologists of religion employ the term "cult" in a morally neutral way, i.e., simply as a religious innovation (typically generated by the claims of a charismatic founder) that deviates markedly from already existing and socially approved religious faiths, rather than defining it as a fraudulent or criminal perversion of "true" religion. For a more detailed discussion of these points, see Gary Shepherd, "Cults: The Social Psychology of," in *The Blackwell Encyclopedia of Sociology*, ed. George Ritzer (Oxford: Blackwell, 2007), 884–87. For sources on orthodox reactions to heresy and heretical movements in Christian history, see David Christie-Murray, *A History of Heresy* (New York: Oxford University Press, 1989); Gillian R. Evans, *A Brief History of Heresy* (New York: Wiley-Blackwell, 2003); and John B. Henderson, *The Construction of Orthodoxy and Heresy: Neo-Confucian, Islamic, Jewish, and Early Christian Patterns* (Albany: State University of New York Press, 1998). For analyses of the tension between new religious movements and establishment religions and government agencies in American history in particular, see Derek Davis and Barry Hankins, eds., *New Religious Movements and Religious Liberty in America* (Waco, TX: Baylor University Press, 2003).

3. For a summary of what social science research reveals about who joins new religions and why, see Lorne L. Dawson, "Who Joins New Religious Movements and Why: Twenty Years of Research and What Have we Learned?" *Studies in Religion* 25 (1996): 193–213.

4. Rodney Stark and William Sims Bainbridge, *The Future of Religion: Secularization, Revival, and Cult Formation* (Berkley: University of California Press, 1985).

sumers who already are predisposed to certain core values and beliefs but are dissatisfied with what currently is offered by established religions. In the second instance, assuming market appeal, we must ask: Exactly what is it that new religions *do* to preserve, and even strengthen, the faith and loyalty of their converted members when faced with concerted opposition to the promulgation of their putatively heretical beliefs and practices? Those socially fostered attitudes, practices, and rituals that serve to reinforce members' compliance with group requirements, in pursuit of group goals, may be called "commitment mechanisms."[5] Effective commitment mechanisms are an essential aspect of the institutional structure of any enduring organization or community; they are particularly important for understanding the survival-fraught careers of new religious movements.

Taking early Mormonism as a strategic case study,[6] we can address the question of how embattled new religions may survive and even flourish by focusing on one complex of LDS beliefs, rituals, and practices in particular—the institution of patriarchal blessings—that emerged as an important compensatory commitment mechanism in the nineteenth-century Mormon restoration movement. Patriarchal blessings were neither the only nor single most important commitment mechanism operating in early Mormon development—far from it. There is a large range of other religious practices, rules, beliefs, and organizational characteristics that elicited Mormon faith and loyalty in the face of opposition, hardship, and doubt.[7] But because both the content and process of obtaining patriarchal blessings combine and emphasize several key elements of Mormon theology—such as revelation and prophetic guidance, priesthood authority, the millennial end times, building the kingdom of God on earth, lineal continuity with the ancient Israelites as God's covenant people, eternal salvation

---

5. The definition and theory of commitment mechanisms we employ in this paper derives from Rosabeth Kanter, *Commitment and Community* (Cambridge: Harvard University Press, 1972).

6. For years, Rodney Stark has prominently argued that the rise and development of Mormonism constitutes the most significant contemporary case for sociological study of successful new religious movements. A compendium of his published arguments and analysis is found in Rodney Stark, *The Rise of Mormonism*, ed. Reid Nielson (New York: Columbia University Press, 2005).

7. In an earlier study we identified a number of major commitment mechanisms that help explain solidarity in both early Mormonism and the contemporary LDS Church. See Gordon Shepherd and Gary Shepherd, *A Kingdom Transformed: Themes in the Development of Mormonism* (Salt Lake City: University of Utah Press, 1984), 103–46.

through sacrificial obedience, and other related themes—we conclude that patriarchal blessings were a particularly potent vehicle for bolstering early Mormon faithfulness. At the same time, patriarchal blessings were also a means of solidifying and reinforcing convert understanding of unique Mormon tenets by articulating these in powerful, personalized, prophetic language.

Securement of faith and loyalty from followers must, of course, be preceded by an initial attraction to join with a group in the first place. The rise and spread of nineteenth-century Mormonism demonstrates a necessary correspondence between the relative success of a new religion and its market appeal to some segment of a religious economy. Those individuals to whom early Mormonism most appealed were Bible-reading Christians who were seeking a restoration of New Testament visionary religion; they were people already primed to accept and be guided by prophetic pronouncements contained in revelations and blessings as God's word to the contemporary world.[8] While the origins of most prophetic new religions like Mormonism naturally draw attention to the character and claims of their charismatic founders, the actual inception, construction, and subsequent development of enduring new religions also need to be understood as the collective result of like-minded collaborators and devoted disciples in interaction, not only with themselves, but also with outsiders and well-entrenched establishment institutions.

Religious Polarization and the Strong Charisma of Oracular Prophecy

The claim of transcendent authority and supernatural power in support of new or alternative doctrines and practices typically is much stronger for religious converts than claims made on mere grounds of reason or any form of human authority. In particular, it is those prophetic religions that attract followers on the basis of *oracular* prophecy that are most likely to be polarizing religions. As a form of communication, oracular prophecy is typically declarative and highly personalized; it aims to have a stimulating and motivational effect on people's thought and action by announcing a divine message. More specifically, oracular prophecies consist of revelatory pronouncements formulated as the literal voice of God or other divine entities, channeled through prophetic oracles, for instructing, ad-

---

8. Richard L. Bushman, "The Visionary World of Joseph Smith," *BYU Studies* 37 (1997): 183–204.

monishing, and rewarding human actors in exchange for their obedience. Obedience in this context of course means compliance with what are construed as God's laws, commandments, and divine principles that typically set adherents apart from non-believers. The Hebrew Decalogue popularly attributed to Moses's Mount Sinai theophany and Muhammad's dictation of the Holy Qur'an are prime examples of oracular prophecy (simulated in Joseph Smith's religious narrative as prophet and founder of nineteenth-century Mormonism). When formalized in writing and officially certified by the recognized authorities of a particular religious tradition, such pronouncements attain the status of holy writ or scripture for both guiding and judging adherents of the faith.

Oracular prophecy can be contrasted with *inspirational* prophecy. Like oracular prophecy, inspirational prophecy may also be canonized in scripture, but its style of communication typically is expository and less personal. It too aims to stimulate and inspire followers to action in God's name but claims only God's sanction and approval. Inspirational prophecy is less radical than oracular prophecy, less strong and demanding; it does not profess to directly dictate God's verbatim words to the people. For example, *ex cathedra* pronouncements contained in Papal Encyclicals issued by the Catholic Church are considered by Catholics to be revelations of God's will to His vicar on earth but are scarcely expressed in the language of oracular prophecy. In contrast to what might be called the *strong charisma of oracular prophecy*, the milder charisma of inspirational prophecy tends to be less polarizing. One common historical pattern among prophetic religions that, like Mormonism, manage to survive the vicissitudes of their origins and become established denominations in the religious economy is to move from their oracular origins to increasing reliance on less radical forms of inspirational prophecy as their chief mode of guidance.[9]

The strong charisma of oracular prophecy is fundamentally supported by what Gary Wills calls *ultra-supernaturalism*.[10] We can employ this term to highlight the beliefs of actors in the religious economy who insist on the ever-present reality of spirit entities that direct human destiny. Prior to

---

9. The distinction between "oracular" and "inspirational" modes of prophecy, with movement from the former to the latter in Mormon history, is a theme that we expound in Gordon Shepherd and Gary Shepherd, "Prophecy Channels and Prophetic Modalities: A Comparison of Revelation in The Family International and the LDS Church," *Journal for the Scientific Study of Religion* 48, no. 4 (2009): 734–55.

10. Gary Wills, *Head and Heart: American Christianities* (New York: Penguin Press, 2007), 16.

the advent of eighteenth-century enlightenment scholarship and science, such a religious specification would seem largely superfluous in Western culture. Both Catholic and Protestant societies were once dominated by such beliefs. Three hundred years ago there was virtual consensus on the proximate reality of an active spirit world—regardless of the governing religion—which sustained a miraculous rather than a naturalistic worldview. It is only from the vantage point of later, more skeptical centuries, in which Christian belief systems have gradually been tempered and much modified in response to scientific naturalism, that adding the prefix "ultra" to supernatural gives us a useful term for retrospectively describing the most emphatic kinds of supernatural beliefs.

Ultra-supernatural beliefs characterize religious cultures like Mormonism that not only posit the existence of supernatural entities and a spirit world that transcend mundane human existence, but *emphasize the permeability of the boundary separating the spirit world from the natural world.* In the ultra-supernatural worldview various spirit entities are believed to routinely breach the veil between heaven and earth, appearing before human actors in dramatic displays of their super-human powers. At the same time, human reports of being transported in time and space to experience contact with and receive verbal instruction or empowerment from transcendent entities are given reverential credence by believers. Ultra-supernatural beliefs serve to explain virtually every aspect of daily life and human history as the result of supernatural intervention in human affairs. In the monotheistic faith traditions of ancient Judaism and early Christianity and Islam, supernatural intervention was portrayed as an integral element in the struggle between good and evil—literalized in ultra-supernatural beliefs as a ferocious spiritual clash between the evil forces of the devil and the godly forces of heaven. Through the lens of ultra-supernatural belief, human conflicts are interpreted as the dramatic unfolding of this cosmic clash by specifying anthropomorphic, spirit entities—both good and evil—who relentlessly labor to achieve their conflicting ends by deploying miraculous powers and recruiting human agents into the struggle.

Nourished by cultures that sustain an ultra-supernatural world view, the members of new religions founded in oracular prophecy typically believe they have been granted privileged possession of ultimate truth and the efficacious (often times esoteric) means for validating it through various forms of studious inquiry, prayer, meditation, ritual, fasting, substance ingestion, hypnotic trance states, etc. All of the latter, with the exception of substance ingestion and hypnotic states, are recommended by Latter-day Saints as efficacious means for validating the exclusive truth claims of their religion. Patriarchal blessings in particular may be understood as a ritual-practice that Mormons believe constitutes a spiritual medium for revealing God's personalized intentions in the lives of blessing recipients, both individually and collectively as God's covenant people.

As we already have noted, the earliest version of Mormonism in America in the 1830s appealed to denominationally disaffected Christians (like Joseph Smith's father) who nonetheless professed ultra-supernatural beliefs and longed for the prophetic authority and spiritual gifts of New Testament Christianity.[11] As a new religious movement, Mormonism was unequivocally oracular in its mode of development and functioning during the brilliantly implausible career of its founder. Smith exercised the strong charisma of oracular prophecy to build the doctrinal foundation of his followers' faith while also providing decisive organizational leadership. At the same time, early Mormonism's cohesiveness and rapid spread did not depend solely on the oracular prophecy of Joseph Smith. Among a variety of additional factors, it also resulted from the organizational authority given to other individuals among his followers to speak and act in the name of God—to pronounce, in the capacity of various lay priesthood offices, what they believed was revelation from God for the instruction, admonition, guidance, and encouragement of Mormon converts. Empowering other men with priesthood authority to speak in God's name and perform miraculous deeds for individual or localized purposes was a significant element in early Mormonism's democratic appeal.[12]

Chief among these additionally empowered oracles were the patriarchs of the Church who, through their delegated sealing authority, vouchsafed blessings to the people redeemable both on earth and in heaven. For Latter-day Saints, to *seal* a blessing or relationship through priesthood authority signifies making a promised result legitimate and permanent, both in this life and in the life to come. Thus, patriarchal blessings became a highly important element in a constellation of emerging LDS practices

---

11. For summaries of Joseph Smith Sr.'s visionary dreams and antipathy towards sectarian religion, see Richard L. Bushman, *Joseph Smith: Rough Stone Rolling* (New York: Alfred A. Knopf, 2005), 23–37.

12. For a detailed discussion of the appeals of "democratic rationalism" offered by Mormon teachings to early nineteenth-century Americans, see Steven C. Harper, "Infallible Proofs, Both Human and Divine: The Persuasiveness of Mormonism for Early Converts," *Religion and American Culture: A Journal of Interpretation* 10, no. 1 (2000): 99–118.

for strengthening converts' ultra-supernatural faith, reinforcing their doctrinal understanding of what outsiders viewed as a Christian heresy, and infusing them with a sense of their transcendent destiny and fulfillment as God's chosen people for restoring what they believed was true Christianity in the last days of human history.

The Compensatory Ritual Character of Early Patriarchal Blessings

Institutionalized group rituals (as opposed to personal rituals) are formally authorized, scripted actions that typically display the characteristics of a performance.[13] As performance, rituals involve authorized actors who through prescribed speech, symbolic gestures, and scripted actions aim to stimulate and shape the feelings of an audience. Religious studies scholar Aldo Terrin defines ritual as "formal and symbolic behavior that leads to the creation or recreation of an emotion in order to obtain or maintain a correct balance between persons and the world."[14] In religious communities rituals are performed in a variety of contexts and are focused on a wide range of particular group objectives correlated with the community's core beliefs and ultimate concerns. Worship rites and sacraments supplemented by numerous rites of passage ceremonies including marriage and funeral rites, atonement and purification rites, ordinations to office, oaths of allegiance, and various dedication ceremonies are but a few examples of rituals commonly performed in religious communities.

Students of ritual are divided in their views as to what aspects of ritual performance should receive priority attention, the principal alternatives being the particular form rituals take (their scripted gestures and sequential actions, including chanting, singing, rhythmic movements, etc.) or their ideational contents (the manifest and/or latent meanings of what is said or symbolized).[15] The stimulation and renewal of feelings of rever-

---

13. *Informal* rituals enacted in face-to-face encounters in daily life are analyzed in Erving Goffman, *Interaction Ritual: Essays on Face to Face Behavior* (New York: Doubleday Anchor, 1967).

14. Aldo N. Terrin, "Rite/Ritual," in *Blackwell Encyclopedia of Sociology*, ed. George Ritzeer (Malden, MA: Blackwell Publishing, 2007): 3933.

15. For an interdisciplinary set of readings on the variegated characteristics of human ritual, see Ronald Grimes, ed., *Readings in Ritual Studies* (Upper Saddle River, NJ: Prentice Hall, 1995). See also Douglas J. Davies, *The Mormon Culture of Salvation* (Burlington, VT: Ashgate Publishing, 2002) for a focus on analytical assumptions regarding religious rituals in general and LDS salvation rituals in particular.

ence, joy, ecstasy, gratitude, responsibility, unity, devotion, and "spiritual enlightenment" that reinforce group commitment and mutual identification are salient products of ritual participation by community members. Is it primarily the physical form or the ideational content of ritual performances that stimulates and shapes participants' feelings in these ways? The conceptual categories of form and content are not, of course, mutually exclusive in the process of striking "a correct balance between persons and the world." At the same time, it is plausible to assume that the relative importance of these two aspects of ritual performance may shift and vary from one ritual context to another.

In the case of LDS patriarchal blessings, the ideational content of the blessing clearly predominates. The scripted form of patriarchal blessings is simplicity itself.[16] The patriarch lays both his hands on the blessing recipient's head and leaves them there until his benediction is complete. The patriarch wears no special garment or regalia to set him apart from the recipient or other onlookers, nor does he conspicuously display or manipulate religious props or sacred symbols. It is the acknowledged authority of his office and the shared belief that through that authority he receives and communicates God's blessing and intentions for recipients which bestows upon the patriarch a revered religious status in the Latter-day Saint community.

Thus, in the performance of his role, the patriarch himself is a symbol of God's beneficence. The one symbolic gesture he employs in bestowing blessings is the laying on of hands, which signifies God's will and power channeled directly through the patriarch to the blessing recipient. There is no rigidly prescribed wording that must be reiterated by the patriarch in all blessings he bestows, but there is a simple format that is routinely followed. The patriarch begins with an invocation in which he addresses the recipient by name and announces that the blessing is being issued in the name of Deity (usually referencing Jesus Christ). At the blessing's end the patriarch also commonly "seals" his benediction in Christ's name. This latter pronouncement is of paramount significance to Latter-day Saints, signifying as it does a binding and eternal promise in the sight of God.[17] In

---

16. The manner in which LDS patriarchal blessings are bestowed is briefly described in Ariel S. Ballif, "Patriarch: Stake Patriarch," in *Encyclopedia of Mormonism*, ed. Daniel H. Ludlow, 4 vols. (New York: Macmillan, 1992), 3:1064–65.

17. As pointed out by Irene M. Bates and E. Gary Smith, "In many of the Patriarch's blessings he uses the phrase 'I seal you up unto eternal life.' At the time the 'sealing power' was associated with the High Priesthood. . . . Elders

between invocation and benediction the patriarch is at liberty to express whatever communicative content he feels inspired to offer. Thus there is an extemporaneous quality in patriarchal blessings that permits the patriarch to personalize his words to each individual recipient. Because they are regarded by Mormon recipients to be inspired utterances, the patriarch's words are attributed the utmost importance, whose present meanings and future portents are eagerly scrutinized and typically reflected upon as a meaningful guide throughout one's life.[18]

While tears of joy may occasionally be induced by the substantive content of the blessing in behalf of particular individuals, reverential concentration on the meaning of the patriarch's words rather than ecstatic expressions in response to performance gestures is the LDS norm. At the same time, there are common ideational themes that appeared repeatedly in early patriarchal blessings, most of which can only be fully appreciated within the context of early Mormonism's doctrinal development. For LDS converts, belief in the latter-day restoration through the agency of a living prophet and the delegated priesthood authority of the patriarch to pronounce God's word and will to the people in blessing were the primary sources of enhanced feelings of gratitude and rejoicing upon receipt of their personal blessings.

Their many trials and ordeals notwithstanding, in the patriarchal blessings of early Latter-day Saints it was the projection of themselves as God's chosen servants in the last days and their transcendent destiny to participate in the realization of the divine plan of human salvation that produced shared feelings of a "correct balance" between themselves and the world. Embattled new religions like nineteenth-century Mormonism must struggle with the discrepancy between their members' convictions of divine mission and special favor in the sight of God and their denigrated, marginal standing in the world. Their material hardships and social marginalization must somehow be compensated by faith in an ultimate reward and shared

---

who were members of the High Priesthood used this sealing power in the early 1830s. . . . The sealing power of the patriarchate became of record in 1841 with the revelation set forth in Doctrine and Covenants 124:93 and 124." Irene M. Bates and E. Gary Smith, *Lost Legacy: The Mormon Office of Presiding Patriarch* (Urbana: University of Illinois Press, 2003), 49.

18. For a discussion of the social science significance of qualitative analysis of "religious talk"—the religious language used by believers—see Robert Wuthnow, "Taking Talk Seriously: Religious Discourse as Social Practice," *Journal for the Scientific Study of Religion* 50, no. 1 (2011): 1–21.

triumph as compensation for their current sacrificial devotion. Themes of ultimate compensation and triumph were, in fact, major motifs in early patriarchal blessings.[19] In part we may thus describe early patriarchal blessings as *compensatory* commitment rituals.[20] Their compensatory functions were further enhanced by the fact that not only were they pronounced orally, they also were recorded by a scribe. Written copies subsequently were given to blessing recipients to treasure in their possession as sacred documents to be pondered, guided by, and even passed on to their children as tangible testimonials of God's power and beneficence through the restored priesthood medium of his chosen servants.[21]

---

19. Shepherd and Shepherd, *Binding Earth and Heaven*, 75–87.

20. The social psychological notion of religious compensators is formally spelled out by Rodney Stark and William Sims Bainbridge in their influential article "Towards a Theory of Religion: Religious Commitment," *Journal for the Scientific Study of Religion* 38, no. 2 (1979): 287–307. In brief, Stark and Bainbridge regard religious organizations as systems that specialize in general, supernaturally-based "compensators." Compensators are defined as intangible substitutes for material rewards that cannot be unequivocally demonstrated but are nevertheless highly valued. Thus, compensators function *as if* they were rewards, and religious adherents are willing to expend costs to obtain them. Employing Stark and Bainbridge's language, the contingent promises contained in patriarchal blessings may be described as supernatural compensators conferred upon blessing recipients in exchange for their faithful commitment to the teachings of the restored gospel and loyal obedience to LDS priesthood authority. It should also be noted that ritual practices are often polysemic in their social and psychological consequences—that is, they may be understood as serving multiple interrelated functions. Thus, in addition to their compensatory commitment function, solidarity and doctrinal functions may also be attributed to patriarchal blessings.

21. While patriarchal blessings are unique in their particulars, other religious faith traditions also offer ritualized blessings (albeit much more generic) to their communicants. See Samuel Balentine, *Prayer in the Hebrew Bible: The Drama of Divine Human Dialogue* (Minneapolis, MN: Augsburg Fortress Publishers, 1993); Joseph Jungmann, *Christian Prayer through the Centuries* (Mahwah, NJ: Paulist Press, 2008); and Thomas Lindgren, "The Narrative Construction of Muslim Prayer Experiences," *International Journal for the Psychology of Religion* 15, no. 2 (2005): 159–74. Likewise, statements included in patriarchal blessings concerning blessing recipients' character and future prospects are superficially similar to "readings" given by astrologers, numerologists, spiritualist mediums, and other kinds of "diviners." But even if electronically recorded, relatively few of these kinds of pronouncements are routinely transcribed and given to recipients as sacred artifacts to treasure and preserve, as is the case with Mormon blessing recipients.

The Communal Character of Early Patriarchal Blessings

Shared feelings evoked through the enactment of ritual performances serve to renew and strengthen the bonds that unite members of a community. This is particularly true when rituals are performed in social settings in which like-minded individuals, who already share core values and beliefs, are assembled together. In his newly ordained capacity as Presiding Patriarch to the Church, the blessings Father Smith (Joseph Smith Sr.) began bestowing on Mormon converts in Kirtland, Ohio, were, in Lavina Fielding Anderson's words, "quasi-public affairs."[22] Blessing meetings in Kirtland initially were conducted in people's homes, with members and family members typically present, as well as other LDS neighbors. At these meetings, multiple individuals would often be blessed in sequence, accompanied by group prayer and hymn singing. The ritual function of producing feelings of community solidarity and shared commitment was undoubtedly amplified when patriarchal blessings were publicly issued in these kinds of group settings.

Blessing meetings were also occasionally combined with "feast" meetings. Mark Staker's account of the early development of LDS Church doctrine and organization in Kirtland, for example, notes that a "pattern developed that combined meetings at which members received patriarchal blessings from Joseph Smith Sr. with a dinner 'for the poor.'" Staker goes on to quote an early convert, Ira Ames, in Kirtland on March 13, 1834, as saying: "I received my Patriarchal Blessing under the hands of Joseph Smith Senior at a feast and blessing meeting which I made at my house for the widows and orphans. . . . [I]t was a very pleasant time, a glorious meeting." Similarly, Staker writes that early Kirtland stalwarts "N. K. and Ann [Whitney] hosted the blessing meeting and feast at which Samuel and Susanna Whitney received their patriarchal blessings along with other individuals. It was a special event, three days of celebrations the likes of which had never before been seen in Kirtland." Staker also quotes Ann Whitney saying of this occasion, "According to our Savior's pattern and agreeably to the Prophet Joseph's and our own ideas of true charity and disinterested benevolence, we determined to make a feast for the poor,

---

22. Lavina Fielding Anderson, "Dreams of Power: The Patriarchal Blessings of Joseph Smith Sr.," paper presented at the 2010 annual meeting of the Mormon Historical Society, Kansas City, Missouri, 14. Copy in authors' possession.

such as we knew could not return the same to us; the lame, the halt; the deaf; the blind; the aged and infirm."²³

Patriarchal blessings given in conjunction with "feast meetings for the poor" further served to reinforce members' feelings of mutual identification and commitment to the egalitarian ideals of Zion. Once the Kirtland Temple was dedicated in 1836, blessing meetings were conducted in the temple assembly hall where Father Smith sometimes presided over meetings of the Kirtland High Council.²⁴ Like religious gatherings in general, blessing meetings served an important community function in which church members' commitments were publicly reiterated and mutually reinforced. As Anderson points out, the sacred character (or supernatural valence) attached to patriarchal blessings undoubtedly was enhanced even more strongly when pronounced in the temple of the Lord, which itself had been ritually dedicated for the purpose of conducting God's work on earth.²⁵ In contrast, today's LDS patriarchal blessings are routinely issued to individual members in private rather than public settings.²⁶ One plausible historical inference to be drawn from the fact that LDS patriarchal blessings have become privatized is that their commitment function has changed (if not weakened) over time, an inference which we address further at the conclusion of this essay.

Anderson also remarks on Father Smith's bolstered status at communal blessing meetings as Church Patriarch and the corresponding prayerful sincerity with which he issued blessings to the faithful. As illustrative examples, Anderson writes that "as a prelude to blessing the forty-two-year-old Jemima Johnson, the venerable sixty-five-year-old Joseph said, 'I pray to show me by his vision his will and his blessing for thee. I want to speak to thee just as God would speak should he now lay his hands on thy head to bless thee.'"²⁷ Similarly, in other blessings the Patriarch prayed: "Sister [Rebecca] Williams, in the name of Jesus Christ of Nazareth I lay

---

23. Mark Staker, *Hearken, O Ye People: The Historical Setting for Joseph Smith's Ohio Revelations* (Salt Lake City: Greg Kofford Books, 2009), 244–45. For documented references to other blessing meetings in Kirtland, see Bates and Smith, *Lost Legacy*, 38–39, 44, 48–49.

24. Bates and Smith, *Lost Legacy*, 43.

25. Anderson, "Dreams of Power," 14.

26. This significant institutional change of the standard social setting in which patriarchal blessings are bestowed is analyzed in Shepherd and Shepherd, *Binding Earth and Heaven*, 108–110.

27. Anderson, "Dreams of Power," 14.

my hands upon thy head, and I ask my heavenly Father to put words and thoughts into my heart, and also, to prepare thee for a blessing,"[28] and, "Sister Mary [Baldwin], In the name of Jesus Christ I pray God the Father, that thou mayest be as Mary at the feet of Jesus that thou mayest be blessed with the ministry of angels."[29] On behalf of Lorenzo Snow, the Patriarch prayed: "I ask God the Eternal Father, who has called me to the office of the priesthood, to open the visions of my mind and give me the Holy Spirit."[30] Such prayerful petitions expressed and reinforced the revelatory premise shared by both the patriarch and his blessing recipients that the veil separating heaven and earth had been made permeable through the agency of God's latter-day oracles, reemphasizing to believers the charismatic authority invested in the office of the patriarch.

Patriarchal blessings were authoritatively pronounced, using first person biblical language as though God, through the agency of the patriarch, was speaking directly and personally to each blessing recipient. The patriarchs' blessings employed prophetic rhetoric similar to the oracular language modeled by Joseph Smith Jr. in his published revelations on Church government and doctrine. While these blessings were limited to individual cases and did not establish official doctrine or Church policy, patriarchal blessings administered to believing Latter-day Saints were nevertheless charged with supernatural valence. Like the prophet Joseph (albeit comparatively circumscribed in the scope and organizational impact of their pronouncements) the Smith patriarchs in their hereditary turn were believed to have revelatory power as authoritative conduits of God's grace and inspiration for His covenant people. Sociologically, we can appreciate how these early blessings served as a powerful compensatory mechanism for reinforcing converts' solidarity and commitment to their new religion and to their leaders' priesthood authority in the face of sustained adversity. They were taken very seriously by early converts, who felt privileged to be blessed by Joseph Sr.—revered as the father of God's latter-day prophet—and later, in succession, by the prophet's brothers Hyrum and William when they assumed the hereditary mantel of Church Patriarch.

In discussing the communal character of early patriarchal blessings, it should also be mentioned that patriarchs, beginning with Joseph Sr., were remunerated financially (as were their scribes and recorders) for the

---

28. Michael Marquardt, *Early Patriarchal Blessings of the Church of Jesus Christ of Latter-day Saints* (Salt Lake City: The Smith-Pettit Foundation, 2007), 44.

29. Marquardt, 84.

30. Marquardt, 94.

blessings they issued.[31] This anomalous practice—Latter-day Saints have always prided themselves on sustaining an unpaid lay clergy—was halted in 1914, and consequently patriarchal blessings have been given gratis to individuals deemed worthy and who seek them in faith and humility.[32] In any event, the modest cost of early patriarchal blessings did not dampen members' anxious desire to obtain them, nor were pecuniary motives commonly imputed by cynics to the Smith patriarchs' exercise of their office.

Hebraic Links: Patriarchal Blessings and Covenental Priesthood Lineage

As we have emphasized, the extemporaneous words pronounced in patriarchal blessings by the Smith patriarchs were received with heartfelt gratitude. They were considered to be the inspired word of God, addressed directly and personally to individual blessing recipients and, in conformity with the ideology of the restoration, constituted an important form of prophetic revelation. The LDS notion of restoration, however, includes far more than a renewal of prophetic communication with God, reaching back, as it does, to incorporate theological and ritual elements from the Hebraic origins of Christianity. LDS patriarchal blessings were modeled on the Old Testament account of Israel blessing his sons.[33] The institution of the office of Church Patriarch and the priesthood sealing authority of his blessings were important elements in the expanding Mormon comprehension of the latter-day restoration, which included literal kinship with the ancient Hebrews as God's covenant people. Thus, in conjunction with his bestowal of personal blessing, the Church Patriarch typically discerned blessing recipients' lineages as descendants from one of the Twelve Tribes of Israel. Increasing Mormon emphasis on lineal descent and identification with ancient Israel appears, at least in part, to have arisen from Joseph Smith's preoccupation with the issue of religious authority—an issue that underlay the justification of virtually every LDS doctrinal and organizational innovation. It is the creative amalgamation of Old Testament and New Testament religious claims in the Mormon restoration that supports Jan Shipps's influential thesis that

---

31. Bates and Smith, *Lost Legacy*, 38.
32. Bates and Smith, 160.
33. Marquardt, *Early Patriarchal Blessings*, vii.

Mormonism is not merely another Christian sect but constitutes a new religious tradition in the world religious economy.[34]

According to D. Michael Quinn, the practice of prophetically confirming Latter-day Saints' Hebraic lineage through patriarchal blessings institutionalized a nascent "tribalism," which already had been developing in early Mormonism, resulting in the formation of sharp moral boundaries separating Mormons from non-Mormons.[35] Congruent with Quinn's analysis, Shipps argues that it was the overlay of a strong Hebraic dimension to Mormonism's Christian restorationist claims that ultimately "would carry the Saints beyond the metaphorical Christian understanding of adoption into Israel to a conviction that the actual blood of Israel coursed through their veins. For the Mormons, this conviction separated humanity into two camps: those who were members of Abraham's family and those who were not. The former (Latter-day Saints and Jews) were God's chosen people; all the rest were Gentile."[36] Correspondingly, in conjunction with the development of temple rituals (including celestial marriage) and the associated doctrines of deification, Shipps persuasively argues that Mormonism's identification with ancient Israel as God's chosen people shifted public perception of the Mormons as merely another contentious Christian sect in the religious economy to being an altogether alien entity.

In heretical contrast to the priesthood doctrines of most New Testament Christians, Joseph Smith argued for a continuation of priesthood authority from the beginning of the Old Testament era to the present day. The priesthood of God, as envisioned in the Book of Mormon and specified in some of Joseph Smith's earliest revelations, was viewed as eternal. Smith and subsequent Mormon theologians maintained that various orders of the priesthood (Melchizedek and Aaronic) were never abrogated, discontinued, or supplanted by a "new priesthood" with the advent of New Testament Christianity.[37] According to Mormon teachings,

---

34. Jan Shipps, *Mormonism: The Story of a New Religious Tradition* (Urbana: University of Illinois Press, 1985).

35. D. Michael Quinn, "Us-Them Tribalism and Early Mormonism," *John Whitmer Historical Association Journal* 29 (2009): 94–114.

36. Jan Shipps, "Difference and Otherness: Mormonism and the American Religious Mainstream," in *Minority Faiths and the American Protestant Mainstream*, ed. Jonathan D. Sarna (Urbana: University of Illinois Press, 1998).

37. A careful textual analysis of the development of early LDS priesthood doctrines can be found in Gregory Prince, *Power from on High: The Development of Mormon Priesthood* (Salt Lake City: Signature Books, 1995).

the eternal priesthood first entrusted to the ancient Hebrew patriarchs and later transmitted by Jesus to his disciples had to be restored directly— that is to say, literally passed on by those who previously possessed it. In the narrative claims of Mormon ecclesiology, both the Aaronic and Melchizedek priesthoods were restored through the laying on of hands by John the Baptist and the apostles Peter, James, and John respectively, who ostensibly appeared to Joseph Smith and Oliver Cowdery sometime in 1829 to delegate them with the authority to restore Christ's church.[38] Here we see a prime example of the kind of supernatural literalism that appealed so strongly to early Mormon converts. To them, accounts of ministering angels, heavenly messengers, and departed spirit agents clinched rather than diluted their enthusiastic acceptance of the restored gospel as proclaimed by Joseph Smith.

As they came to understand Smith's revelations, the restored priesthood signified divine authority *and* a covenantal relationship with the God of both the Old and New Testaments. Congruent with the Calvinistic theology of their New England ancestors, Mormons construed themselves as a "covenant people," both collectively and individually. The notion of sacred covenants between God and His children, in which the deity proffers blessings in exchange for solemn promises to obey His laws, informs virtually every aspect of LDS doctrine and corresponding religious practices. Mormons contend that God's proffered covenants, and the proper ritual means by which they are to be symbolically enacted (as in baptism or marriage), must come through revelation and the authority of the restored priesthood.[39] Thus, belief in the literal restoration of the priesthood through the supernatural intervention of agents from the spirit world not only meant Mormon converts were properly authorized to act in God's name, it also signified to

---

38. In his 1838 personal history (elaborating on his earlier 1830 and 1832 accounts), Joseph Smith gave the date of John the Baptist's visitation, returning to earth as a celestialized being, as May 15, 1829. See Joseph Smith et al., *History of the Church of Jesus Christ of Latterday Saints*, ed. B. H. Roberts, 7 vols., 2nd ed. rev. (Salt Lake City: Deseret Book, 1948 printing), 1:39–41. In 1830 Smith avowed that he and Cowdery had received the Melchizedek Priesthood and been ordained to the Apostleship by Peter, James, and John—also now celestialized beings—but gave no specific date for this event, which reportedly occurred sometime in May 1829 subsequent to the restoration of the Aaronic Priesthood through John the Baptist. See Doctrine and Covenants 27:12.

39. On LDS covenant making, see Rex Cooper, *Promises Made to the Fathers: Mormon Covenant Organization* (Salt Lake City: University of Utah Press, 1990).

them that they were covenantal heirs of God's promises to the children of Abraham, Isaac, and Jacob. And in particular, through the lineage of Jacob's favored son, Joseph, they were proclaimed heirs of the promises to the Tribes of Ephraim and Manasseh, who formed the House of Joseph. Quite literally, in fact, early Mormons believed they were descended from the fabled "Ten Lost Tribes" of Israel, whose members were presumed to have dispersed throughout the world dating from the Babylonian Captivity in 721 BCE (hence the designation of one's lineage given in patriarchal blessings to recipients). A major impetus of early Mormon proselytizing was to gather Israelite descendants from among the nations and bring them together as a people again to build up Zion and receive at long last their promised blessings in the latter days of human history.[40]

Thus, in doctrinal tandem with the institutionalization of patriarchal blessings was the LDS elaboration of Christian restoration theology, which very quickly went beyond mere revival of spiritual gifts and the New Testament apostolic church. What increasingly set the Latter-day Saints apart theologically from other restorationist groups was their insistence that, through the restored priesthood, God had authorized Joseph Smith to usher in what they believed was the "last dispensation of the fullness of times." The last dispensation was designated as the end-time or latter-days of human history in which the "fullness" of God's plan of salvation would be revealed as part of the "restoration of all things" (D&C 6:3; 50:2).[41] The restoration of all things significantly included Old Testament covenants and institutions, such as patriarchal priesthood authority, prophetic guidance, temple worship, and—most controversially—plural marriage, as well as the promise of an inheritance in Zion, where God would dwell with His covenant people.[42] These distinctively Mormon restorationist claims dovetailed with the emerging sealing ceremonies performed in

---

40. For a definitive discussion of LDS lineage beliefs and their wide-ranging implications and consequences for modern Mormonism, see Armand Mauss, *All Abraham's Children: Changing Mormon Conceptions of Race and Lineage* (Urbana: University of Illinois Press, 2003).

41. For commentary and exposition by one of Hyrum Smith's grandsons (and tenth president of the LDS Church), see Joseph Fielding Smith, *The Restoration of All Things* (Salt Lake City: Deseret Book, 1945). See also Steven Harper, "The Making of Modern Scripture: Latter-day Saints and the Book of Commandments and Revelations," *Mormon Historical Studies* 10, no. 2 (2008): 31–39.

42. For a historical account of the institution of plural marriage, see Richard S. Van Wagoner, *Mormon Polygamy: A History* (Salt Lake City: Signature Books, 1989).

LDS temples and the corresponding doctrines of "exaltation" and eternal life in God's celestial kingdom.[43]

In oracular voice and approaching the end of his meteoric life, Joseph Smith expounded on the sealing power of the restored priesthood and the "keys" of this power which made delegation of authority in the Church possible (including, by inference, the patriarch's authority to bless the people):

> All covenants, contracts, bonds, obligations, oaths, vows, performances, connections, associations, or expectations, that are not made and entered into and sealed by the Holy Spirit of promise, of him who is anointed, both as well for time and all eternity, and that too most holy, by revelation and commandment through the medium of mine anointed, whom I have appointed on the earth to hold this power . . . are of no efficacy, virtue, or force in and after the resurrection of the dead; for all contracts that are not made unto this end have an end when men are dead. (D&C 132:7)[44]

The purported sealing power of the restored priesthood and the delegated keys to its exercise have become the central doctrines which, in conjunction with fundamental belief in contemporary revelation, bind the faith and commitment of Latter-day Saints in compliance with the directives of both their local congregational leaders and the general authorities of the LDS Church.

Excerpts from Early Patriarchal Blessings Illustrating Prophetic Commitment Language

To illustrate the prophetic mode of language and some of the doctrinal themes commonly contained in early LDS blessings, we have selected portions of blessings issued by the first three Church patriarchs, Joseph Smith Sr., Hyrum Smith, and William Smith, in the years between 1834 and 1845. All of these blessings, and over 700 others, can be found in Michael Marquardt's compilation *Early Patriarchal Blessings of the Church*

---

43. For a chronological analysis of the development and adaptive change of LDS temple practices in conjunction with other developments in Mormon history, see Devery Anderson, *Development of LDS Temple Worship, 1846–2000: A Documentary History* (Salt Lake City: Signature Books, 2010); and David John Buerger, *The Mysteries of Godliness: A History of Mormon Temple Worship* (Salt Lake City: Signature Books, 2002).

44. This disquisition on priesthood sealing power was prefatory to the lengthy revelation Joseph Smith announced in justification of the doctrine and practice of plural marriage; see the remainder of Doctrine and Covenants 132:15–66.

of Jesus Christ of Latter-day Saints. Through the delegated sealing power of their patriarchal office, the Smith patriarchs' compensatory blessings were considered by church members to be efficacious both on earth and in heaven, for time and eternity.

The following excerpt is from the patriarchal blessing of Charles C. Rich, pronounced by Joseph Smith Sr. on April 2, 1836, in Kirtland, Ohio.[45]

> Brother Charles, in the name of Jesus Christ of Nazareth, I lay my hands upon thy head and seal blessings according to the power of the holy priesthood. . . . Thou art a Son of Zion and have been willing to lay down thy life for thy brethren. . . . Thou art a son of Joseph, an Ephraimite by blood. The Lord hath looked on thee from the beginning and chosen thee from the foundation of the world to be a polished shaft in his quiver. . . . [T]hy name is sealed in heaven, never to be blotted out. . . . Satan shall have no power over thee. . . . [T]he Lord is thy deliverer, and thy life is hid with Christ in God and shall be kept from the destroyer. . . . [T]hou shalt preach the gospel till the Savior comes in the clouds of heaven. . . . Thy posterity shall be blessed after thee and thy blessing shall reach unto thy children . . . and they shall reign with thee in the kingdom of heaven on earth, for thou art one of the hundred and forty and four thousand, which will stand upon Mount Zion with white robes. . . . Thou shalt gather thousands to Zion. . . . Thou shalt weep over them when thou seest their calamities and seek them out and send them up to Zion. . . . Thou shalt be a blessing to all wherever you shall go . . . and thou shalt have all the power of the holy priesthood. . . . These blessings I seal for thee in the name of Jesus.

This next excerpt is from the patriarchal blessing of Susanna White, pronounced by Hyrum Smith on September 8, 1841, in Nauvoo, Illinois.[46]

> Susanna, I lay my hands upon your head, in the name of Jesus of Nazareth, to bless you . . . for your benefit and the benefit of your posterity and kinsfolk, that you might have a name in Israel, as a daughter of Abraham in the lineage of Joseph . . . and as a mother in Israel . . . to receive the honor of that blessing in the fullness of time. . . . I seal upon your head the gift of eternal life . . . in connection with one who holdeth the keys for the knowledge of God . . . even the fullness of the revelations of Jesus Christ in these last days. . . . The Lord has looked upon your integrity . . . and called you from your

---

45. Marquardt, *Early Patriarchal Blessings*, 68. Charles C. Rich was an early Mormon convert (1831) who, subsequently, in 1849, was called by Brigham Young to be a member of the Quorum of the Twelve Apostles.

46. Marquardt, 205–6. Biographical information on Susanna White does not appear to exist beyond this recorded blessing, which identifies her as a probable British convert and a member of the Church in good standing at the time.

native country, from your kinfolk, in answer to the prayers of your fathers. . . . Notwithstanding . . . tribulation awaits you, trials, sorrowing. In them you shall be sustained and supported by the grace of God in the hour of your deepest affliction . . . the truth of these promises shall have this sign . . . another Comforter, that when you read these lines you will feel glad in your heart, which Comforter is the promise of eternal life. Your children shall have the priesthood and their names shall be honored in the midst of the princes of Israel. . . . [Y]our years shall be many and you shall receive an inheritance in time and eternity.

The last excerpt is from the patriarchal blessing of Levi Runyan, pronounced by William Smith on July 30, 1845, in Nauvoo, Illinois.[47]

Beloved brother, I lay my hands upon your head in the name of the Lord Jesus Christ. . . . [T]he priesthood after the holy order with all the powers and privileges shall be sealed upon thy head, with appointments and ordinations greater than thou hast yet received . . . even that exaltation that belongs to the servants of the most high God. . . . [T]he Holy Spirit shall be given unto thee. . . . [T]he heavens shall be opened. Angels shall be sent to administer unto thee, and by visions and dreams the will of God shall be unfolded. . . . Unto thee is appointed to a great work. . . . [E]nemies may deride thee and scoff . . . yet thy courage shall increase . . . and by wisdom that cometh from on high none can resist the power of thy testimony. . . . [T]hese are the days of tribulation, the time of wars and rumors of war. . . . [T]hou shalt rise up like Melchisedec of old to establish peace in the land and gather out the lost sheep of the house of Israel. . . . [T]hou shalt see Zion go forth . . . and all who battle against it shall be brought to naught. . . . [A]nd *if thou art faithful* . . . thou shalt come up on Mount Zion as a Savior of many of your brethren who are of the seed of Joseph, whose blood thou art. . . . [T]his shall be thy ministry, thy glory, thy power, and thy salvation, for I seal it upon thy head in the name of Jesus Christ.

While the general substance and form of early patriarchal blessings given to thousands of blessing recipients were often repetitious, they were pronounced extemporaneously and therefore displayed a certain range of idiosyncratic variation, as can be seen in the above excerpts. At the same time, the overall thematic unity of these early blessings is also evi-

---

47. Marquardt, 366–67. Levi Runyan was a relatively new Mormon convert at the time of his blessing. He subsequently joined the Mormon flight from Nauvoo, Illinois, in early 1846 and, while en route with those refugees that followed Brigham Young, was among the five hundred men recruited by the US Army in 1847 to serve in the short-lived Mexican War as a member of the "Mormon Battalion."

dent. They were permeated with the religious hopes and aspirations of the Mormon restoration and employed phrasing and concepts that resonated with and reinforced specific Mormon doctrines.[48] In spite of their lack of formal rhetorical training, all three Smith patriarchs had a good command of religious language and were even capable of eloquence in the blessings they bestowed upon the Latter-day Saints. This, no doubt, was additional evidence to blessing recipients that the words of the patriarchs were inspired of God, and the ultimate veracity of their blessings was accepted with humility and gratitude as a transcendent beacon of hope and inspiration in their lives.

Conclusion

It is both the commitment and doctrinal exposition functions of these blessings in the lives of the early Latter-day Saints—Mormonism's original converts—with which we are concerned in this essay. To what extent *current* patriarchal blessings continue to serve these functions in modern Mormonism is, we would say, an open question.

Over time, humanly constructed institutions, including religious institutions, are subject to a wide assortment of interrelated changes in which the stabilizing authority and functions of venerable group practices may be modified, supplemented, or superseded by new institutional forms. This elementary fact of human social life is highlighted in the history of the office of Church Patriarch and the ritual-practice of bestowing patriarchal blessings in the LDS Church. In the Presiding Patriarch's stead today, hundreds of stake patriarchs administer thousands of blessings annually to church members residing in LDS stakes throughout the world.[49] No longer under the general jurisdiction of a Presiding Patriarch, stake pa-

---

48. The twenty most salient blessing themes in our statistical content analysis of early patriarchal blessings from 1834 to 1845 were, in order of their relative salience: salvation and eternal life; lineage; posterity; Zion; priesthood; faith; spirit; afflictions; husbands; material blessings; spiritual blessings; knowledge and understanding; end times; Israel; good name and reputation; power; Kingdom; gospel; covenants; and angels. See Shepherd and Shepherd, *Binding Earth and Heaven*, 75–87.

49. As of 2012 there were 3,005 LDS stakes organized throughout the world with local jurisdiction over a total of 29,014 wards/branches. See "Statistical Report, 2012," Church of Jesus Christ of Latter-day Saints (website), https://www.lds.org/general-conference/2013/04/statistical-report-2012.

triarchs are subject to the local authority of LDS stake presidents and have been given standard guidelines to follow in administering their blessings.[50]

We see in the institution of LDS patriarchal blessings a clear example of the routinization of charisma in the development of new religions that not only survive the hazards of their origins but, over successive generations, grow and even flourish by making accommodating adjustments in their doctrines and organizational practices. In the Mormon case this process prominently has featured a transition from the strong charisma of Joseph Smith's early oracular revelations to increasing reliance on the milder and less polarizing charisma of inspirational guidance, which is closely regulated by an ecclesiastical hierarchy. Diminution and eventual elimination of the office of Presiding Church Patriarch and increasing standardization and regulation of patriarchal blessings has been a significant part of this transition process.[51]

Institutional routinization and current organizational controls notwithstanding, patriarchal blessings issued privately by local stake patriarchs are still considered by devout Latter-day Saints to be inspired of God. As was true for their nineteenth-century forebears, LDS members continue to take them seriously as an enduring source of comfort and religious guidance in their lives. Even though their relative salience as a ritual means for uniting the faithful and promulgating prophetic doctrines has diminished, patriarchal blessings today, as in the past, continue to serve as a meaningful anchor of personal commitment in the religion of the Latter-day Saints.

---

50. Irene Bates, "Patriarchal Blessings and the Routinization of Charisma," *Dialogue: A Journal of Mormon Thought* 26 (1993): 1–29. Also see Ballif, "Patriarch: Stake Patriarch," 3:1064–65; and Carlfred Broderick, "Uses and Abuses of Patriarchal Blessings in Therapy," talk given at the annual conference of the Association of Mormon Counselors and Psychiatrists, Salt Lake City, Utah, 1995. Transcript in authors' possession.

51. The history of the origin, development, decline, and ultimate suspension of the office of Presiding Church Patriarch is detailed in Bates and Smith, *Lost Legacy*.

CONTRIBUTORS

Brian D. Birch is the director of the Religious Studies Program and Center for the Study of Ethics at Utah Valley University where he teaches philosophy of religion, ethics, and Mormon Studies. He is the founding editor of *Element: The Journal of the Society for Mormon Philosophy and Theology* and co-editor of the *Perspectives on Mormon Theology* series. He is a senior fellow at the Foundation for Religious Diplomacy and has served on the Board of Trustees of the Parliament of the World's Religions and *Dialogue: A Journal of Mormon Thought*.

David Bokovoy holds a PhD in Hebrew Bible and the Ancient Near East and an MA in Near Eastern and Judaic Studies, both from Brandeis University. He has published articles on the Hebrew Bible in the *Journal of Biblical Literature*, *Vetus Tetamentum*, *Studies in the Bible and Antiquity*, and the *FARMS Review*. He is the co-author of *Testaments: Links Between the Book of Mormon and the Hebrew Bible* (Heritage Press, 2003) and author of *Authoring the Old Testament: Genesis–Deuteronomy* (Greg Kofford Books, 2014).

Claudia L. Bushman is a social and cultural historian of the nineteenth-century United States, holds degrees from Wellesley College, Brigham Young University, and Boston University, and has taught most recently at Columbia University and Claremont Graduate University. She writes widely on women and Mormonism. She is the author of *Going to Boston: Harriet Robinson's Journey to New Womanhood* (University Press of New England, 2017) about life in 1870. Bushman is also the author of a forthcoming autobiography entitled *I, Claudia*.

Richard Lyman Bushman is Gouverneur Morris Professor of History Emeritus at Columbia University in New York City. From 2008 to 2011, he was visiting Howard W. Hunter Chair of Mormon Studies at Claremont Graduate University. He earned an A.M. in history and a Ph.D. in the history of American civilization from Harvard University. His first book, *From Puritan to Yankee: Character and the Social Order in Connecticut, 1690–1765* (Harvard University Press, 1967), was awarded the Bancroft Prize. He has also published *Joseph Smith and the Beginnings of Mormonism* (University of Illinois Press, 1984), *King and People in Provincial Massachusetts* (University of North Carolina Press, 1985); *The Refinement of America: Persons, Houses, Cities* (Knopf, 1992); *Joseph Smith: Rough Stone Rolling* (Knopf, 2005); and *The American Farmer in the Eighteenth Century* (Yale University Press, 2018). He and his wife Claudia Bushman live in New York City.

James E. Faulconer is Resident Senior Research Fellow at the Wheatley Institution at Brigham Young University. He has held the Richard L. Evans Chair of Religious Understanding at BYU and served as Director of the BYU London Centre. He received his PhD in philosophy from Pennsylvania State University and was the founding editor of *Epoche': A Journal for the History of Philosophy*. Faulconer publishes extensively on Mormon thought, including *The Life of Holiness: Notes and Reflections on Romans 1, 5-8* (Maxwell Institute, 2012) and his co-edited volume entitled *Perspectives on Mormon Theology: Scriptural Theology* (Greg Kofford Books, 2015).

Paul C. Gutjahr is Ruth N. Halls Professor of English at Indiana University. Among his numerous books and articles, he is the author of *An American Bible: The History of the Good Book in the United States, 1777–1881* (Stanford University Press, 1991), *Charles Hodge, Guardian of American Orthodoxy* (Oxford University Press, 2011), *The Book of Mormon: A Biography* (Princeton University Press, 2012), and the editor of *Bestsellers in Nineteenth-Century America: An Anthology* (Anthem Press, 2016) and *The Oxford Handbook of the Bible in America* (Oxford University Press, 2017).

Grant Hardy is Professor of History and Religious Studies at the University of North Carolina at Asheville. He has authored *Worlds of Bronze and Bamboo: Sima Qian's Conquest of History* (Columbia University Press, 1999), *The Establishment of the Han Empire and Imperial China* (Greenwood Press, 2005), and *Understanding the Book of Mormon: A Reader's Guide* (Oxford University Press, 2010). He has also edited *The Book of Mormon: A Reader's Edition* (University of Illinois Press, 2005), the *Maxwell Institute Study Edition Book of Mormon* (Maxwell Institute, 2018), and co-edited the *Oxford History of Historical Writing, Vol. 1* (Oxford University Press, 2018).

Brian M. Hauglid is Associate Professor and Visiting Fellow at the Neal A. Maxwell Institute for Religious Studies at Brigham Young University. He completed his PhD at the University of Utah in Arabic and Islamic studies in 1998. He is on the Academic Advisory Board for *Intermountain West Journal of Religious Studies* and is the former editor of the *Journal of Book of Mormon Studies* (2013–17). His publications include *Traditions about the Early Life of Abraham* (FARMS, 2001); *Astronomy, Papyrus, and Covenant* (FARMS, 2005); and *A Textual History of the Book of Abraham: Manuscripts and Editions* (Maxwell Institute, 2011). He is also a co-editor with Robin Scott Jensen for the Joseph Smith Papers volume *Revelations and Translations: Book of Abraham and Related Manuscripts*, Facsimile Edition (Church Historian's Press, 2018).

David Frank Holland is the John A. Bartlett Professor of New England Church History at Harvard Divinity School. He also serves on the faculties of Religion and American Studies at Harvard University. His is the author of *Sacred Borders: Continuing Revelation and Canonical Restraint in Early America* (Oxford

University Press, 2011) and his research has appeared in the *New England Quarterly, Law and History Review*, and in a variety of other scholarly collections, including a recent essay in *Secularization and Religious Innovation in the Atlantic World* (Oxford University Press, 2017). He is currently at work on a comparative biography, *A Particular Universe: Ellen Gould White, Mary Baker Eddy, and the Nineteenth Century United States* (Yale University Press, forthcoming).

Boyd Jay Petersen is the Program Coordinator for Mormon Studies at Utah Valley University and Editor of *Dialogue: A Journal of Mormon Thought*. He is author of *Hugh Nibley: A Consecrated Life* (Greg Kofford Books, 2002) and *Dead Wood and Rushing Water: Essays on Mormon Faith, Culture, and Family* (Greg Kofford Books, 2013) and has been published in the *Journal of Mormon History, Voices for Equality: Ordain Women and Resurgent Mormon Feminism*, and *The New York Review of Science Fiction*. He served as Book Review Editor for the *Journal of Mormon History* and is past president of the Association of Mormon Letters.

David W. Scott is a Professor of Communication at Utah Valley University and associate editor of *Dialogue: A Journal of Mormon Thought*. His publications include "Dinosaurs on Noah's Ark: Multi-media Narratives and Natural Science Museum Discourse at the Creation Museum in Kentucky" in the *Journal of Media & Religion* and "Communicating Jesus" in *Dialogue: A Journal of Mormon Thought*. He is a contributor to the *Encyclopedia of Religion, Communication, and Media* and *Religion & Mass Media*.

Gary Shepherd is the former department chair of sociology and anthropology and Professor Emeritus at Oakland University. With Gordon Shepherd, he is co-author of *Mormon Passage: A Missionary Chronicle* (University of Illinois Press, 1998), *Talking with the Children of God: Prophecy and Reformation in a Radical Religious Group* (University of Illinois Press, 2010), *Binding Heaven and Earth: Patriarchal Blessings in the Prophetic Development of Early Mormonism* (Penn State University Press, 2012), *A Kingdom Transformed: Early Mormonism and the Modern LDS Church* (University of Utah Press, 2015), and, also with Lavina Fielding Anderson, co-editor of *Voices for Equality: Ordain Women and Resurgent Mormon Feminism* (Greg Kofford Books, 2015).

Gordon Shepherd is Professor Emeritus of Sociology at the University of Central Arkansas. With Gary Shepherd, he is co-author of *Mormon Passage: A Missionary Chronicle* (University of Illinois Press, 1998), *Talking with the Children of God: Prophecy and Reformation in a Radical Religious Group* (University of Illinois Press, 2010), *Binding Heaven and Earth: Patriarchal Blessings in the Prophetic Development of Early Mormonism* (Penn State University Press, 2012), *A Kingdom Transformed: Early Mormonism and the Modern LDS Church* (University of Utah Press, 2015), and, also with Lavina Fielding Anderson, co-editor of *Voices for Equality: Ordain Women and Resurgent Mormon Feminism* (Greg Kofford Books, 2015).

Ann Taves is Professor of Religious Studies at the University of California at Santa Barbara where she teaches courses on religious experience, new religious movements, and comparative worldviews, along with supervising the interdisciplinary Religion, Experience, and Mind Lab Group. She is the author of numerous books and articles, including *Fits, Trances, and Visions: Experiencing Religion and Explaining Experience from Wesley to James* (Princeton University Press, 1999) and *Religious Experience Reconsidered* (Princeton University Press, 2009). Her most recent book, *Revelatory Events: Three Case Studies of the Emergence of New Spiritual Paths* (Princeton University Press, 2016), analyzes the emergence of three new spiritual paths: Mormonism, Alcoholics Anonymous, and *A Course in Miracles*.

Grant Underwood is Professor of History at Brigham Young University. He received a PhD in history from the University of California at Los Angeles. He is the author of *The Millenarian World of Early Mormonism* (Illinois, 1993) and editor of *Pioneers of the Pacific* (Brigham Young University, 2005). Underwood is a co-editor of three volumes in the Documents series of *The Joseph Smith Papers*.

Blair G. Van Dyke is an independent scholar and instructor at Utah Valley University where he teaches courses in philosophy and religious studies. He is a Senior Research Fellow at the Foundation For Religious Diplomacy and is the Custodian of the Mormon Chapter of the Foundation. He is on the Editorial Board for *Dialogue: A Journal of Mormon Thought* and holds a Doctorate in the philosophy of education from Brigham Young University. Van Dyke is the co-author of *Holy Lands, A History of the Latter-day Saints in the Near East* (Covenant Books, 2005) and co-editor of *Perspectives on Mormon Theology: Apologetics* (Greg Kofford Books, 2017).

INDEX

A

A Holy Sacred and Divine Roll and Book, 14–15, 77
Adi Granth, 80
Aquinas, Thomas, 52–53
"Articles and Covenants," 172, 179

B

Ballard, M. Russell, 194
Barlow, Philip, 185
Bednar, David A., 187, 200
Benedict XVI, 32–33
Benson, Ezra Taft, xiii, 20–21, 210–11
Berger, Peter, 221
Bible
    in American culture, 160–61
    Joseph Smith Translation. *See* Joseph Smith Translation.
    privileged text, 125
    sovereignty of. *See* sola scriptura.
    women in, 59, 61
Bloesch, Donald G., 11
Book of Mormon
    1981 edition, 165–67
    2013 edition, 189, 201–5
    and *Adi Granth*, 80
    on Bible, xii, xiii, 78–79
    biblical language, 161–62
    borrows from Bible, 80
    canonization of, 74–75
    does not claim finality, 82
    electronic, 167–69, 189–91, 201–5
    Emma Smith on, 69–70
    enhanced by Orson Pratt, 163–65
    equal to Bible, 77–78
    first publication, 158
    fixed text, 75
    golden plates. *See* golden plates.
    keystone of Mormonism, ix
    Liverpool editions, 163
    lost manuscript, 87–88
    most correct book, xiv–xv
    preceded Church, 76
    primary devotional text, 85
    publication of, ix
    and Quran, 79–82
    skepticism of, 95–96
    small plates, 88
    as theological exposition, 74
    truth of, 17–18
    uniqueness of, 86
    and women, 61
Book of Abraham
    and Egyptian artifacts, 149–50
    Imagination Position, 151–52
    papyrus, 151–52
    Revelation Position, 153–54
    serial publication of, 150
    translation issues, 144
    translation of, 140–41, 150–51, 154–55
Book of Commandments, 172
Book of Commandments and Revelations, 171, 174
Book of Moses, 123–24
    and 1 Enoch, 135
    criticisms of, 149
    inclusio, 124
    as midrash, 133
    serial publication of, 147–48
    third-person narrator, 131
Bott, Randy, 25–26, 45
Brodie, Fawn, 95–96
brother of Jared, 105–7
Brown, Hugh B., 4–5
Brownson, Orestes, 13–14
Bushman, Richard, 94–95

C

Cannon, Elaine S., 6–7
Cannon, George Q.
    on prophetic fallibility, 23, 30–32
    on testing prophets, 5–6
canon, 47–48
    in Catholicism, xi
    meaning of, 76–77

open, ix
in Protestantism, xi
canonization, 22
of Book of Mormon, 74–75
Carr, David, 128
Catholicism
and canon, xi
deposit of the faith, 29–34
magisterium, 30
papal infallibility, 34–35
revelation in, 30
Chicago Statement on Biblical Inerrancy, x–xi
Chillingworth, William, 12, 18
Christofferson, D. Todd, 31
Church Handbook of Instructions, 198–99
Clark, J. Reuben, 31–33, 216
Congregation for the Doctrine of the Faith, 36
continuing revelation, x–xi
creed, 13

D

Dead Sea Scrolls, 132
delusion, 109–12
doctrine, 39–40, 43–44
Doctrine and Covenants
Consensus Earliest Wording, 175
earliest known texts, 174
early editors. *See* Literary Firm.
edits to, 173–80
types of edits, 175–80
Documentary Hypothesis, 126–28
Dreyfus, Hubert, 114

E–F

Ehrman, Bart, 135
electronic scriptures
1997 LDS editions, 190
2013 LDS editions, 189, 201–5
in other traditions, 186
spiritualizing of, 197–200
First Vatican Council, 34–35
First Vision, xii
Flake, Kathleen, xv
Fluhman, Spencer, 2–3
folk belief, 110

G

Gadamer, Hans-Georg, 51
Gardner, Brant, 103n40

Gates, Susa Young, 70–71
gender roles, 210–11
Givens, Terryl, 94–95, 204–5, 207–8
golden plates
accusations of fraud, 108
description of, 98–99
discovery of, 97–98
and the Eucharist, 108
existence of, 95–96
given to Joseph Smith, 103
made material, 104–5
materiality of, 98–103
seen in vision, 102–3
simulation of ancient artifact, 116
witnesses of, 100, 102–3
Graeber, David, 114–15

H–J

Harris, Martin, 102
Heavenly Mother, 66
Hinckley Gordon B.
introduces Proclamation on the Family, 210
on modern revelation, 28
and technology, 191
Holland, David, xii, 76, 143
Hooker, Richard, 7–8
Iron Rod saints, 207–8
John Paul II, 32
Joseph Smith Translation, xv, 122–25
Josephus, 132

K

Kelly, Sean, 114
Kimball, Sarah N., 67
Kimball, Spencer W., 3–4
lifts priesthood ban, 27
Kirtland Revelation Book, 171
Kung, Hans, 37

L–N

Lee, Harold B., xiv
Liahona Mormons, 207–8
literacy, 129–30
Literary Firm, 172, 180–81
"Living Christ, The" 220
Madigan, Daniel, 81
materialization of the sacred, 105, 108–9
Mauss, Armand, 40–44
McConkie, Bruce R., xiv

McDannell, Colleen, 221–22
midrash, 131–33
Miner (Mrs.), 67
Monson, Thomas S., 61, 199
Morgan, David, 221
National Coalition of the Protection of Children and Family, 191–92
Nephi, 89–90

O

O'Dea, Thomas, 27–28
Oaks, Dallin H.
   on Church handbooks, 198–99
   and electronic scriptures, 200
   on prophetic authority, 4
Official Declaration 2, 201–3
Okazaki, Chieko, 71
Olupona, Jacob K., 1–2
ordinary and universal magisterium, 35–38
Outler, Albert C., 8–9

P

Packer, Boyd K., 213
patriarchal blessings
   based on Israel's blessings, 241–42
   as compensatory commitment rituals, 237
   communal character of, 238–41
   early, 238–41, 245–48
   importance of, 236
   language of, 240
   performance of, 235–36
   privatized, 239
   and restoration of all things, 244
   and sealings, 245
   and tribalism, 242–43
patriarchs, 233
   and financial compensation, 240–41
Pearl of Great Price
   first publication of, 145, 148
   and Joseph Smith, 144
   and Orson Pratt, 145–46
Pentateuch, 127–29
Perry, L. Tom, 199
placebos, 114–15
Poll, Richard, 207
pornography, 188, 191–93
Proclamation on the Family
   authority of, 215–17
   in Church curricula, 217–19
   definition of proclamation, 208–10
   design and presentation of, 219–21
   and gender roles, 210–11
   in General Conference, 216–17
   given to state leaders, 213–14
   history of, 210–15
   previous proclamations, 209–10
   and same-sex marriage, 212–13
   use in Mormon homes, 223–25
   use in politics, 214–15
Pratt, Orson
   and Pearl of Great Price, 145–46
   on prophetic authority, 6
   publishes enhanced Book of Mormon, 163–65
priesthood and temple ban, 40–41, 45
   based on revelation, 41
   defense of, 41–42
prophecy, 230–31
prophets
   authority of, 6–7, 20–21
   fallibility of, 3–6, 23, 30–31, 43
pseudepigrapha, 135–37
publishing technologies, 158–60

Q–R

Quran, 79–81
"Race and the Priesthood," 45
racism, 40–41
Radden, Jennifer, 109
Rahner, Karl, 37–38
Rakove, Jack, 10
Reed, Annette Yoshiko, 137
Reeve, Paul, 42
Relief Society, 64–66
revelation
   basis for priesthood ban, 41
   bureaucratic, 27–29
   charismatic, 27–29
   in Catholicism, 30
   continuing, 26–29
   lack of, 28
   lifting priesthood ban, 27, 40
   personal, 17–19, 239
Rich, Charles C., 246
Richards, Franklin D., 145
Riter, Levi (Mrs.), 67
ritual, 234
Runyan, Levi, 247

S

Schoolhouse Rock, 1
Scott, Richard G., 196–97
scripture
  authority of, 48
  electronic. *See* electronic scriptures.
  and history, 48–52
  literal reading, 52–57
  meaning of, 47–48
Second Vatican Council, xi, 35
seer stones, 113
Shakers, 14–15, 77
Sheppard, Gerald, 74–76
Smith, Emma, 69–70
Smith, Jesse, 96–97
Smith, Joseph
  accused of fraud, 108
  acquires Egyptian artifacts, 149–50
  acquires golden plates, 103, 158
  and biblical authority, xii
  and biblical criticism, 122
  on Book of Mormon, xiv–xv
  creates pseudo-ancient text, 138–39
  and delusion, 109–12
  and folk belief, 110
  and Genesis opening, 131
  materializes golden plates, 140–5
  and Pearl of Great Price, 144
  on prophetic fallibility, 30
  on revelation, 26–27
  seer, 112–13
  and translation, 140–41
  translates Bible, xv, 122–25
  treasure seeker, 113
Smith, Lucy Mack, 62–63, 101
Snow, Eliza R., 66–67
sola scriptura, x, 11–14
Staker, Susan, 112
Standard Works, ix–x
  canonization of, 22
Stewart, Philemon, 14–15

T–V

technology
  in church meetings, 192
  divine source of, 187–88
  fear of, 188, 191–93
  and LDS leaders, 194
  and LDS members, 193–94
  and local leadership, 193
  love of, 187
  and missionary work, 195–96
  and pornography, 188, 191–93
  in publishing, 158–60
translation, 140–41
Tullidge, Edward W., 68–69
Uchtdorf, Dieter F., 31
ultra-supernaturalism, 231–32
Underwood, Grant, xvi
United Firm revelations, 138–39
Vanhoozer, Kevin, 11
Vogel Dan, 96

W–Y

Welch, John W., 2
Wellhausen, Julius, 125–26
Westminster Confession of Faith, x, xiv
Whitaker, William, 11–12
White, Susan, 246–47
Williams, Elisha, 12–13
women
  in Bible, 59, 61
  in Book of Mormon, 61
  in Paul's epistles, 59
Women of Mormondom, The, 68–69
Wuthnow, Robert, 222
Young, Brigham, xiii, 5
Young, Harriet Cook, 67

Also available from
GREG KOFFORD BOOKS

Authoring the Old Testament: Genesis–Deuteronomy

David Bokovoy

Paperback, ISBN: 978-1-58958-588-1
Hardcover, ISBN: 978-1-58958-675-8

For the last two centuries, biblical scholars have made discoveries and insights about the Old Testament that have greatly changed the way in which the authorship of these ancient scriptures has been understood. In the first of three volumes spanning the entire Hebrew Bible, David Bokovoy dives into the Pentateuch, showing how and why textual criticism has led biblical scholars today to understand the first five books of the Bible as an amalgamation of multiple texts into a single, though often complicated narrative; and he discusses what implications those have for Latter-day Saint understandings of the Bible and modern scripture.

Praise for *Authoring the Old Testament*:

"*Authoring the Old Testament* is a welcome introduction, from a faithful Latter-day Saint perspective, to the academic world of Higher Criticism of the Hebrew Bible.... [R]eaders will be positively served and firmly impressed by the many strengths of this book, coupled with Bokovoy's genuine dedication to learning by study and also by faith." — John W. Welch, editor, *BYU Studies Quarterly*

"Bokovoy provides a lucid, insightful lens through which disciple-students can study intelligently LDS scripture. This is first rate scholarship made accessible to a broad audience—nourishing to the heart and mind alike." — Fiona Givens, co-author, *The God Who Weeps: How Mormonism Makes Sense of Life*

"I repeat: this is one of the most important books on Mormon scripture to be published recently.... [*Authoring the Old Testament*] has the potential to radically expand understanding and appreciation for not only the Old Testament, but scripture in general. It's really that good. Read it. Share it with your friends. Discuss it." — David Tayman, The Improvement Era: A Mormon Blog

Mormon Women Have Their Say: Essays from the Claremont Oral History Collection

Edited by Claudia L. Bushman and Caroline Kline

Paperback, ISBN: 978-1-58958-494-5

The Claremont Women's Oral History Project has collected hundreds of interviews with Mormon women of various ages, experiences, and levels of activity. These interviews record the experiences of these women in their homes and family life, their church life, and their work life, in their roles as homemakers, students, missionaries, career women, single women, converts, and disaffected members. Their stories feed into and illuminate the broader narrative of LDS history and belief, filling in a large gap in Mormon history that has often neglected the lived experiences of women. This project preserves and perpetuates their voices and memories, allowing them to say share what has too often been left unspoken. The silent majority speaks in these records.

This volume is the first to explore the riches of the collection in print. A group of young scholars and others have used the interviews to better understand what Mormonism means to these women and what women mean for Mormonism. They explore those interviews through the lenses of history, doctrine, mythology, feminist theory, personal experience, and current events to help us understand what these women have to say about their own faith and lives.

Praise for *Mormon Women Have Their Say*:

"Using a variety of analytical techniques and their own savvy, the authors connect ordinary lives with enduring themes in Latter-day Saint faith and history." --Laurel Thatcher Ulrich, author of *Well-Behaved Women Seldom Make History*

"Essential.... In these pages, Mormon women will find *ourselves*." --Joanna Brooks, author of *The Book of Mormon Girl: A Memoir of an American Faith*

"The varieties of women's responses to the major issues in their lives will provide many surprises for the reader, who will be struck by how many different ways there are to be a thoughtful and faithful Latter-day Saint woman." --Armand Mauss, author of *All Abraham's Children: Changing Mormon Conceptions of Race and Lineage*

As Iron Sharpens Iron: Listening to the Various Voices of Scripture

Julie M. Smith

Paperback, ISBN: 978-1-58958-501-0

**2016 Best Religious Non-fiction Award,
Association for Mormon Letters**

Our scripture study and reading often assume that the prophetic figures within the texts are in complete agreement with each other. Because of this we can fail to recognize that those authors and personalities frequently have different—and sometimes competing—views on some of the most important doctrines of the Gospel, including the nature of God, the roles of scripture and prophecy, and the Atonement.

In this unique volume, fictionalized dialogues between the various voices of scripture illustrate how these differences and disagreements are not flaws of the texts but are rather essential features of the canon. These creative dialogues include Abraham and Job debating the utility of suffering and our submission to God, Alma and Abinidi disagreeing on the place of justice in the Atonement, and the authors Mark and Luke discussing the role of women in Jesus's ministry. It is by examining and embracing the different perspectives within the canon that readers are able to discover just how rich and invigorating the scriptures can be. The dialogues within this volume show how just as "iron sharpeneth iron," so can we sharpen our own thoughts and beliefs as we engage not just the various voices in the scriptures but also the various voices within our community (Proverbs 27:17).

Beholding the Tree of Life: A Rabbinic Approach to the Book of Mormon

Bradley J. Kramer

Paperback, ISBN: 978-1-58958-701-4
Hardcover, ISBN: 978-1-58958-702-1

Too often readers approach the Book of Mormon simply as a collection of quotations, an inspired anthology to be scanned quickly and routinely recited. In Beholding the Tree of Life Bradley J. Kramer encourages his readers to slow down, to step back, and to contemplate the literary qualities of the Book of Mormon using interpretive techniques developed by Talmudic and post-Talmudic rabbis. Specifically, Kramer shows how to read the Book of Mormon closely, in levels, paying attention to the details of its expression as well as to its overall connection to the Hebrew Scriptures—all in order to better appreciate the beauty of the Book of Mormon and its limitless capacity to convey divine meaning.

Praise for *Authoring the Old Testament*:

"Latter-day Saints have claimed the Book of Mormon as the keystone of their religion, but it presents itself first and foremost as a Jewish narrative. *Beholding the Tree of Life* is the first book I have seen that attempts to situate the Book of Mormon by paying serious attention to its Jewish literary precedents and ways of reading scripture. It breaks fresh ground in numerous ways that enrich an LDS understanding of the scriptures and that builds bridges to a potential Jewish readership." — Terryl L. Givens, author of *By the Hand of Mormon: The American Scripture that Launched a New World Religion*

"Bradley Kramer has done what someone ought to have done long ago, used the methods of Jewish scripture interpretation to look closely at the Book of Mormon. Kramer has taken the time and put in the effort required to learn those methods from Jewish teachers. He explains what he has learned clearly and carefully. And then he shows us the fruit of that learning by applying it to the Book of Mormon. The results are not only interesting, they are inspiring. This is one of those books that, on reading it, I thought 'I wish I'd written that!'" — James E. Faulconer, author of *The Book of Mormon Made Harder* and *Faith, Philosophy, Scripture*

Perspectives on Mormon Theology: Apologetics

Edited by Blair G. Van Dyke and Loyd Isao Ericson

Paperback, ISBN: 978-1-58958-580-5
Hardcover, ISBN: 978-1-58958-581-2

This volume in the PERSPECTIVES ON MORMON THEOLOGY series is an exploration of Mormon apologetics—or the defense of faith. Since its very beginning, various Latter-day Saints have sought to utilize evidence and reason to actively promote or defend beliefs and claims within the Mormon tradition. Mormon apologetics reached new levels of sophistication as believers trained in fields such as Near-Eastern languages and culture, history, and philosophy began to utilize their knowledge and skills to defend their beliefs.

The contributors to this volume seek to explore the textures and contours of apologetics from multiple perspectives, revealing deep theological and ideological fissures within the Mormon scholarly community concerning apologetics. However, in spite of deep-seated differences, what each author has in common is a passion for Mormonism and how it is presented and defended. This volume captures that reality and allows readers to encounter the terrain of Mormon apologetics at close range.

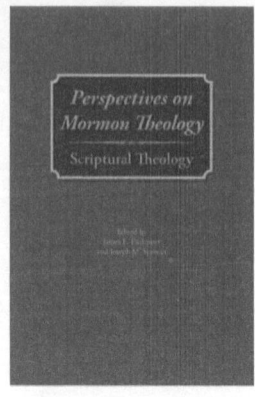

Perspectives on Mormon Theology: Scriptural Theology

Edited by James E. Faulconer and Joseph M. Spencer

Paperback, ISBN: 978-1-58958-712-0
Hardcover, ISBN: 978-1-58958-713-7

The phrase "theology of scripture" can be understood in two distinct ways. First, theology of scripture would be reflection on the nature of scripture, asking questions about what it means for a person or a people to be oriented by a written text (rather than or in addition to an oral tradition or a ritual tradition). In this first sense, theology of scripture would form a relatively minor part of the broader theological project, since the nature of scripture is just one of many things on which theologians reflect. Second, theology of scripture would be theological reflection guided by scripture, asking questions of scriptural texts and allowing those texts to shape the direction the theologian's thoughts pursue. In this second sense, theology of scripture would be less a part of the larger theological project than a way of doing theology, since whatever the theologian takes up reflectively, she investigates through the lens of scripture.

The essays making up this collection reflect attentiveness to both ways of understanding the phrase "theology of scripture." Each essay takes up the relatively un-self-conscious work of reading a scriptural text but then—at some point or another—asks the self-conscious question of exactly what she or he is doing in the work of reading scripture. We have thus attempted in this book (1) to create a dialogue concerning what scripture is for Latter-day Saints, and (2) to focus that dialogue on concrete examples of Latter-day Saints reading actual scripture texts.

Dead Wood and Rushing Water: Essays on Mormon Faith, Culture, and Family

Boyd Jay Petersen

Paperback, ISBN: 978-1-58958-658-1

For over a decade, Boyd Petersen has been an active voice in Mormon studies and thought. In essays that steer a course between apologetics and criticism, striving for the balance of what Eugene England once called the "radical middle," he explores various aspects of Mormon life and culture—from the Dream Mine near Salem, Utah, to the challenges that Latter-day Saints of the millennial generation face today.

Praise for *Dead Wood and Rushing Water*:

"*Dead Wood and Rushing Water* gives us a reflective, striving, wise soul ruminating on his world. In the tradition of Eugene England, Petersen examines everything in his Mormon life from the gold plates to missions to dream mines to doubt and on to Glenn Beck, Hugh Nibley, and gender. It is a book I had trouble putting down." — Richard L. Bushman, author of *Joseph Smith: Rough Stone Rolling*

"Boyd Petersen is correct when he says that Mormons have a deep hunger for personal stories—at least when they are as thoughtful and well-crafted as the ones he shares in this collection." — Jana Riess, author of *The Twible* and *Flunking Sainthood*

"Boyd Petersen invites us all to ponder anew the verities we hold, sharing in his humility, tentativeness, and cheerful confidence that our paths will converge in the end." — Terryl. L. Givens, author of *People of Paradox: A History of Mormon Culture*

Textual Studies of the Doctrine and Covenants: The Plural Marriage Revelation

William Victor Smith

Paperback, ISBN: 978-1-58958-690-1
Hardcover, ISBN: 978-1-58958-691-8

Joseph Smith's July 12, 1843, revelation on plural marriage was the last of his formal written revelations and a transformational moment in Mormonism. While acting today as the basis for the doctrine of eternal nuclear families, the revelation came forth during a period of theological expansion as Smith was in the midst of introducing new temple rituals, radical doctrines on God and humanity, a restructured priesthood and ecclesiastical hierarchy, and, of course, the practice of plural marriage.

In this volume, author William V. Smith examines the text of this complicated and rough revelation to explore the motivation for its existence, how it reflects this dynamic theology of the Nauvoo period, and how the revelation was utilized and reinterpreted as Mormonism fully embraced and later abandoned polygamy.

Praise for *Textual Studies*:

"No Mormon text is as ritually important and as fundamentally mysterious as Doctrine and Covenants 132. William V. Smith's work is a fine example of what a serious-minded and meticulous blend of source and redaction critical methods can tell us about the revelations produced by Joseph Smith. This is a model of what the future of Mormon scriptural studies should be."
— Stephen C. Taysom, author of *Shakers, Mormons, and Religious Worlds: Conflicting Visions, Contested Boundaries*

www.ingramcontent.com/pod-product-compliance
Lightning Source LLC
Chambersburg PA
CBHW020235170426
43202CB00008B/97